Roman Ingarden
Man and Value

Philosophia Resources Library

Reprints, Translations and Commentaries
Relating to Austrian Intellectual History

Philosophia Verlag München Wien

Roman Ingarden

Man and Value

Translation by Arthur Szylewicz

The Catholic University of America Press
Washington, D.C.

Philosophia Verlag München Wien

CIP-Kurztitelaufnahme der Deutschen Bibliothek

Ingarden, Roman:
Man and value / Roman Ingarden. Transl. by Arthur Szylewicz. – Washington, D.C.: Catholic University of America Press; München, Wien: Philosophia Verlag, 1983.
(Philosophia Resources Library)
ISBN 3-88405-042-7 (Philosophia Verlag)
ISBN 0-8132-0592-1 (Catholic Univ. of America Press)

Library of Congress Cataloging in Publication Data

Ingarden, Roman, 1893–
Man and value.
(Philosophia resources library)
Includes translation of: Książeczka o człowieku and Über die Verantwortung.
Includes index.
1. Responsibility-Adresses, essays, lectures. 2. Man-Adresses, essays, lectures.
I. Ingarden, Roman, 1893– . Książeczka o człowieku. English. 1983,
II. Ingarden, Roman, 1893– . Über die Verantwortung. English. 1983,
III. Title. IV. Series.
BJ 1453.149 1983 170 83-15245
ISBN 0-8132-0592-1

Available in North and South America from The Catholic University of America Press, Washington, D.C.

Translated from the Polish and German by Arthur Szylewicz
Originally published under the titles
Książeczka o człowieku
Wydawnictwo Literackie, Cracow: 1972
and *Über die Verantwortung*
Philipp Reclam Jun., Stuttgart: 1970

ISBN 3-88405-042-7
ISBN 0-8132-0592-1

Printed in Germany 1983

This translation is dedicated
to my parents

Table of Contents

Foreword to the Original Polish Edition*

Some words about the genesis of this volume

It was the author's intention to have it published at some future time. This intention was born at the beginning of 1969, when it was necessary to make a final decision as to which works (including some previously published and scattered in various periodicals and conference acts) were to be included in vol. III of *Studies in Aesthetics*, the next in the series of Roman Ingarden's *Collected Philosophical Works*, issued by the Polish Scientific Publishers (PWN). Several very small papers fell into the author's hands at the time (primarily, the first four contained in the present little volume) which he did not want to include in the projected volume (*Aesthetics* III), due to its cohesive composition. A somewhat different thematic thread ties these papers together: the nature of man.

To this day I still remember perfectly (as it happened in my presence) that lightly jocular tone of the author, who was accustomed to putting out lengthy volumes, when he said: "How about if I some day put out a *Little Book on Man*?" Several of the Professor's students enthusiastically endorsed the idea, and an understanding was reached with the publisher (Wydawnictwo Literackie, Cracow). For the time being, however, the matter fizzled out – the composite bulk of these four little papers was too small for even a 'booklet', and attaching the very brief article "On Fruitful Discussion" would not in any way change the situation. Obviously, the prospective little volume could have been supplemented with new discussions, for this sphere of problems had attracted Ingarden since his youth (after all, the topic which he first proposed for his doctoral dissertation read: "The Structure of the Human Person"). But for the next several years pressing work in other realms of philosophy did not allow him to seriously think about such a supplementation. He had to finally bring to completion and publish an important work on the methodological foundations of epistemology which he had repeatedly taken up over the years. There loomed ahead also the preparation of the volume *Issues in the Theory of Language and the Philosophical Foundations of Logic*, which he had promised to PWN. The author was indeed just finishing a sizable essay, written in German, entitled "On

* *Książeczka o człowieku* (Little Book on Man), Cracow: Wydawnictwo Literackie, 1972.

Responsibility. Its Ontic Foundations", which was commissioned by the publishing house Reclam, Stuttgart. It consisted of an expanded version of a paper read in 1968, at the 14th International Congress of Philosophy held in Vienna. This work, as he himself admitted, would be very well suited for inclusion in a little volume of works on man: responsibility is, after all, a phenomenon which appears only in the human world, and the psycho-physical structure of man is one of the fundamental ontic conditions for its possibility. But the author refused to agree to the proposal that the *Little Book* be at once complemented with this essay. He had neither the time nor the desire to translate "On Responsibility". To be sure, he intended to write this piece in Polish some day, but only after having taken it to task once more in order to develop it, and give it more depth. Perhaps the same thing would then happen to it that had frequently happened before when he took up anew a topic previously laid to rest: sometimes a wholly new, sizable work was born as a result. And this theme was undoubtedly very dear to him; he thought about its possible link-up with a working over of materials for lectures on ethics that he gave: once, before the War, at the Jan Kazimierz University in Lwow, and a second time at the Jagiellonian University in Cracow, during the academic year 1961/62.* But all this could only happen in the more distant future, and there was no more talk concerning the *Little Book on Man*.

Roman Ingarden's sudden death in June, 1970 changed the situation completely: an expanded Polish version of "On Responsibility" could no longer be expected; the original German version, as Ingarden's last work to be published in his lifetime, had meanwhile gone out of print. Prof. Wladyslaw Tatarkiewicz' professional opinion reached the public that the printing of this culminating treatise by Reclam dictates the "acknowledgment of its author as a classic philosopher". Interest in the essay grows; the German copies are almost inaccessible in Poland. A clamour begins for its Polish translation. Dr. Adam Węgrzecki, a student of the Professor's, launched the translation. Thus, a new substantial essay was being appended to Ingarden's collection of studies on man. Wydawnictwo Literackie, with great kindness, agreed to its publication.

And so, Roman Ingarden's fleeting wish is today being realized: the reader receives his *Little Book on Man*, which, without popularizing gimmicks, so foreign to the author's spirit, can, owing to the appropriate arrangement of the studies contained in it, lead even someone who is entirely unacquainted with its domain into the realm of the most serious and difficult problems of philosophy.

D. Gierulanka
Cracow, August 1971

* Ingarden's *Lectures on Ethics* were projected to comprise one of the forthcoming volumes in his *Collected Works*.–Tr.

Foreword to Man and Value

This book has come about as the translation of a collection of six of Roman Ingarden's essays which were issued in 1972, in Poland, in a volume entitled *Little Book on Man*, to which the translator attached three essays devoted exclusively to the problem of values.

In this form, the book as a whole acquires a peculiar character which marks none of Ingarden's Polish publications. Thus, when I was asked to provide an informative Preface to it, I decided to do so in two steps: first, to offer in unaltered form the Foreword once written for the *Little Book on Man*; secondly, to attach a separate, supplementary text, prefacing the present publication.

Let the first of these serve as a living trace, fixed on the spur of the moment, of the author's own intentions with regard to these fragments of his work, which can be relegated to philosophical anthropology. Let it at the same time call the reader's attention to the goal of the editors of the *Little Book* (noted in the last sentence of its Foreword): to take advantage, through their very arrangement in the proper sequence, of what apparently could have threatened the cohesiveness of that collection of essays (namely, the diverse degree of substantive difficulty of the individual pieces and the differences in style of the analyses contained in them), in order to open access to Ingarden's philosophy to a wider public, in a form unadulterated by popularizing gimmickry – a goal that has been fully realized in Poland (a fact which is attested to by three consecutive sold-out printings of the *Little Book on Man*).

Another feature of Ingarden's philosophy emerges in the whole presented here, which requires that another particular be brought to the attention of the reader who has not been able to come in contact with the entire scope of the author's philosophical creativity. By annexing the last three essays, the anthropological current of the author's philosophical thought is presented in conjunction with its axiological aspect. On the one hand, this unquestionably represents an enrichment; on the other hand, however, it disrupts the type of dynamic unity with which the *Little Book* was endowed owing to its gradation in the difficulty of the successive essays – with the result of imperceptibly drawing the reader into the most serious philosophical analyses. The tension of this build-up is characteristically resolved by closing the collection with the very brief article "Some Words Concerning Fruitful Discussion", which can at the same time be regarded as an expression of how moral responsibility extends for the author to include the sphere of purely intellectual endeavours.

How, then, is this link of thought-currents, the anthropological and axiological, manifested in Ingarden's creative work? From the very content of the essays composing the *Little Book*, the reader must be struck by the fact that the author assigns to values a very important role in human affairs. In this, however, he is no different from most philosophers, nor does he diverge from popular intuitions. What, in contrast, is peculiarly characteristic of Ingarden's conception of this theme is the way in which it leads him to problems concerning values, as well as his manner of posing these problems and his attempts to solve them. It may be stated briefly, if not rigorously, that these are problems concerning (1) the *essence* of values and (2) the material in which values are *realized* and *manifested* and the *manner* in which this manifestation is accomplished.

The three last major essays of the collection primarily illustrate Ingarden's approach relative to problems of the first group, i.e. problems concerning the essence of values. As with the pieces that made up the *Little Book*, these essays differ in their analytical style (from the attempt at a conceptual ordering of the relevant issues in "Remarks on the Relativity of Values", through a setting out of the general approach to fundamental problems in "What we do not know about Values", to an attempt at specific phenomenological analyses in "An Analysis of Moral Values") and make up a small but representative selection of the author's approach, a fragment of his researches in the domain of axiology. Ingarden never tried systematically to develop axiological investigations in complete generality – in accord with the standpoint of axiological pluralism that emerges in these essays, which dictates that we reckon with the need for separate investigations in each sphere of values. It may be worthwhile to mention, however, for the orientation of the reader interested in these matters, that the fullest and most systematic of Ingarden's researches in the realm of axiology appeared toward the end of his life[1], as the coronation of his probing and extensive investigations in the realm of aesthetics, which comprise the best known facet of his philosophical output.[2] It is no accident that such researches occurred so late, and precisely with respect to a realm to which the author devoted so many ground-breaking works in his lifetime. For Ingarden had already concerned himself in the late twenties with works of art (for other reasons, about which I shall add a few words later) as examples of so-called *purely intentional objects*, created in a certain manner owing to the artist's acts of consciousness, on the basis of material drawn from the natural world and transformed in a specific way. Never losing perspective of the goal that bestows meaning on the creation of such works – the embodiment of a particular type of values – he patiently refrained from making pronouncements on the theme of these values until he had acquired a more thorough familiarity with what he sometimes calls the 'anatomy' of a work of art and with the essence of the processes of its reception. Such a genealogy of the conception of aesthetic values finally allowed him responsibly to assert something within aesthetics itself about the manner of realizing values, and to pose in a new way (with the promise of the possibility of solution) the fundamental and hitherto unresolved problem of the objectivity of aesthetic values.

Returning, after these particulars, to the collection of essays at hand, I would like to impress on the reader that precisely the initial three pieces – bearing on the question of what makes up the essential characteristic feature of man's humanity – are quite strongly rooted in the very context of problems within which Ingarden's aesthetics flowered. I have in mind here the problematic of purely intentional objects in general, which comprise the peculiar sphere that man creates around himself (the author calls it "man's reality" in the title of one of the essays) – and he creates it by appropriately moulding a basis extracted for it from the world of nature and incarnating it with various sorts of values, not only aesthetic ones. The author's most fundamental ontological investigations ultimately lie behind these suggestively and rather freely written essays: rigorous and detailed analyses of the basic formal structures and mode of existence of that intentional sphere which so greatly differ from the structures and mode of existence of the real world. Moreover, in these 'innocent essays' the reader, perhaps without realizing it, brushes against fundamental problems that form the keystone of Ingarden's 'heavy philosophy', the subject of the main and deepest current of his philosophical thought, set forth in his *Der Streit um die Existenz der Welt*[3]; this work opens up a new path for approaching the age-old problem of idealism vs. realism, a problem which was unsettling to the author from his youth. It also needs to be mentioned now that one of those 'other reasons' due to which Ingarden undertook investigations into works of art was the desire to come up with a better account of the formal structure of objects whose mode of existence is that of a *product of consciousness*, i.e. that mode of existence which a particular type of idealism is inclined to ascribe to what we naively regard as the real world. With his realistic intuitions, Ingarden nurtured the hope that, by contrasting the formal structure of the world with that which is typical of those unquestionably intentional objects, he would manage to acquire a cogent argument against the idealistic solution of the problem of the existence of the world.

In the foregoing I have indicated links which, though otherwise clear, must be very indirect for someone uninitiated in the totality of Ingarden's corpus. They justify the statement that even these first little 'essays' strike their roots into the main, ontological current of his philosophy. On the other hand, rootedness in this current is quite distinct and direct in "On Responsibility". The subtitle of the essay: "Its Ontic Foundations" points to this explicitly. In this way the author makes reference to a series of conceptions elaborated in his *Streit*. Of principal importance here are the formal structures of objects belonging to the world, the structure of the whole world in general as a region of objects (*gegenständliche Region*), and, in particular, the conception of its causal structure – to which all of vol. III of the *Streit* is devoted[4] – and, within the framework of this causal structure, a refinement of the sense and conditions of a determinism that can be acknowledged as obtaining in the real world without thereby excluding free will, which constitutes a necessary condition of responsibility. But the conception of time, e.g., as a factor co-determining the real mode of existence, is also a main issue. The style of thought in the expositions of "On Responsibility" is also not without significance; these expositions (especially in the later chapters) lead the reader into a climate characteristic of the researches of the *Streit*.

It so happens that thus far I have not mentioned the essay "Man and Time", the fourth piece in the collection. In a certain sense, more so than all the others, it speaks for itself. It speaks both through the way it was written (most vibrant, and perhaps most fascinating to the reader) and the 'existential' (as some are wont to say today) commitment of the author, especially in that part of it that was added on during the War, a part that is most fervently searching and culminates in a solution. This solution, indeed, strikes the most perspicuous chord in the whole book, which binds what is perhaps of the greatest importance to man – the self-realization of his person, threatened by the annihilating experience of passing on – with the relation of man to values.

D. Gierulanka
Cracow, June 1981

Notes

[1] Signaled already in 1956, at the III International Congress of Aesthetics in Venice, September 3–5, 1956. (cf. "La valeur esthéthique et le probléme de son fondement objectif", in: *Atti del III Congresso Internazionale di Estetica, Venezia, 3–5 Settembre 1956*, Torino, 1957, pp. 167–73). (German trans. in (4) of footnote 2, below. Tr.)

[2] The following works primarily come into question here:

1) *Das literarische Kunstwerk. Eine Untersuchung aus dem Grenzgebiet der Ontologie, Logik und Literaturwissenschaft*, Halle, Niemeyer, 1931. (*The Literary Work of Art*, trans. by George G. Grabowicz, Evanston, Northwestern U.P., Evanston, 1973).

2) *Untersuchungen zur Ontologie der Kunst. Musikwerk, Bild, Architektur, Film*, Niemeyer, Tübingen, 1962.

3) *Vom Erkennen des literarischen Kunstwerks*, Niemeyer, Tübingen, 1968 – expanded version of the original Polish edition of 1936. (*The Cognition of the Literary Work of Art*, trans. by Ruth Ann Crowley and Kenneth R. Olson, Evanston, Northwestern U.P., 1973)

4) *Erlebnis, Kunstwerk und Wert. Vorträge zur Aesthetik 1937–1967*, Niemeyer, Tübingen, 1969.

[3] Written in Polish (and simultaneously in German) during the War, 2 volumes of this work were published (in Polish) for the first time in 1947/48, and only considerably later in German by Ingarden's ever loyal publisher (Niemeyer) as

1) *Der Streit um die Existenz der Welt, Bd. I, Existentialontologie*, Tübingen, Niemeyer, 1964.

2) *Der Streit um die Existenz der Welt, Bd. II/1, Formalontologie, 1. Teil, Form und Wesen*, Tübingen, Niemeyer, 1965.

3) *Der Streit um die Existenz der Welt, Bd. II/2, Formalontologie, 2. Teil, Welt und Bewußtsein*, Niemeyer, Tübingen, 1965.

[4] Written in German in the years 1951–54, issued posthumously under the title *Über die kausale Struktur der realen Welt, Der Streit um die Existenz der Welt, Bd. III*, Tübingen, Niemeyer, 1974.

Translator's Preface

All the essays in this collection, with the exception of "On Responsibility", have been translated from the Polish. "Remarks on the Relativity of Values" (which first appeared in a briefer French version) and "What We Do Not Know About Values" have also appeared in a German version (in *Erlebnis, Kunstwerk und Wert. Vorträge zur Ästhetik 1937–1967*, Niemeyer, Tübingen, 1969). These vary slightly in particulars (tighter sentence construction, greater precision and rigour, larger sentences broken down into smaller ones) from the originals, are in places amplified with more examples, but do not – according to this translator – differ in substance, though some commentators have disagreed. In view of the lack of consensus on this last point, it seemed all the more prudent to make available an English translation from the less accessible language for those scholars who might wish to discern significant differences between the two. The remaining six essays have previously been available in their entirety only in Polish.

Commonly accepted translating conventions have been followed; numbered notes belong to the author, asterisked ones to the translator; bracketed insertions belong to the translator, those in parentheses to the author. Where responsible translating practice called for citing a word from the original Polish, I have replaced it with Ingarden's counterpart German.

I wish to express my deepest gratitude to Mr. Janusz Ingarden for his cooperation in setting up the project, and to Profs. D. Gierulanka and A. Półtawski for their unstinting generosity in guiding me through Ingarden's texts and their gracious hospitality during my stays in Poland. I also wish to thank my colleague, Fred S. Hofman for helping me unravel some of the intricacies of the German text, Dr. Thomas Peterson for some finer points of English syntax, and Denise Hardie for a scrupulous typing of parts of the manuscript.

My greatest debt is to Prof. Izchak Miller for having introduced me to Ingarden's writings, and for offering encouragement when it was most needed – at the very beginning.

Arthur Szylewicz
Thousand Oaks, California 1982

Man and Nature*

I agree with the speaker, Prof. Lotz, that man transcends nature, and that by the "power of his essence" he "projects (*entwirft*) a world, which, despite its always self-sustaining, fundamental form, takes on countless historical guises." It is also true that his "conscious activeness [*Wirken*] is expressed primarily in three basic forms: as the cognition of what is true, the doing of good and the shaping of beauty." But it still remains to be explained what makes up his creative activeness, and the relation between the world created by man and the nature in which he finds himself at the inception of his activity. The essence of man can be clarified by explicating, among other things, the sense and mode of existence of his works, which find their support in nature. It is not important for this problem how one conceives nature itself: whether as the totality of things, or as the totality of what is visible or, finally, as the totality of what is [*Gesamtheit des Seienden*]. The only important thing is the fact that nature exists prior to any activity by man and that it changes within itself, for the most part independently not only of man's activity, but also of his existence. Nature is also the ultimate foundation of his being, as well as of the existence of his works. This is apparent not so much in the fact of human knowledge as in the intrinsic content and mode of existence of the products of human culture.

Today, man finds himself all too rarely face to face with original nature; e.g., on a solitary expedition into high mountains or during a powerful hurricane at sea or, finally, when he is witness to the relentless spread of a fatal disease in a friend, feeling totally impotent in all efforts to save him. In such instances man is perhaps at awe at the beauty and greatness of nature, or maybe terrified by the undaunted force of a hurricane, or feels that things are moving irrevocably in the direction ordained by nature itself and that nothing can evade doom. However, he is always saturated by a very special, doubly-complexioned feeling. On one side, he feels quite alien to everything that happens in nature independently of him, and he sees himself deprived by it of any kindly help, so that he almost loses trust in fate. On the other side, however, in his pure and

* A contribution to the discussion of the problem "Man and Nature" during the plenary session of the XII. International Congress of Philosophy, Venice, 1958. The main speaker on this theme was Professor Johannes B. Lotz, S.J.

autonomous essence he feels himself to be something that stands out above nature, something that is so much more dignified than purely physical processes or what transpires in animals, that he cannot feel in solidarity with nature and live fully happily by being united with it in its domain. When from time to time man discovers in himself something of original nature, he feels not only extremely abased, but even completely alien to himself, and thus becomes unintelligible to himself. He cannot, and refuses to, admit that he comprises a fragment of primordial nature and that he is an animal which is in no respect better than the beasts, neither as natural reality nor as an individual entity, nor is there anything about him that is radically different from the rest of nature. Though science tells him so, man cannot admit in the recesses of his heart that the life-processes occurring in his body, and even in his soul, are not in principle of a different sort than the processes going on in animals. And in the depths of his heart he does not believe in his own death, and convinces himself that his soul is immortal, even though he daily witnesses the deaths of friends and working colleagues. He does not really understand the death of other people and is horrified at the sight of a decomposing body, which is why he buries it deep underground. He is deeply upset if in some situation he feels himself reduced to the level of an animal, or when he sees that bringing all his powers and efforts to bear on truly crossing the bounds prescribed by nature proves futile. He then begins to live in excess of his powers and innate nature: he creates for himself a new world, a new reality around and within himself. He creates the world of culture and endows himself with the aspect of humanity.

Man changes nature by subjugating it (in agriculture, or in technology) and confers upon it at the same time a certain sense which it does not possess of itself; he creates works that differ completely in their essence from anything to be found in the world as product of nature alone. These works are made to respond to his soul and comprise his completion. Once they have been created, he encounters them in the world as if they were something actual in it. He creates works of art (literature, music, etc.), creates science, philosophy, religion as well as his own history, and that of mankind. He also creates in some sense his own family and other families, his own nation and other nations, which in turn lays on him obligations with respect to his family and nation, and also brings about obligations of nations with respect to humanity. A whole wealth of diverse values then spreads before his eyes, and commits him to various deeds towards his relatives, friends or enemies. His life begins to have some purpose and goal, and acquires a particular sense and meaning which it would not have in brute nature. This life becomes responsible. He acquires virtues and is burdened with sins. Man lives in a world different from nature and forgets almost completely that at the basis of this whole, new reality is concealed a nature indifferent to every value, and insensitive to his happiness or discontent. He forgets also that his humanity consists of only a thin layer on his surface, and that it is this layer which changes the whole sense of his life and fortunes. He now becomes a person who plays a particular role in the human world, and who seems to have his autonomy and freedom in this very world. Even when he is subject to a specific legal system, this law is absolutely different from laws which hold sway in nature, and is a law established by man. A man who lives in this way can be a happy and good person, and can gain contact with something that seems to him greater and more perfect than he and all of humanity, and which exceeds all ideas and noblest ideals of man, as well as all perfections of finite being in general – he can win communion with God. He is therefore prepared to sacrifice his life, and even his very existence, for the realization of ideals, and to do so with a sense of full accountability toward God. He forgets that his being and life depends on what happens in nature, and thinks he can exceed and vanquish nature itself. And only once in a while does he recall to himself his own animal nature, in which he cannot recognize himself.

But the creative power with which man creates a specifically human world is not unbounded; it is not even sufficiently creative to be able to realize truly that new world, to endow it with autonomous existence. Man's creative power can only evoke those changes in nature that are indispensable for the phenomenal presence of works and specifically human characters, but which do not suffice for guaranteeing the latter autonomous existence. The products of culture created by man are nothing more than a certain sort of shadow of reality, in that they are merely intentional formations [*Gebilde*]. They wear that mere semblance of existence which characterizes all of man's spiritual works, such as works of art and various other products of human culture, be they the works of a particular man or those of a whole human community. These products of human culture are constituted on the basis of the things and processes of the natural world, and are made suitable to that end by man; and the properties of the former surpass the bounds of qualitative endowment of material things, covering them with a new layer of sense and new phenomena. In transcending these natural things, they lose the fullness and autonomy of existence, and do not have the force of a reality independent of man and his spiritual acts. These cultural products can gratify man's aspirations to a life elevated above nature only under the condition of his extraordinary spiritual activeness, and they fall back into total oblivion as soon as man loses the will to transcend his simple, inborn nature, and surrenders the creative activeness of his consciousness. Nonetheless, they are not merely present to man, who opens himself, as it were, to objects of this sort and tries to understand them; they also affect him and sometimes deeply modify his spiritual life, and also, to some extent, his corporeal life. They condition his specifically human existence, though they are of course unable, truly to influence that real individual entity which is a constituent of nature, and which, in particular, makes up man's natural physical basis.

Man exists and lives on the boundary of two different essences, only one of which seems to comprise his humanity, and the other – unfortunately more real than the first, so to speak – stems from his animality, and conditions the first. Man finds himself on the boundary of two regions of being: nature and the specifically human world. And he cannot live without the latter, but it also does not suffice for his existence, nor is it capable of assuring it to him. Man is forced therefore to live on the substratum of nature and within its framework, but owing to his peculiar essence he must cross its bounds; yet he can never fully appease his need for being human.

Such is the tragedy of man's fate. But precisely in this is manifest his true nature; his geniality and the finitude of his being. He has, in principle, at his disposal only two possibilities of triumphing over nature. On the one hand, he can come to know himself and the surrounding nature in its own, true and original essence. On the other hand, with his endeavours – through his victories, even defeats – he realizes the values of good and beauty, which do, to be sure, appear in merely intentional works, but which at bottom have for him a higher reality than the world of sheer nature. And man remains in the service of realizing these values. When he has managed this, he rests assured in his soul that he does not live in vain.

On Human Nature*

It is surely difficult to define the nature of man. Through his deeds, sometimes heroic but at times horrifying, through the immense diversity of his character and the goals he strives to realize, through the inexhaustible novelty of his works and admirable capacity to regenerate after almost every fall – man transcends the confines of every imposed definition. All efforts at comprehending the plenitude of his essence with a satisfactory and adequate definition have proven vain. Every feature we find in his essence can be juxtaposed to concrete facts appearing to demonstrate something diametrically contrary. And it is certain that there are many irrefutable facts of man's reality, in the annals of humanity as a whole, which, though real and in fact actualized by him, are still something less than his true nature. But at the same time, there is occasionally in man's life an occurrence so lofty and exceptional that it could not possibly mark anything but some direction along the path of his noblest evolution, and not a commonly realized goal.

Though we are well aware of the great difficulties inherent in the attempt to grasp man's very nature, to make the attempt once more is, after all, something enticing – even at the risk of giving, at best, only a partial definition, or one which points to features that are only very seldom realized. The following thoughts then occur to us:

Egoism most certainly dominates the greater part of human deeds, be they individual, social or national. Yet it is something specifically human to act with the welfare or success of another exclusively in mind, and in exceptional cases to give one's own life to save the life of another, sometimes even that of a complete stranger. Man is capable of frightful, cruel and inhumane deeds, but at the same time he is the sole creature to feel humiliated by his evil deeds, and to try to atone for his sins. In the limit, he is prepared to kill himself in order to salvage his honour, and he is surely the only creature for whom honour, and the denigration of this honour, exists at all. Only man, too, feels responsible for his life-style, especially when he is unable to realize those values which in his opinion are indispensable for his inner well-being. And whilst, finally, it is true

* This article contains the theses of a paper read at the XI. Congress of the French Philosophical Societies held in Montpellier in September, 1961; the paper was published in the Acts of that Congress (Paris, 1961) under the title "*Nature Humaine*".

that in the majority of cases utility is the decisive motive in his affairs, it is also true that man is the only creature which can create works and situations that are in no respect useful. He creates them, rather, only for their beauty and to enrich through their existence a specifically human world.

Briefly speaking: there is a certain set of special values which man fixes for himself and tries to realize, and even feels a calling to realize. It is hard to say what kind of values these are. And it is possible that the totality of these values changes within well-defined limits, depending on the particular type of man and on the historical era. But despite this possible change there exists a certain basic stock of values which is characteristic of any given human epoch. This basic stock of values does not, however, depend on particular values, but on an assortment of the basic categories of values. Still, it is not so much the basic traits of this stock of value-categories that is essential to man's nature, but rather the fact that man experiences the need at all, and even feels the necessity, to have and to come to know values as well as to realize them to the extent that is possible in general, and in the world surrounding him in particular. Man is deeply unhappy without an immediate and intuitive contact with values, without the joy that such contact affords him. The actualization [*Verwirklichung*] of values, on the other hand, makes him happy and he is spellbound by their peculiar attraction. It is not in this case a matter of relative values, at least not primarily; neither those values that are relative with respect to his purely vital needs (such as nourishment, for example), nor those relative to his pleasure (such as, e.g., delight and rapture) are here at issue, but values that are absolute in their immanent quality, irrespective of the fact that their realization depends on man's creative power, in a word – moral and aesthetic values.

But man does not stumble onto these values in nature, in the material world. He must create the real conditions for bringing them into existence and getting them to appear in the world. Owing to a special faculty of foreseeing the quality of such values he creates a new world – a world in which values are manifest, the world of human culture – and he does so on the basis of the real world by an appropriate transformation of some things and by an evocation of certain processes.

This new world would not exist without the genius and creative activity of man, and it would be incapable of concretization without creating the physical basis of its existence, which is made by man to conform to the function of manifesting new objects and their values. In its intrinsic content, however, this new world transcends the world of nature in an essential way, and at the same time clads it somehow with a particular veil of the most diverse, unique qualities, which bestow on some things a distinctive meaning and a certain importance that does not accrue and is alien to them if they are merely regarded as things of nature. This new reality belonging to man consists for him of a certain kind of atmosphere that is necessary for endowing his life with a new sense and a new meaning, a meaning which transforms every one of his deeds, and his entire role in the world, in such a way that, were they deprived of that meaning, man could not accept his own existence.

In the face of this new reality man forgets to some degree his true, original, purely animal nature. He also forgets about that countenance of the real world which is independent of his creative activity, a countenance radically different from the face of culture imposed by him on a nature alien, even hostile, to his ideals and most dignified objects of affection. He feels happy to be aware of the presence of values created by himself or those close to him. This specifically human reality is more enduring and longer lasting than the life of a particular man, and – even though it depends for its existence on the creative power of consciousness – is, for each of us, a certain kind of legacy that we encounter in our world, as a gift of predecessors, as a revival or restoration of past historical epochs and as a meeting with people who have long since ceased to live. And we try not only to preserve the treasure of values received from previous ages, but also to enrich and transform it with our creative acts and new works. But only the fact of managing to create values bearing our own personal imprint can afford us full satisfaction in life. And, peculiarly enough, we ourselves are transformed under the influence of the works we have created and with which we maintain direct, intuitive contact; and – irrespective of our wishes or knowledge – we are reborn and transformed by our very effort of remaining in the service of realizing values. We enrich ourselves by giving our best efforts to the creation of a reality for mankind as a whole.

But the creative power of man is limited. It is incapable of creating works that are autonomous in their existence and independent of our consciousness. It is too weak to be able to actually transform primordial nature into the reality of man. This reality is only a certain stratum that is intentionally created and, as it were, laid over the substratum of real nature. And it is never so opaque and so impermeable that nature's reality-aspect would never again be able to shine through and unveil for us its amazing, savage countenance. The works of spiritual, human culture never find in material things a support so secure that it would enable them to exist completely without the aid of human action and consciousness. When man's spiritual power weakens or recedes, the stratum of human reality in the world appears to blur and disappear, whereas man uncovers the original face of primordial nature in the world surrounding him and even in himself; and he then feels himself abandoned in a world strange and terrifying to him. He falls into true despair, severed from all sense, a sense which turned him from beast to man.

Human nature depends on an incessant effort to surpass the animality inherent in man and on rising above it through humaneness and man's role as a creator of values. Without this mission and without this effort of rising above his very self, man reverts, without deliverance, back to his animality – which portends his death.

Man and His Reality*

I once heard a paper by an eminent biologist concerning man's status on earth. One of the paper's main theses was the assertion that man was able to conquer nature to a greater extent than any other species of animal and that his exceptional status among living beings on earth is based precisely on this fact. I then entertained the question whether the unquestionably higher degree of man's dominion over nature, and for that very reason his greater independence of what happens in it, is really what distinguishes him from beasts in an essential way. This would perhaps be true only if the conception of man defined as *homo faber* had to be employed as the basis of this contrast. But such a conception does not indeed touch on what is essential for his humanity. Man's exceptional status in the world does, in fact, depend on something else, so that the fact of his domination over nature and beast is only a certain phenomenon which is, if not altogether derivative, still not the most important. I wish to share a few thoughts with the reader on this topic.

Man is distinguished from the beasts in that, among other things, he not only dominates nature within limits that are incomparably wider than those attainable by animals, and even transforms and adapts it to suit his needs and demands, but more importantly – and in this lies his essential feature – in that he creates for himself an entirely new reality or, one might say, *quasi*-reality. Once created, it becomes a significant constituent of the world surrounding him.

Man works the earth and cultivates plants, erects houses, builds roads and tracks, regulates rivers, etc. However, at least some animals – beavers, ants, termites – do the same sorts of things in their manner and on their scale, though certainly to a much lesser degree of perfection and universality. But, above and beyond these, man creates objects such as: works of art, scientific theories, metaphysical or theological systems, and languages to serve as the various means of preserving and conveying to others what had once been thought[1]; countries, public institutions (universities, for example); legal systems, money, etc. Thus, by

* This sketch is a radio address, aired in the Spring of 1939. I do not think that it contained anything drastically new, but it may serve to introduce the reader to that tiny segment of "man's reality" which consists of literary works of art. First printed in the periodical *Tydzień Polski*(Polish Week), I, no. 6, February 24, 1935.

cultivating and transmitting knowledge about his own past and about the past of works created by his predecessors, man creates a historical reality, owing to which the currently living generation becomes the continuation of already acomplished historical processes and events.

"To be sure", the reader will say, "but all this is only possible due to man's having succeeded in conquering nature and vanquishing the beasts which at one time continually threatened him. It is therefore this fact that ought to be regarded as decisive and essential for man."

I reply: there is no doubt that this fact at least facilitated man's creativity along the direction indicated. It does not appear so certain, however, that it made creativity altogether possible for him. For we could ask conversely whether it is not the fact of man's having created certain objects which had not previously existed in the world that made possible, or at least facilitated, the conquest of nature and struggle with the beasts. After all, with what did man once vanquish the animals? That he did not accomplish this simply by the strength of his limbs, but with the aid of tools seems highly probable. The invention of tools became at any rate a decisive factor in the battle between man and brutes. These tools were indeed at first only certain things found by man ready-made. However, having been used to perform specific tasks, these things became something entirely novel through this very function, something which had not been present in nature prior to man. They later became objects that were produced by man deliberately, in order to attain with their aid states of affairs that he deemed to his advantage. Also, these manufactured tools make up just a certain special case among the products of human work in general, especially since man was able to invent master-machines capable of producing other machines and tools with much greater precision than man was ever able to attain with the labour of his hands. But the interesting and essential fact is precisely that man was not satisfied with the invention of tools for the sole purpose of his purely biological functioning, but that already during 'prehistoric' times he began to create various objects that from a physico-biological point of view were of little or no use and yet were necessary to him and to his mental life, objects representing not only the manifestation of the discharge of certain of his spiritual energies, but at the same time also enriching enormously the world in which he lives. We already find the first works of painting on the walls of caves that man once inhabited, works that tell us a great deal about the good taste and the vital artistic needs of their creators.

It is not of paramount significance whether these products of human activity are all 'real' in the same sense as the world of 'nature' surrounding us. It may well be that arguments could be presented in favour of recognizing works of art, for example, or aesthetic objects, as 'real' in a sense different from that of, for example, the building (the museum) in which they are housed. It may be that some scholars would not agree to ascribe reality to works of art or (to take an example from another realm) to a sort of object like the Polish State or the Jagiellonian University – not even metaphorically. These are issues that are too difficult and complicated to discuss, or indeed resolve, here. It cannot, however, be denied that all the objects just enumerated do exist in some fashion, and go into making up the world in which we live and with which we comport daily. For let us imagine that suddenly all works of art were to vanish from this world, all scientific and philosophical theories, all countries, private and public institutions, etc., and that we would at the same time be unable to learn in any way about what once was in our own life and in the life of generations and nations which had already passed away. Would what would then remain be for us essentially this world in which we in fact live? Would it not be something tremendously more meagre, and different? And would not we ourselves have to change – to some extent degenerate – in order to be able to live in this impoverished world, and live in it in such a way as not to create new works of art after awhile, new sciences, new countries etc., – as not to return anew to a world in which alone we do not feel as strangers?

Would not the long chain of all our previous ways at once lose all sense, would it not become something entirely needless and without purpose, and at the same time something completely unintelligible? From this day on we would not read poems, go to the theatre, or listen to symphonies. We would carry on no disputes concerning literary movements and values; we would not spend years, sometimes decades, of our life on conducting laborious and subtle experiments in physics and elsewhere; we would not fight over so-called ideas, that is to say, over the truth or falsity of scientific or philosophical doctrines, the correctness or incorrectness of ethical or legal norms; we would not struggle for this or that social or national order; we would not give our finest efforts for the good and honour of the country whose citizens we are; we would not conform our conduct to the traditions and intentions of our predecessors or, to the contrary, would not clash with their ideas, with their world of art and their science; we would not feel at all as anyone's progeny, not as heirs of the goods and ideals of bygone generations. We would not do all these things that play such a decisive role in our life, because there would not be within the scope of our experience, according to this assumption, all those objects towards which our actions could turn. They would all vanish from our purview, and along with them everything that is good, beautiful, noble and true. And then would not whoever chose to continue fighting over legal ideals, for example, or over the values of this or that artistic movement, despite the nonexistence of the given objects, whoever would wish to be enthralled by (altogether non-existent) works of art, or defend the honour of his country or nation, would he not, under these circumstances, have to pass in our eyes (still truly 'ours'?) for someone mad?

And how different our life would then be – if it were to be at all human. Perhaps we would even be well off, have something to eat and wear and somewhere to live, perhaps we would have more convenient railroads and faster airplanes than thus far (though this is highly doubtful, for would we know how to do all this, and be able to do it, without science and art and all those things which were alleged to surpass the framework of the real world?), but would we then still be able to live like human beings? Would abundance of food, sensual pleasure and comfort, be enough to bind us to life to such an extent as to make it worth our while to bear its hardships, dangers and sufferings?[2]

What, in the final philosophical reckoning, *are* all these strange objects which somehow go into making up the world man lives in: are they reality or fiction? – that is a problem not so easily resolved.[3] But the very existence and sensibleness of this problem has at its foundation the assumption that in our daily affairs we somehow have dealings with many objects which by their very nature differ *toto coelo* from things and events existing in so-called 'nature'. It is also a fact that the domains of art, sciences, laws and technologies invented by us human beings, along with the historical reality we have created, have such a bearing on our life and so influence its course, that we ourselves change under the influence of having to do with this (according to some) *quasi*-reality; we are shaped by it, we acquire new character traits, new likes or dislikes, infatuations and objects of affection. From childhood we grow into a certain ready-found world of products of the human spirit. This world surrounds and influences us, moulding our body, our thoughts, feelings and desires, before we begin to transform it and augment it with new works. It makes us into the heirs of past generations; it is owing to it that we are not forlorn in the world, each one of us apart from others, that we have a common world of the products of mind (and of the bodily[4] functions that are guided by it); and for this reason we ourselves – man with man – grow together, to a lesser or greater extent, into a single human organism, as it were. And when, in turn, we become creators or co-creators of new works of art, new laws, new social or moral ideals, new history, new machines and devices, all this – as if in a backlash – returns to affect us. We live in a different world as a result, and we ourselves are different. Not only are our works offsprings of ours, but to a certain extent we become ourselves the progeny of these works and – once we have created them, and have to do with them – no longer know how to live and be such as we were when they were not yet around. For we change both bodily and spiritually under the impress of the world of works we have produced. Having railways and airplanes we are no longer able to walk the way our forefathers did. And our eyes are adapted to electric lights and microscopes. And we feel the ebb of time differently, and all movement, and life's tempo. And once we have listened to the works of Beethoven or Chopin, we no longer want to listen to a barrel-organ. When "Paradise Lost" or "The Love Song of J. Alfred Prufrock" or the lyrics of Verlaine or Rilke, dazzled us with their beauties, many a previously prized composition became dull because our artistic sensitivity had by then already been altered, and so had our criteria of poetic beauty. And if our works are of high value, beautiful, spiritually rich, high-minded and intelligent, then we ourselves become better for it; but if they bear the traces of evil, ugliness and impotence, sickness or dementia, then, under their influence we become worse, impoverished, weaker or sick. But it is when for some reason we do not know how to properly comprehend our own works (regardless of which realm of human reality they may belong to) and do them justice in our experience, when we do not measure up to their subtelty or intensity, to this or that perfection, that we feel how unavoidably we fall below our own level, our power, our deepest essence: we cease to be the human beings who had created them and who were worthy of them. We feel degraded, more degenerate; we regress to a certain extent toward the boundary at which the difference between ourselves and the brutes would be effaced.

And let us now ask: do we not come to be human beings who are radically different from the beasts, precisely because we have created some new reality out of the surrounding – more than that, out of *our* – world? And how diverse that reality is, for which the realm of so-called 'nature' is just a necessary substratum. Moreover, we differ from them not only by the gains we have made in the course of our evolution, but also through the losses we have suffered by living in a world different from theirs. We are human beings because we live in a certain sense 'beyond our means', because above and beyond what is necessary for sustaining our physiological life with its lesser or greater well-being, we create certain 'things' that are a luxury for that physiological life, but which are also indispensable for our wanting to bear the pleasures and sorrows of that life, and for doing homage to our inner dignity, without which we would be altogether unable to live. We are human beings because we surpass the biological conditions in which we have found ourselves, and build on their foundation a new, different world.

But let us take one more, decisive step: All those things we call values – such as goodness, beauty, truth, justice, etc. – are not found in the physico-biological substratum of our human world, but indeed emerge only in that superimposed reality we have created, a reality appropriate to man; or, at least – like goodness in the moral sense – these values become manifest through that reality, or demand its creation for their embodiment.[5] Man creates this reality with his utmost effort, sometimes with the toil and sacrifice of a lifetime, with the sheer quintessence of his genius. But had man simply done this for the sole purpose of accommodating his nature, of having an outlet and creating for himself the conditions of a pleasant spiritual existence, he would not yet thereby fulfill his most essential function, he would not yet, in his deepest core, measure up to his calling, to that which makes up his idea or essence, as man. He first attains to his genuine stature as a human being because, and only because, he creates a reality which manifests or embodies in itself the values of goodness, beauty, truth and law; because in his life, or at least in that in it which is of sole importance, he remains in the service of realizing values within the reality he has created; only thus does he attain to the mission that tells of his humanity: he becomes a man who mediates between what is merely 'nature' and what he can divine only crudely, as if in a reflection, through the values he has disclosed and embodied.

Man stands at the fringe of two worlds – one world out of which he originated and which he surpasses with the greatest exertion of the spirit, and the other, to which he approaches through his most prized creations – not being truly 'at home' in either. Wishing to balance himself on this fringe, continually fettered anew by the inertia of the physico-biological world and constrained by his nature in regard to his possibilities, while at the same time feeling the inadequacy and unresponsiveness of this fringe to his human essence, man draws from out of himself the power of creative living and surrounds himself with a new reality. It is this reality which first unveils for him a perspective onto entirely new dimensions of being; but in this new, presaged world he encounters forces that are just as alien to him as the world from which he comes, and which are on a level much higher than anything to which he will ever manage to reach. In this lies his special role in the world, and at the same time the source of his tragic, solitary struggle, his many defeats and his few, almost never decisive, victories.

Notes

1 It is likely that even some select species of animals have their 'language' of sorts – a system of signals, with the aid of which they communicate in communal life. Yet, as far as we know, no trace has been found among the beasts of the existence of *written* language, which first makes possible the fixation not only of literary works, but also, e.g., of public documents.

2 I wrote these words a few years before the war. Could there be a better confirmation of them than the experience brought on by the war? As soon as the cannons went silent in Poland in 1939, the Germans threw themselves into destroying everything that comprised our cultural achievement; they also tried to make it impossible for us to have any contact with our culture,

and to nullify all output of cultural works. They knew that the existence of this cultural world attests to our existence as a separate nation. And we preferred to risk imprisonment and persecution than consent to a non-productive, inhuman life.

[3] The situation is quite curious. Philosophically untrained readers will hold that I am needlessly 'breaking through an open door.' For who could possibly doubt the existence of all these products of man's activity? At the same time, however, these same readers, under the influence of psychologism and psychologistic relativism (which among Polish, academically trained people is still [1935] sustained as a special sort of *opinio communis*), will hold that these products are nothing other than certain human 'apparitions' or, more generally, something 'psychical'. But if all these objects were essentially 'psychical', they would be in ourselves, and not in the world around us. Yet, when we have to do with these objects in everyday living it seems to us that they make up one of the constituents of the surrounding world, and a constituent, at that, which is neither material nor psychical, but something of an entirely different nature, even though it appears within the framework of the material-psychical world (if we may put it that way). When we become aware of all this, and if at the same time we realize that we are generally inclined to ascribe real existence only to material objects and individual psychophysical entities, we will then also have to recognize that the existence of the products of human activity of the kind enumerated is not at all as self-evident as may appear to us in daily life, and that arguments need to be found which would confirm this existence, or deny it definitively. But these arguments ought to beware of one thing: of ascribing to these objects properties which are alien to them, and which are never ascribed to them in either pre-philosophical considerations or through the experience we gain by dealing with them. This is precisely what is always done in a psychologistic treatment of the products of man's culture.

[4] We do not meander in the world with a mind alone, and had we not had our sprite and nimble hands, and our keen, sensitive eyes and finely attuned ears, many of our works would not have come to be at all.

[5] This is not yet tantamount to saying that values are themselves created by man. To ask what their source is, or whether we can speak at all of their having been created, is an entirely new perspective of questioning which is no longer within the scope of the problem of man's essence. The only thing that is of crucial importance for man is that he is able to attain to that sphere of being which is comprised of values.

Man and Time*

We all live in time, and we know it. There are, however, two fundamentally different ways of experiencing time and ourselves in time. According to the first it seems that what 'truly' exists is *we ourselves*; time, on the other hand, is only something derivative and merely phenomenal (*erscheinungsmäßig*). But according to the second it is *time* and the *changes* occurring in it which make up the sole reality; we, on the other hand, are, as it were, subject to complete annihilation by these changes. At best we sustain ourselves in existence as a pure phenomenon, as a certain kind of phantom produced by the changes occurring in the present.

The extreme polarity of these experiences and their apparently equal claim to veracity makes them the ultimate (sometimes unarticulated) basis of mutually opposed metaphysical standpoints. Thus for example at the very beginning of European philosophy the view of Heraclitus on the one hand, and the metaphysics of the Eleatics on the other, have their origin in these experiences. In modern philosophy, the conflict between realism and transcendental idealism is a manifestation of this opposition. More detailed historical analyses could likewise show how two different experiences of time play their role in the particular views concerning time which have appeared in the course of the history of European philosophy. Yet, perhaps the difference between the two experiences of time is most acutely reflected in the problem of the essence of the self, in the conception of the human being in general, and makes this essence into the central problem of philosophy. Let us examine this matter in greater detail.

I

In the constant passage and incessant newness of time I continually feel myself to be *this same* human being and I live in the primordial sensation

* Parts I and II of this article comprise the content of my address at the IX. International Congress of Philosophy in Paris, in 1937, and were published, along with part III in vol. XLI (1938) of *Przegląd Filozoficzny*. They offered no solution at the time. Not until my further researches into the essence of time–carried out within the framework of my other work–did I arrive at a stage where I could (already during the War) write the conclusion (parts V and VI) of the piece.

that I shall remain myself in the future. My self-identity thereby designates two different matters: 1) that in the course of my life I am *one* individuum; 2) that in the course of that very life I *remain this same* human being, in *his full qualitatively invariant*, determinate *nature*. Both these issues are inseparably linked together. The following are capable of being discriminated, in direct experience, in the whole which I am: (a) changing, ever new conscious experiences; (b) variable psychic *states* and *processes*, as well as psychical[1] and physical *properties*; and (c) a certain completely unrepeatable and specific permanent *qualification* (*Qualifizierung*) which determines the whole of me as a human being. It is this qualification that I call my nature – thus, for each other person, e.g., Adam Mickiewicz or some Joe Doe, I call this qualification, in each case, his nature. All changes, continually new experiences, states and processes notwithstanding, this nature of mine appears immutable through the course of my whole life, and it is thanks to it that I have the feeling of always being myself. To put it differently: my having the feeling of being always myself means nothing other than that I feel myself to be a person constituted by this specific nature. The moment this nature would suffer change – for example in cases of so-called destructuration of consciousness – I would cease to have the feeling of being myself, the same self as I was yesterday. I would not even be able to recognize my own self from yesterday, nor to identify myself with it. I would have the feeling of being the self of my actual 'now', and my self of yesterday I would regard as someone *other* who could never be 'myself'.

Neither the very occurrence of changes in my psychic structure and in my body, even deep and multi-faceted ones, nor even the consciousness of such changes having taken place hinders me in the least in this feeling of being myself through the course of my entire life. To be sure, sometimes the effected changes of which I become aware are very important, and if indeed they occurred in the distant past it may happen that I become a stranger to myself, that I cease to be in solidarity with myself, that I set myself in opposition to myself and judge myself harshly, moreover, that I cease to understand my self from the past. But none of these phenomena in any way disturb my more or less distinctive feeling of being myself, of being the same as I once was.

Secondly: I as a human being (along with all my original and permanent, as well as changing, properties and states) am, and have the feeling of being, a real entity, real to a higher degree, as it were, than my experiences. That is to say, I am, in accordance with this feeling, a *lasting or abiding being*, whereas my experiences are merely *transient externalizations* or manifestations of me myself. I alone comprise the source and ultimate substratum of the experiences which on their side are something grounded in me, derived from me, which, in other words, are *my* experiences. Their passage and content are not in fact without influence on me, as a human being. They too are actual. But when I become aware of myself, or of something in myself, and as a result have an effect on and shape myself in this or that way, this happens not because certain life processes have transpired, but because I, as a human being, effect actions in a real mode. Surely, the fact that certain experiences occur in me has its real impact on me and on the further course of my life. That also my experiences – though derivative – are something real, is likewise manifested in this influence. But my action is not consumed in the experiencing itself, but also in attacking a certain actuality with my powers. And if, similarly, through my experiences I secure knowledge about other people, animals or events, if I am affected by their action or live together with them, and if through co-habitating I change, then this happens, once again, not because, or at least not primarily because, certain experiences have occurred in me but because certain of my real powers found their outlet through them. My conscious experiences merely comprise the mode of my living, a mode which does not contain everything that happens in me and in my life. I, as a human being, also appear to be independent of my conscious experiences in the sense that I can *be* even when they are not. After a period of being unconscious or after a dreamless sleep, I awake not only as the same human being that I was *prior* to falling asleep, but also as someone who existed *whilst* I was asleep (in a state of being unconscious). In a word, as a human being I am *transcendent* in relation to my experiences.[2] And precisely that which is transcendent with respect to them is what comprises my actual, 'true' being.

A certain special type of time-experience is closely related to this. Namely: whilst continually feeling myself to be the same human being, I at the same time in my innermost being feel myself to be *independent* of time; I do not feel threatened by its passage; it is as if I were not 'cognizant' of time and of the incessant passing of all actuality. I do not take time into account; I do not bother with it. No abstract *knowledge* about the constant passing of events in the world surrounding me, and in me myself, can in any way change the feeling that time is entirely without significance for me myself. For, it then appears that passing does not stem from the essence of time, but rather from the nature of *happening* (of becoming).

I, however, who am not a happening, but am something *existent, remain* in time. And although through its passage time forces out of actuality everything which is merely a happening, it can do nothing to *me myself*: it washes over me, as it were, leaves me undisturbed.[3]

And not I alone, as I believe, remain the same in time. It seems to me likewise with respect to other people that they, too, are continually the self-same individuals, though I do not at all thereby ignore what happens to them, nor that they change in this way or that as a result; and similarly with *things*: these same houses, streets and cities, yesterday and today, and these same pieces of old furniture surrounding me since my childhood years, known to me in their silence and passivity. I have grown accustomed to them in the same way as to old friends, whose aging I do not perceive for a long time when we see each other daily. Despite all events, occurrences and changes to which I am witness, the world seems to me to be one and identical and to remain the same, as do I in it. It is as if all changes wash over it, as if there were no time, as if it were only some phantom, a mere 'phenomenon'. This is how it seems to me. Furthermore: I apprehend myself and my environment to be such.

On first impression – in this type of experience – time is not anything which would exist separately in itself. It is at best some derivative phenomenon owing its existence to something else existing – some real being – and time, or better stated, the passage of time, manifests itself to me because this something is how it is in some special way. But this something is at the same time itself qualitatively indeterminate, even though always identical. In my original life-attitude I do not ponder on how to reconcile all of this; it seems natural to me that it is in fact so.

A certain relation to the time which is lived through by me stems from this type of experience. In a certain sense I feel myself to be master over it, I vanquish it. This is so, first of all, to the extent that what is past, what once had in fact really *occurred*, does not seem to me completely dead, is not entirely annihilated for me. One has the impression as if it were merely not present and as if it were becoming more and more distant from me. However, I can once again summon it 'toward myself' and animate it to some degree. Conceived *from the side* [from a standpoint outside the time in which we are entrenched] this 'toward myself' is strictly tantamount to 'toward myself *such as I feel myself to be in the actually lived-through present*'. However, within an experience of time of the presently discussed type, and so long as I do not extricate myself from the current of time (as when I try to reflect on it 'from the side'[4]), I do not, in speaking and thinking about myself and in feeling myself as myself, grasp my 'I' in its relation to and dependence on the time flowing away. Rather, I seem to myself in the flowing away of time as always the same, as if there were no time, as if it had no influence on me. So also the 'I' toward which I call forth past facts which were experienced by me once upon a time is not only the same in immediate experiencing (generally, as long as some catastrophe has not occurred meanwhile, which has changed me 'beyond recognition'), but is also in its nature the same as that 'I' which was once witness to the recalled facts.

I also live under a distinct weight of the past; I am bound by it to a greater or lesser degree. I bend what I do 'now' to adjust to events and occurrences, which, though they had passed, still *were*, and which, once having occurred and been revivified by memory, *weigh* on my present. Today, I act as I do because this or that had once *happened*, because, e.g., certain definite occurrences had taken place between myself and my friends or acquaintances. If the entire past were to vanish completely for me, I would be free in many respects in regard to which I feel constrained not only because this or that once happened, but because it still exists for me today in some remarkable way (though not in the same way as what happens *now*) – and exists for me even though I do not specifically recall it to myself in separate acts. I simply feel myself bound by, for example, obligations and promises once made. Likewise, deeds once performed by me (victories or defeats) obligate me toward myself. There is a certain special '*noblesse*' of my own past, '*qui m'oblige*' still today, just as there is a so-called 'curse of the past', an anathema of my culpabilities long ago perpetrated and past, yet still determining the course of my present life. Thus I (and other people) not only survive in time, but I moreover *conserve*, as it were, that which, as occurring in time, has passed, and which, in passing, was ousted from the actuality of existence and somehow returns into this actuality thanks to me. My past *is* in each instance of my present to such an extent that it requires a separate act in order to be liberated from its impress; as though what is past did not pass, as if there were no time.

Simultaneously, I also live in an almost constant orientation toward the future. I continually somehow plunge into it; I become intimately acquainted with it. My present is under the influence of a future which proclaims itself in some manner precisely because my plans reach into the future, because what I expect announces itself as something that *will arrive*, that *will happen* – and this frequently *despite*, or *independently* of, my will. What is in the future influences me and can transform me already *now*, and sometimes even when it does *not* depend on me. What is future (better: my future) *is* now, though it is not yet itself present, but only, 'awaits' me or ('waits') for me. To be sure: only my expectations, hopes, apprehensions or fears of what I anticipate exist 'now' *actualiter*; what will be does not yet exist *actualiter*, but it nevertheless becomes an influential factor in my life, on my actual state, on my plans and decisions, and even on me myself, by announcing itself as something which will become actuality with certainty, or with only a lesser or greater degree of probability.

Hence, I overcome time by living naturally and straightforwardly (*ursprünglich*), so that *I do not feel restricted* by the boundaries of the present, by constantly *crossing over* them. I, who am transcendent in relation to my fleeting conscious experiences, constantly transcend what exists in each instant of the present, as if not only what is present exists in some manner, but also what is past and future. In this, indeed, the phenomenal (*erscheinungsmäßig*) character of time manifests itself: it has the kind of appearance-mode that enables me to meander over an actuality which is, as it were, all-pervasively present.

II

There is, however, another way of experiencing time, where time appears in a radically different manner. This way of experiencing time also leads to a wholly different conception of me myself. I arrive at this experience along two paths: 1) by becoming aware of the destructive role that time has for my existence; 2) by arriving at the conviction that as a person I am myself constituted only in multifarious temporal perspectives of experiences.

The first path leads through the apprehension of the fragility of all actual being, that is, through becoming aware of the fact that whatever is actual can, the instant it has come to exist, just as well cease to be. For, *the existence of what is actual does not follow from its essence, and is not necessary*. The existence of what is actual – and therefore of me myself – always seems to be merely some gift of good grace, since that which is real is always conditioned in its being and qualitative endowment by something else, irrespective of what that something else might be. By the same token, it can always be annihilated by withdrawing the conditioning object or state of affairs.

Not every epoch grasps in a direct experience the conditionality and contingency of everything actual. And not all of us today realize it; and even if we do, we are not aware of it throughout the span of our life. Only when we are witness to how the powers which appeared immutable fall into ruin, how human works which manifested the genius of the human spirit through generations nonetheless inescapably age with the passage of time and cannot be revived, how values which have guided a succession of generations some day turn out to be a deception after all and when, finally, we discover the possibility of non-existence within ourselves – only then do we see that this lasting being, which we had appeared to ourselves to be is after all transient and infirm and in its innermost core *demands* some *support*, some foothold. Then, we also discover that everything actual (we ourselves included) comprises, as if by sheer accident, only the filling out of some ever new temporal phase and that it has room to exist, as it were, only in a limited period of time. Then we finally know that it is not we who are the masters of time, but that time rules over us: what we do and how we try to mould ourselves has no ultimate significance – time goes by, and we age in it and pass, forlorn, to its ebb. For the moment the possibility of the non-existence of what is actual, as well as the fact of the destruction of real objects, unveils itself to us directly; the *essence* of time also shows itself, as it seems – an essence which constrains everything temporal to being in the present, and at the same time does not allow what is present to *endure*, since it ousts it from being into the past and non-being, through a continually new present.

Irrespective, therefore, of how much we transcend every instance of our present and consider ourselves as beings who abide and are independent of time, we always find ourselves as if on the edge between two abysses of non-being. The present, instead of being a phase which is univocally determined by its filling out, is transformed into a *punctual* 'now' devoid of any qualities, which can contain nothing within itself since it has no extension whatever.

What, indeed, are *we ourselves* in this ever new 'now' about which Bergson once said that even it 'is' not, since it continually becomes and, once having become, ceases to exist? Can we still be something that exists *enduringly* in this incessant passage of continually new presents, something which would be *transcendent* in relation to the passing experiences and which, as an ego always determined by its nature, would comprise the ultimate basis of these experiences?

This is (or seems) impossible for the presently considered experience of time, since no real being can exist which would be independent of time and would overcome the non-being of past and future. If this experience of time had its full legitimacy (*Rechtmäßigkeit*), then we would have to *identify* ourselves, it seems, either with ever new phases of conscious experience, which under these conditions we have become accustomed to calling 'pure', or with the so-called 'pure ego', whose existence and full qualitative endowment is exhausted in possessing experiences. (See, e.g., E. Husserl, *Ideen zu einer reinen Phänomenologie*.) And under these conditions this pure 'transcendental ego' would also have to be conceived as a present ego which continually originates itself anew.

We may concede that in considerations of a transcendental theory of knowledge it may be necessary to resort to such a transcendental, traitless ego as an ultimate and indubitable being. It is no less true, however, that as a human being I cannot identify myself with that pure ego, nor can I be reduced to it (about which even the transcendentalists agree). But in that case, if the experience of time just sketched were fully and finally legitimate, we would have to agree that I, as a human being, do not exist at all, though it may be true that the pure ego (the subject) exists.

I am not, however, as easily prepared to admit that I, as a human being, do not exist at all. In the face of an eternally fluid time which constrains being to the actual present, I therefore appeal to the invariant qualification (*Qualifizierung*) of me myself, to my nature, which comprises the basis of my identity through ceaseless changes. Certainly, one might say; but what is that *invariant ego*? It seemed to me that I know what it is – through an original, immediate sensation. But this will not here suffice. For now I stand before two different, incongruous experiences of time, the second of which also casts in doubt the way of understanding our ego, a way which seems natural on the basis of the first manner of experiencing time. Thus I must now clearly and distinctly *know* what my ego is, and I must also know how to *determine* exactly what it is on the basis of a distinct experience of me myself. But how do I experience my very self; what is the final, immutable basis for grasping my unique, identical ego?

When I ponder this matter I realize that this ego in its qualification, as well as in immediate cognition, is itself entwined in time. What I now *am* is – as I discern in an immediate sensation, without asking for substantiation – unambiguously determined by everything that I was before and that has affected me heretofore. But I will not know about what I am now until the present now belongs to the *past*, hence, when I will no longer be what I now am. If I *now* feel myself to be an ego, endowed in its personal being with determinate properties, this happens only because I have secured for myself certain knowledge about myself as I was in the more or less distant past, and because I apprehend myself in the present under the aspect of a *past* qualitative endowment of my ego. Thus, I apprehend myself as I was in the past, either in the *recollection* of everything through which my ego manifests itself in its various kinds of properties, or in the vivid *remembering* ('preserving in memory') of the immediate, not yet decayed past. Both modes of knowing about the past, however, exhibit it to me – as I tried to show elsewhere[5] – 'in foreshortenings' of temporal perspective. What is past takes on a countenance, in the past, which deforms it in a necessary and lawfully governed manner: what once belonged to the present does not show itself to me in every detail in my immediate knowledge of the past in that form which it once had as something present, but shows itself through transformations and aspects which are dependent on the relevant *type* of knowledge about the past, and which have their cognitive value only within the associated *framework*. It is thereby not only a question of the kinds of 'shifts', the shortenings or lengthenings of temporal phases and of the processes taking place in them, and not only of a different look of the dynamic character of something which is happening or, finally, of the greater or lesser *distance* at which what I recall stands from me, and therewith of its greater or lesser distinctness; what is above all at issue is that what was once present *shows* itself as past through *other properties*, sometimes even through an *essence* other than that which was its own, and proper to it, in the past present. And this not due to incidental considerations, such as blunders or simple deceptions of recall, which, by the way, are also possible; it is a consequence of necessary transformations of temporal perspective. What in a bygone present *was* love may necessarily unveil itself in knowledge about the past as a 'false' pseudo-love, if certain facts attesting to this have been ascertained in the period of time between its occurring and the moment of my recall; what in the past present was a defeat and flight from threatening dangers sometimes assumes, in a recalled past, the Gestalt of inner victory; what in our earlier life was extremely important and dominant over us, turns out to be an insignificant event when juxtaposed against our later life – the latter, likewise, disclosed through knowledge about our past, etc. My ego also assumes properties and characteristic features with regard to all these aspects which differ from those which characterized it in a past present. And these other, new features now have for me the guise of a genuine actuality.

In short: the 'I' which I once was, and which I believe myself still to be, assumes a Gestalt *dependent* on the content of each successive instance of my 'now', and one that is appropriately adapted to this content. I apprehend myself under this relative aspect of temporal perspective as a human being who still exists at this moment and who is qualified accordingly. Even when I oppose myself to my past ego, for example in condemning 'myself' and my past, this opposition, too, is not without influence on the content of my feeling of being myself in the present – I may feel myself to be considerably better and more dignified precisely because I set myself against, and condemn, myself. But, that I grasp my past self in aspects of temporal perspective that are relative to the actual present, and that, on the other hand, I grasp myself in the actual present only in conjunction with such a perspectivally transformed self, considered as something real – even this I know only from the perspective of a *later* present, from a perspective which is once again relative to this new present. Who, therefore, am I through all these changes and varying temporal perspectives? What is this ego which despite everything transcends all these changes and perspectives, and which despite the crampedness of the present and of the two chasms of non-being nevertheless appears to endure and exist. Is it, in the last reckoning, nothing other than a mere *phantom*, an *apparition* created by my living in the present and by my knowledge of the past with its multifarious aspects of temporal perspective? And even though these aspects refer, in their content, to an ego that is continually one and the same, is this not in fact a merely illusory, though perhaps necessary, semblance? And perhaps the ego is (as the transcendental idealists claim) essentially nothing other than merely an experiential process limited to the present, which incessantly fancies forth an apparition of me myself – an apparition of that other 'I' which would transcend the present, and which would be determined by the same nature and endure despite all changes and constraints of time?

For this reason, Descartes' words are alive and valid even today: "*Hoc pronuntiatum, ego sum, ego existo, quoties a me profertur, vel mente concipitur, necessario esse verum, Nondum vero satis intelligo, quis nam sim ego ille, qui iam necessario sum* ..." But still, the problem of the essence of our ego as a human being living in time needs to be posed anew on the basis of the different experiences of time, and new solutions of it need to be sought.

III

An appeal, therefore, to the way in which the constitution of my self is accomplished for me against the background of the second experience of time, also does not allow us a resolution of the difficulty into which the existence of two dissimilar, incompatible experiences of time had landed us. For a contemplation of how my 'I' is constituted for me indeed strongly undermines my belief that I exist as a human being who transcends his actual experiences and his actual present. But at the same time this contemplation is not capable of banishing this belief entirely, nor of working up in me the conviction that this way of learning about me myself and about the constituting of my human ego (rules out) the existence of this ego in itself and its being such as it represents itself to me in experience. Thus, all sources of knowledge about oneself need to be scrupulously examined, and we need to consider whether and within what limits the results of this knowledge are capable of assuring us about the existence and the properties of we ourselves as people transcending experience. It is a problem for the solution of which we are as yet unprepared. For no matter how much effort has been expended in the history of European epistemology upon the investigation of the process of sensory perception and of the cognitive results acquired on its basis, still, by strange coincidence, the problem of how we cognize our own selves continues to lie fallow. Today, we do not even have the essential beginnings of a theory of inner experience, since it is difficult to regard as such a beginning a small number of scant generalities on the topic of so-called inner perception which can be found in the literature. I do not however intend to deal with this matter here in any greater detail. On the other hand I do still want to point out some consequences which suggest themselves to us on the basis of the second of the experiences of time presented here and the views already sketched out. For these consequences may cast a certain light on the problem of the existence and essence of the human ego, so strongly linked with the experience of time.

How does this come about? By living within time we begin to seem to ourselves as a mere intentional product of experiences in the present. The experience of time unveils to us two voids of non-being: the annihilation of what once was and the non-existence of what is yet to be. The present is on the boundary of these two voids. But as St. Augustine already emphasizes, it is not merely on the boundary: it is itself the boundary. It is not a phase, but a sharp cut. By what? By something which is not there (*ist nicht da*). This and only this boundary, this punctual section is supposed to be that which exists. And at the same time there is supposed to fit in this very sharp cut not only our actual life, (and our human ego [*Ichlichkeit*] is supposed to achieve constitution in it), but also all those complex and mutually conditioned processes which, creating a variety of perspectives, are somehow supposed to simulate my ego which, in its existence and qualitative endowment, transcends both the course of conscious experience itself and my actual present. That conscious living-through that exists in the boundary cut of the present, however, would have to effect still more, as has been repeatedly claimed from St. Augustine to Husserl. For in it would have to lie also the source of the constitution of time itself; hence, not only of the present but also of both past and future. If, however, it were to be true (and of this I am of course not yet convinced, but it needs to be presupposed for our further arguments) that my human ego, conceived as an abiding being that transcends the present and that somehow evades annihilation in the past, is to be merely a certain kind of *fictum* of consciousness-like processes, then why should the past itself and the future not be the *same* kind of *fictum*, and thereby also that ceaseless passing, the transformation from the non-being of the future into a momentary actuality and of the latter in turn into non-being? Putting it differently, why should time itself, under these conditions, not be a purely intentional product of particular consciousness-like processes, a product to which nothing corresponds, as we say, "in actuality"? There have been several attempts in the history of European philosophy to realize this thought, – in several different ways, for example in the work of Kant who, as we know, saw in time only a form of intuition (or, stated differently, a certain transcendental product of an 'inner sense'); or in that form in which Husserl attempted it, according to which time is constituted in a system of retentions; or even in the manner of Bergson, according to whom homogeneous time is only a certain formal schema which is relative to the exigencies of acting. One may finally say that the form of time described by me, as correlate of the first of the experiences distinguished here, is also nothing other than merely such a purely intentional product of this experience.

I do not want to engage here in a critique of these varied views; I mention them only in order to underscore the fact that in the theoretical situation in which we find ourselves it is ultimately quite irrelevant how we shall conceive 'time', which is supposed to be one or another kind of *fictum*-product of the experiences contained in the momentary present. The only essential question is: how would it be possible for these experiences, which are so complex and which lead to the constitution of multifarious transcendent formations, including the past and the future, to occur in the crampedness of the momentary present? Could existence be adduced to these experiences under the given circumstances? Should we not rather concede that they do not occur at all? For could anything *be* – it makes no difference whether it be experiences or something that would transcend them – which would, in the *same* instant in which it becomes, simultaneously *cease to be* at that same instant which is only supposed to be a punctual boundary between two non-beings? How can anything whatever be somehow *qualified*, if this qualification arises and vanishes 'simultaneously', if it cannot *endure* as *the same*?

If on the contrary we had to agree that experiences exist, and that time – and in particular the past – is to be first constituted in them, would we not at the same time have to admit that each of these experiences must, as *one and the same*, reach *beyond* that 'punctual' now, that a continuum of such punctual nows must *conserve* itself *as one and the same*, and thereby in its being step beyond, transcend *each* of those 'punctual' nows and endure somehow, in spite of the punctual appearance and disappearance of each of them? But in that case, should we not rather relinquish conceiving the present as a 'cut', a 'boundary', or a 'temporal point' and say (as has been attempted more than once) that there is nothing of this kind? Such a *punctual* now does not emerge at all in concrete experience. Rather, it is a purely theoretical conception which is suggested to us on the one hand by the second of the discussed ways of experiencing time and on the other hand by an understanding of time as, to use Bergson's words, a point-continuum.

But if we concede that the present is not a punctual boundary between the non-being of the past and the non-being of the future, should we not place in doubt that experience of time in which this non-being is unveiled to us? We could certainly never accept that the 'past present' continues to exist in *the same way* as it once had as the present present (and similarly with reference to the future). But do we have to admit only this *one* mode of being – and precisely that one which is proper to being in the actual present?

There is, however, a still further possibility which presents itself. Namely, if we concede that the experiences in which the constitution of time and of other transcendent formations is to be accomplished must themselves transcend the punctual present then, having at the same time accepted that the present *is* a punctual boundary between past and

and future, we should have to posit that this punctuality of the present in no way lays to waste the existence and identity of the experiences which transcend the present. But in that case, would we not have to posit that the punctuality of the present is similarly 'powerless' over against the being and qualifications of other transcendents, and in particular against my human ego, which according to the first experience is supposed to overcome time?

To forestall our making any decisive step prematurely, let us not resolve how things ultimately stand with these issues. Better that we ponder over yet another matter. If past and future are nothing other than *non-being*, then to conceive of what is as 'present' loses all sense. To speak of 'the present' makes sense only when we agree that the past and the future are not simple, total non-being, but rather that they are special forms or modes of existing which differ specifically from being in the actual present. Otherwise, we should speak only of being and non-being, and time vanishes altogether from the purview of consideration.

Let us suppose once more, however, that past and future were to be only intentional products of experiences belonging to the now and, at the same time, that both are pure non-being. The question then arises, why we should ascribe an absolute character to precisely *this* product, in contrast to other, presumably also merely intentional products of experiences belonging to the now; that is to say, why should we assert that this pure non-being comprises a state of affairs independent of the operations of consciousness? Should we not rather consequently concede that also this entire void of non-being of the past and the future is merely a certain intentional *fictum*, i.e., that there 'truly' *is no such void*? And is not the whole matter then reversed? Should we not then say that living on the sharp edge of two non-beings is just a singular kind of illusion stemming from a special way of living through experiences, which illusion, by the way, is neither necessary nor unique? Should we then not say that things are 'really' completely otherwise? But in that case should we not assign greater weight to the first of the two different experiences of time, and thereby incline toward the view that the human ego is not a simple intentional product of a certain way of living through experiences, but something in principle dissimilar from this?

I do not want to deliberate upon all of these questions here. Having animated the problem itself, I believe that in order to come closer to a solution of it, many different matters still need to be thought through and that what is given in experience as well as the progress of these experiences need to be analyzed in greater detail. At present my only thesis is that there are two different experiences of time, as described above, and that a tight bond obtains between them and the problem of the essence and existence of our personality.

IV

There are also, however, certain practical consequences of living in the second experience of time. The following are the most important of these:

Immersed in time, the human being, eternally longing for himself as for a being immune to time, feels himself threatened by his passing on and by the unknown nothingness of tomorrow. Not having made himself aware of this, he wants to flee from himself, to forget about himself. He tries not to know that he passes on inescapably, that with each instant he nears his end, like an ember which is burning itself out. He 'kills time': he contrives ways of occupying himself so as to 'fill' time, and he concentrates his total attention on work which he could do without. In order not to feel forlorn and a stranger in the world, he creates for himself the fiction of being obligated toward something which is in fact not there, something which is unimportant, but which he himself had created for himself and to which, without admitting it, he confers the semblance of importance and existence. He neglects himself in order to serve something else. Instead of *being* by remaining with himself, by grasping himself through every pain and every joy, and through every effort and victory, he abandons himself irrevocably. He does not know how much he loses. He thinks he is building a world around himself and shaping himself in this world, but meanwhile he is only quelling his own fear of the void which threatens him. And for this reason he is today already becoming ever emptier.

And when one day the circumstances in which he finds himself demand of him a decision that bears no reference to ready-made models, external prescriptions or norms, but rather a decision made according to his own knowledge, grown out of his own deliberate effort, then he suddenly returns to himself and feels like a child–incompetent and stupid. He finds a void where he expected to encounter himself; he lacks not only the power to resist, but even the capacity of being transported, the capability of being moved and enraptured. And then he also discovers with surprise that despite the eternal passage of time, despite continually finding himself between what no longer is and what has not yet come about, he could have *remained* himself in the course of the changes, annihilations and originations had he only known how to defy the destroyer 'time' and had he not engrossed himself in a life 'beyond himself'.

Sometimes a human being lost in time tries to preserve himself by enclosing himself in his work. He falls prey to the misguided belief, born of the yearning for permanent being, that only he himself, suspended on the boundary between two non-beings, passes on; that only he himself cannot truly *be*; that the world surrounding him, on the other hand is immune to time, endures, exists. He then tries to embed his work – work in the fields of art, or science, or technical work – in this world which is presumably independent of time, and to embody in it himself, or that which he considers best in himself: his deepest thought, his purest feeling, his ideals.[6] All may still be well so long as he does not see through the fact that he will neither succeed in embodying himself in this work nor manage to make it permanent. He situates his works in reality only in the historical course of time and submits them to the train of incessant and irreversible transformations in which they sooner or later age and decay, or become mute. When, some day, he comprehends this, then he will also understand that he has sacrificed his life in vain to the pursuit of an illusion.

And sometimes man strives to preserve himself in a still different way: he lives in the conviction that he and his deeds and works of today will some day remain for others in the future in the same way as he, with the power of his responsiveness and style of life, makes the already past past enduring and current. But in order to make it lasting and his own, similar to himself, he forgets or tries to forget about the still more removed, more distant, past as if it did not exist at all. For this reason (apparently) he extracts from the torrent of time what he counts as belonging to his present, to his 'today'. He then says: 'today's' people, 'today's' art, 'today's' science. Those 'remote' ages, peoples, works, cultures of old which no longer belong to 'us' do not count for him any more 'today'. They are not there. He does not feel as their descendant or successor. He prizes only *his own* age, *his own* achievements, *his own* works. He forgets that man has many times already attained the same cultural peaks and, having attained them, has once again left them behind, passed on. He lives with a steadily attendant belief that sometime in the darkness of the past there was at most a preparation, merely beginnings, that there was as yet no one like himself who would be (or only feel himself to be?) the procurer, the culminator or the epitome of a culture which would be destined to *remain*. He lives beyond time. And he forgets that on his tombs, on the ashes of his culture, about which some day no one will any longer know anything, *others* will build their works.

The boundedness of historical time and the extendedness of 'our' epoch, the epoch of 'today'; the belief that only our culture and ourselves possess a singular value or maturity – all this germinates from the same source: from man's desire to escape his forlornness in time, from eternal passing.

But all these attempts at killing time, at overcoming or veiling it are incapable of annihilating the knowledge which above and beyond everything flickers in man (living on the basis of this experience of time), that he is losing himself in time. On the contrary. This knowledge, or rather this feeling, is the source of an ever renewed unrest and of man's repeated attempt at fleeing from himself. This unrest will surely be allayed by whoever feels in himself the traces of a being which is not subject to the passage of time. In order to discover these traces in oneself one needs to know how to *remain with oneself* without fear of being lost in time and without falling prey to the semblance of being a thing in the world. To remain with oneself, however, means not only to enhance the self-knowledge of one's own ego on its various levels, but moreover *to have oneself at one's command* and, in skirmishes with the adversities of fortune, with oneself and with life's problems, to shape *one's own self* as a continually growing inner power; to trust oneself and one's own existence.

Then also the countenance of time alters. It becomes only an opportunity that allows man to ground his spirit in himself.

V

But the following thought, which may contribute toward clarifying the matter, still obtrudes:

There are my free and responsible deeds which I perform in life's difficult moments – sometimes in the face of death – and which spring forth from the deepest interior of the ego, as it has become in the past and sustains itself to this day, to the moment of the deed. These deeds can be accomplished only insofar as I, who have previously become as I am, remain such to this day. From this strength engendered in the past, and accumulated from the beliefs which I fostered, from the attachments with which I lived and from the desires which I tried to realize, is born the power which must be *alive* in me if I am to succeed in accomplishing the deed. In my innermost essence, which at any rate is not ordinarily manifest to me and which finds its outlet in this deed, I must *remain* such as I have become in the past; and time, despite all the changes which it evokes in me, can do nothing to me, is powerless in the face of my deepest essence, runs over me like water. And there are such deeds of mine, the actuality of which attests to the actuality of my abiding ego.

What are the limits of remaining oneself in time; how long can I be 'young'? Whether I am, or can be, *entirely* independent of time or independent only within certain limits, these are already different, further questions, which depend in turn on other questions. But the fundamental possibility of overcoming time is given by the fact of such free deeds of mine, accomplished in full awareness of the responsibility for them that weighs upon me, deeds sometimes accomplished against the greatest obstacles and under the menace of suffering the most dire consequences, and yet performed out of a deep conviction that only they can protect me from an extermination of my inner unity, from a breakdown through the loss of faith in myself, in the ultimate basis of all living. My ego, the durability of my existence, manifests itself in such deeds. Their performance simultaneously *enhances* my powers, shapes me for the future and *makes me independent of time*. Its passage becomes insignificant to me to a higher degree than it was prior to accomplishing the deed. (There are also other deeds of mine, likewise positive, which, however, 'wear me down', which usurp my powers. But it is not time, not the passage of days which thereby annihilate me; it is I myself who 'burns out' through these deeds. That is a perspective on a new set of problems, which I must waive here).

To be sure – and here is certainly a source for various new difficulties – such a representation of the matter opens up a perspective upon a whole gamut of variations of my attitude or of the relation of my ego toward time. I can behave variously in life, proceed variously; for example in such a way that 'with time' I *succumb* to the action of time, that I become subject to destruction by its passage. If I am too weak, if I do not measure up to the task of correctly solving the problems which life poses before me, *practical* problems which demand certain *moral* resolutions and decisions, if I do not know how to 'collect' myself, if I 'lose' myself in the insignificance of life's everyday trivia, if I allow myself to be 'effaced' by the various trivial adversities of living, if I 'squander' my powers on worthless matters or spend myself in a deceptive pursuit after illusory values, if I am inwardly a coward or a lazy so-and-so who does not feel like expending any effort, who prefers to lie in langour, to persist in indolence instead of forging ahead through effort and exposure to dangers, toil and perseverance through fear and suffering, if, finally, *I betray myself* – then I slowly *disintegrate in time.* Then, its passage alone destroys me; 'from day to day' I become increasingly 'nothing'.

All this can have various degrees and modes, so that consequently there are not only differing *experiences of time*, but also, if one may put it so, different variants of *time itself*, correlative to the different modes of my living and conduct. And in fact in this connection new theoretical difficulties and quandaries emerge. For, *different times* would have to be accepted *as the different modes of the enduring of psychic subjects*, or at least as different *correlates* of man's ways of enduring and behaving. But on the other hand it does not seem as if man could play such an important role in reality, could have such power over it, that different times could actually correspond to him *realiter*. And so the most obvious thing to do would be to accept only *one world time* for everyone and everything.

It may be that this whole train of thought ultimately comes from Bergson, although this only occurred to me after I had already thought it.

Still, the direction of the solution would be the reverse of Bergson's: the free deed would confirm the existence of time according to the first experience, which Bergson would rather consider as corresponding only to a certain kind of *fictum*, not to a 'real duration'. The description of the given in either of the two experiences of time does not accord for me with what Bergson says about time and duration. But even if it were true that the attempt at a solution just presented should derive from Bergson, I would still have to say that, until now, I had not really understood Bergson's thought (in *Les données immédiates de la conscience*) and that I had arrived at this not through an analysis of Bergson's texts, not through theoretical reflection, but through a sudden discerning in the reality of my own life, of what might serve as a key to the solution of the problem – though these initial flashes still have to be elaborated in greater detail.

The essential thought in all this is that time is a *derivative* phenomenon, *dependent* on the behaviour of the human person and, more generally, of what exists. Its form or mode, if this were true, would be a *manifestation* of the mode of being of that which exists. But at the same time, if the above thoughts were correct, there would also be the influence of time, of its passage, on what exists, and in particular on the inner cohesion and distinctness of man, on his inner power, on what ultimately matters in reality. Time, as something derived, would at the same time be something before which one would need to defend oneself, even though it is not always possible to do so. It would then certainly not be, as Kant, for example, would have it, a pure *form* of experience, but a certain real force, as it were, within the realm of what is actual. At the same time, however, it would not and could not be something *separate, alongside* of what exists in the actual world; it would have to be something which settles over what exists, and which at the same time comprehends it in some peculiar way so that what exists *is in time*. And it would be different depending on how that which exists is, how it behaves, lives, how it is squandered or concentrated and strengthened in itself. *How* it would differ is already a matter to be considered on its own.

VI

With all this, this whole thought – that through my free deed I persist in time as the same, hence, that the passage of time does not annihilate me – can be posited only insofar as the ego, my person, is not the same as the stream of consciousness, as the course of ever new experiences incessantly flowing by and perishing with no essential trace, only, therefore, insofar as consciousness is merely an *outlet* for my ego, merely a *manifestation* of myself. Who am I – Descartes' question returns once more – who persist in time, who shape myself in it by my deeds, or fall apart as soon as I release the tension of inner exertion as soon as I give myself over even for an instant to the vicissitudes of fate without making an effort to maintain a grip on myself? Who am I, who hide somewhere behind my experiences and yet live within them, find an outlet in them, attain to an expressiveness of my being through them, develop myself through them? Who am I, not that chunk of flesh and bones, but I, the acting *human being* grown out of my blood and bones?

Having once arisen, as a result of whatever forces and on whatever kind of basis, I am a power which magnifies itself, develops, and outgrows itself – if it is able to collect itself rather than to become dispersed in tiny moments of suffering or submission to pleasure. I am a power – living in a body and making use of it – which bears the tracks of this body on itself and is sometimes subject to its action. But at the same time, once having subjugated this body, this power turns all its possibilities toward enhancing itself. I am a power which, once having been cast into a world alien to me, makes this world its own and creates new works – indispensable for its living – in addition to what it encounters. I am a power which wants to fix itself in permanence – in itself, in its works, in everything which it meets – feeling that a single moment of relaxation or forgetfulness suffices to shatter itself, to forsake or annihilate itself. I am a power which longingly envisions for itself the greatest treasures of rapture and happiness and aspires to actualize them, but is ready to renounce them all for the mere capacity to perdure. I am a power which survives the adversities of fortune when it feels and knows that through its free deed it will elicit out of non-being what will remain when it itself has already burnt out in the struggle. I am a power which wants to be free. And it will even sacrifice for freedom its continuing to exist. But everywhere living under the stress of other forces it finds the seeds of bondage within itself, should it relax or neglect its efforts. And it will lose its freedom if it becomes attached to itself. It can last and be free only when it voluntarily gives itself over to the creation of goodness, beauty, and truth. Only then does it exist.

Notes

[1] According to accepted terminology, the expressions "conscious experience" and "psychic state" are used interchangeably or synonymously. As is apparent from my manner of expression here, I employ these expressions with significations which imply the mutual exclusion of their domains: no psychical state or process is a conscious experience, and conversely. Conscious experiences (though not in every case) only *manifest* psychical states

and processes (e.g. a state of inner breakdown or of concentration, the process of the growth of a man's inner strength, and the like). We cannot go deeper into this.

2 This term has become ambiguous as a result of various historical influences, and can give cause for misunderstandings. I employ it here exclusively in the sense that whatever is transcendent with respect to a conscious experience comprises no element or moment of that experience. This does not at all mean, as Kant believes, that what is transcendent with respect to an experience is inaccessible to cognition.

3 In connection with this, two different kinds of time, as it were, have been distinguished by the Scholastics since St. Thomas: the time of processes and the duration of substances.

4 This 'looking from the side' can also be an intervention into the course of experiences of a second and different manner of experiencing time.

5 See, *The Cognition of the Literary Work of Art*, ch. II. Vivid memory should not be identified with the so-called retention about which Husserl speaks, nor with the so-called *souvenir du present* which Bergson considers.

6 P. Valéry's or Lavelle's conception of art, for example, grows out of this substratum. It is the correlate of the attitude to life sketched above and of a one-sided commitment to only one experience of time. Then art *appears* to be a conquest of time. But it does not follow from this that it really is such. Its essence and sense in human life is something quite distinct.

On Responsibility
Its Ontic Foundations*

I

Main Thesis of the Study

The problem of responsibility has heretofore been treated primarily as a special problem of ethics, without any more precise investigation of its wider contexts. The main contention of the present discussion is that this is insufficient and that other underlying factual matters (*Tatbestände*), that lead into deeper problems, have to be taken into account before we can discover the conditions under which one can speak of responsibility in a meaningful way. It also seems that responsibility comes up in realms other than the moral. Moral responsibility is only a certain special case. Thus, the range of cases and examples to be taken into consideration has to be expanded.

II

Differentiation of Various Situations Involving Responsibility

To begin with, we need to distinguish four different situations in which the phenomenon of responsibility emerges:
Someone

1. *bears* responsibility for something or, differently put, *is* responsible for something,
2. *assumes* responsibility for something,
3. is *called* to account[1] for something,
4. *acts* responsibly.

The distinctiveness of the first three situations is demonstrated in the first place by their factual independence of each other, although determinate interconnections of sense undoubtedly obtain between them. One can be

* This treatise is based on a paper read at the XIV. International Congress of Philosophy in Vienna on September 4, 1968. It has been published in a German version as *Über die Verantwortung. Ihre ontischen Fundamente*, Stuttgart, Reclam, 1970.

responsible but neither be called to account, nor assume responsibility ("take it upon oneself", as Nicolai Hartmann puts it). And conversely, one can be called to account for something without being in fact responsible for it. One can also factually assume responsibility for something, without being actually responsible for it. Given that someone is responsible for something, he should both assume responsibility and be called to account for it. If one does not assume responsibility, or even evades doing so, despite the fact that one is responsible for something, then one is (also) responsible for behaving in such an [irresponsible] manner. But even the very assumption of responsibility for something that one is not responsible for appears to fall under the proviso of responsibility. Still, an essential interconnection of sense appears to obtain between these factual states of affairs, irrespective of their mutual independence in fact. Hence, this likewise remains a problem to be clarified.

III

Bearing Responsibility

The bearing of responsibility is a factual state of affairs which is somehow automatically imposed on someone who performs a determinate kind of deed. We *become* responsible for the deed as soon as it has been undertaken and performed, and we continue to *remain* responsible for it, whether we want to or not. Responsibility *burdens* the agent. It remains to clarify on what this 'burden' depends, and why it issues of itself (*von selbst*) out of the deed performed. What is essential is that the agent can indeed 'relieve' himself of this burden with a new deed of an appropriate type, but no one else can do that for him. This 'bearing' of responsibility for something differs from the other situations involving responsibility in that it is a factual state which is passively borne by the agent. To be sure, the assumption of responsibility is itself not yet an active mode of behaviour on the part of the agent, yet it depends on a certain active taking of a position (*Stellungnahme*) out of which his determinately structured mode of behaviour can, or should, ensue. This assuming of responsibility is a real psychic act (*Akt*) of the person, not a mere experience, and leads to a fundamental inner readiness for undertaking steps toward relieving the agent, steps the conscious aim of which is not this relief itself, but first and foremost the fulfillment of requirements which stem from responsibility and are directed at the agent. The legitimate fulfillment of these requirements brings with it the exoneration of the agent only peripherally.

Both the bearing and assuming of responsibility lie within the ontological orbit of the agent, although both transcend this orbit owing to their foundations and their consequences. On the other hand, 'calling someone to account' has its source, and also takes its course, outside the agent, but it is directed at him and is supposed to elicit certain changes in him. It unfolds in a definite kind of action which certainly concerns the agent, but cannot automatically relieve him of responsibility. It is causally independent of the agent's deed, but it empowers whomever is so authorized to call the agent to account. A justified 'calling to account' presupposes that the deed was really initiated and executed by the (alleged) agent himself. It, therefore, calls for a preliminary investigation of the actual matters of fact and circumstances. It can either exonerate the agent of responsibility, or ascertain its holding in force and lead to a calling to account.

Responsible action is carried out by the agent in a special manner. The agent undertakes and performs it with an understanding insight, more or less complete, into both the situation brought about by his action, considered in its value aspect, and the value of the motives which compelled him to act. During all phases of his action the agent realizes its connection with the positive or negative value of its result, and undertakes or continues it with a conscious affirmation of the value of its outcome and thereby also of the correctness and propriety of the action. Thus he does not *blindly* fall into an action the consequences of which he does not foresee, but is fully aware of these consequences and adjusts his actions accordingly. How this 'responsible' acting proceeds, and to what extent the agent actually succeeds in bringing it to completion, depends not only on whether he is capable of assuming responsibility but also on whether he is capable of realizing it. In order to gain clear insight into this matter, we have to characterize in greater detail what it is to bear responsibility.

In the phrase 'someone bears responsibility for something', beside the word 'bears' there also appear the following expressions: 'someone', 'responsibility', 'for something'. Their sense must be clarified.

This 'someone', the agent who is to bear responsibility for something, can only be some human being[2]. But not just any human being, and not in just any situation. Only that human being is at issue who, as a truly responsibility-bearing agent, is aware of his action at the moment of acting and is in possession[3] of all the 'normal' faculties indispensable for exercising control over the situation, and who finally does something or foregoes doing it, at the instant he was going to do it. In particular, it must be a person who is properly qualified to act at the moment of acting. However, the views on what a person is vary greatly. So, as a preliminary, I mention only that trait which is of foremost importance. It is constitutive of a person that he is a point of origin [*Quellpunkt*] for the possible decisions which are founded on rational insight into situations involving values, and at the same time that he is capable of realizing what he has himself resolved. This being-a-person of the human individual comprises a necessary but not sufficient condition of his being able to bear responsibility for something that he does, or foregoes doing. Further conditions must attach: on one side, a more detailed qualification of the person himself; on the other side, the qualitative determination of that for which the person is to be responsible.

That for which the agent is responsible is of a twofold kind: first, it is a certain behaviour; secondly, it is whatever is brought forth, in particular, realized, by this behaviour, i.e., the result. The first is, as regards its form, a process, a happening, but not of an arbitrary kind. It must be an actively undertaken acting; not a purely passive tolerating of something that happens[4] to the agent, or some involuntary, automatically induced reaction (as, for example, when a blow instantly elicits a counterblow, a counterblow from which the given person cannot refrain and whose peculiar nature he cannot apprehend). Yet it would be too much to say that this action must have been consciously and deliberately undertaken. In the latter case, of course, the acting person would certainly be responsible for his action.

It would be proper to ask, however, if the range of that for which one can be responsible is not then being conceived too narrowly. For there is left over a whole domain of actions which are, indeed, performed consciously, but which lack that clear intention to be executed, and for which one nevertheless appears to be responsible. Moreover, this being-conscious still allows for various grades of clarity and modes of concentration in the course of executing the action, or at least at its inception. To be sure, these grades of clarity and modes of concentration no longer comprise the optimum [criterion] for responsibility to obtain in force but they nonetheless comprehend some knowledge about that action which in a given case would be sufficient to arrest, or at least modify, the initiated action. If the modifying or arresting action is not effected then even though the person who is already cognizant of the nature of the unfolding action is not in solidarity with it, he is still responsible for it, and all the more so if he senses the burden of responsibility but still persists in his action. Of course, an essential difficulty is posed by the question of how to determine that threshold of consciousness where the adopted action still lies within the scope of the agent's accountability. The fact that in court proceedings a great deal of emphasis is placed on establishing the degree of consciousness [*Bewußtheitsgrad*] of the agent during his action shows best that we have before us an essential limiting condition of responsibility, albeit one difficult to determine unambiguously. It is, at any rate, once again insufficient.

The action for which the agent may eventually be held accountable need not always be a simple action performed at a single stroke. Sometimes it consists of a complicated process which is composed of several qualitatively different steps and is stretched out over an extended period of time. The extent of conscious awareness of the experiences in which this action unfolds can be quite varied. Thus activities can be involved in the complete execution of the process which require for their success that they take place rather automatically, i.e. that they are not performed consciously. The requirement that the action for which one is to be held responsible be performed consciously must, therefore, be treated with care, and properly adapted to the nature and circumstances of the action.

But the nature of the action seems to be the most decisive factor with respect to whether this action can encumber the agent with responsibility. Meanwhile, we encounter here equally great difficulties. It becomes quite clear that these are not and cannot be completely arbitrary actions as soon as we think of actions which belong to the primitive life-function of a human being. Is, for example, normal eating, which also happens with full intent and awareness, something for which one can be responsible? Or the journey home from the place of employment, or the playing of children with their toys? It seems that special circumstances must come into play before such actions (or concerns), which are in themselves harmless, can burden someone with responsibility. So, also, if one merely adds that the action performed by someone be laudable or deplorable, this need not always entail responsibility on the part of the acting agent, just as, e.g., eating is doubtless beneficial to the eater (it is after all life-sustaining), but this alone leads neither to the credit of the eater nor to his discredit. Eating gets drawn into the purview of the eater's responsible behaviour only when [for example] someone ill is deprived of nourishment that is given to someone healthy and strong in order fully to satisfy the latter. On the other hand there also appear to exist actions which through their very nature are of themselves destined to burden the agent with responsibility, for example the killing of a human being. Do not certain circumstances thereby have to be taken into account, circumstances which play at least some role with respect to the sense in which the agent is responsible? The consideration of this problem, which at first glance appears easily solvable, thereby leads us into situations in which the role played by the nature of the action with respect to the emergence of responsibility is very opaque.

The second thing for which one is or can be responsible is the outcome of an action. The outcome is with respect to its form first of all a factual matter [*Tatbestand*] or state of affairs [*Sachverhalt*], such as for example the death of an assailant due to a defensive action, or the destruction of a town by an aerial bombardment, or the cure of someone seriously ill thanks to surgery. It can also be some object, in particular a thing. Every work created through action, be it a highly valued work of art or an object of use, for example a bridge, is assessed as to its faults or merits whenever the agent's or creator's responsibility becomes an issue.

But once again the question arises as to whether any result is a factor which always encumbers the agent with responsibility, irrespective of its distinctive material nature and of the circumstances under which it came about, or whether it is its special nature that led to this. The first answer to suggest itself is the following:

The accomplished action and its outcome contribute to the appearance of a definite responsibility on the part of the agent only when they are carriers of some positive or negative value or when they at least indirectly lead to the emergence of a factual state bearing a value character. If they are absolutely value-neutral (in any realm of values whatever, i.e. not only in the sphere of moral values), then the agent is still their originator, to be sure, but this alone is not enough for the question of his responsibility to arise. The latter is bound up with the essence of responsibility for something, which still remains to be clarified. At any rate, it seems clear that no one can be called to account for playing solitaire in his free time. Only if it turns out that in order not to interrupt this otherwise harmless recreation he is shirking some duty he is obligated to carry out (for example, if he is a doctor and does not want to attend to a sick person or refuses him help), does the question of his responsibility arise. But then the responsibility weighs on him not for the harmless playing of solitaire, but for the neglect of his medical duties and for valuing a leisurely respite more than the fulfillment of his obligations in the service of other people.

Of course, in the case of making decisions, and of the actions which follow from them, actions for which one is or can be responsible, it happens for the most part that, prior to the deed or at the instant of choosing to effect it, there are other possibilities[5] whose results have differing values, possibilities not all of which are simultaneously realizable but all of which are to a certain degree within the agent's purview and within his range of realization. After the decision and the execution of the deed he is not only responsible for realizing a specific positive (or negative) value, but at the same time for failure to realize, or for the destruction or negation [*Vernichtung*] of other values that compete with the latter. The situation involving responsibility then becomes markedly more complicated, and responsibility depends heavily not only on what value the outcome possesses, but also on how it was arrived at. Was the agent's decision made in simple ignorance of the other values, or did he have all the values in view as possibilities, or finally did he wage a struggle for justly realizing one of them because of a correct insight into the requirement of its realization, – or because he was more strongly drawn to it and succumbed to its power of persuasion, or because he was driven to it because it was more convenient to realize? The magnitude and kind of responsibility are not dependent on the value of the result in some simple way, but are a resultant, frequently quite difficult to survey, of the total situation, taken in its value-aspect, which existed both before and after a decision in favour of a given deed. But it is precisely this dependence, at first not easily surveyable, of the magnitude and kind of responsibility on the values of the possible results which strengthens our conviction that without any value attaching to the result itself, and also to the action itself, there could not be any responsibility at all.

The agent is responsible for the deed performed by him and for its result if and only if it is his *own* deed.

To begin with, we have to clarify what it means for some action to be someone's *own* deed, and secondly we have to demonstrate *why* the agent is responsible only for his own deeds. The first question ties in with both the problem (already touched upon) of being conscious when performing some action and the problem of the requisite degree of consciousness of this consciousness [*Bewußtheit dieses Bewußtseins*]. We now have to elaborate: if a sufficiently lucid consciousness were not operative when performing an action (or exercising a deliberate decision), then the agent could not have command over his action, and in particular could not direct or control it, thus he could not take it upon himself that it has come to pass; it would proceed just as though he had not been present. On the other hand the requisite that the action be the agent's own deed is linked to the age-old problem of the freedom of the human individual. This freedom has always been demanded whenever the question of responsibility for an action, and of its moral value, has been raised in any specific instance. But the question concerning the possibility of 'free' action is almost without exception bound up with the so-called problem of determinism. For freedom of action or, as we also ordinarily say due to a shift in the problem context, the decision of a 'free will',[6] is interpreted in the sense of 'lacking a cause'. This is considered incompatible with the determinacy which, in the real world, reigns universally. This is also at bottom Kant's position, who in fact introduces into the world of things in themselves a certain 'causality inherent in freedom' and distinguishes it from the 'causality of nature' (in the phenomenal world). In some remarkable way, however, Kant allows this 'causality inherent in freedom' to break into the seamless web of causal interconnections in the phenomenal world and to initiate in it new causal chains. This chain is itself not supposed to have any cause in nature, yet it is supposed to appear in it and to affect its course. In the world of appearances therefore 'freedom of the will' is tantamount to 'lacking a cause'. How Kant can speak about a causality inherent in freedom in the world of things in themselves – in which, after all, no categories whatever have a place –, and how he can suppose that it can penetrate into the uninterrupted, causally determined manifold of events in the phenomenal world are matters concerning the Kantian philosophy itself which we need not delve into here. We should not forget however that the Kantian determinism in nature tacitly presupposes a causal ('natural') order of the world in the sense of Laplace. In this context two things need to be undertaken: 1) not to interpret freedom in the sense of absence of cause, but to set in its place the concept of one's own deliberate decision and of one's own action; 2) to consider whether Laplace's conception cannot be replaced by some other conception of the causal structure of the real world. I shall not go into the latter until later.

Nicolai Hartmann, who does not accept Kant's transcendental idealism and his two-world theory, has already emphasized in a noteworthy manner that it is impossible to demand that the free volitional decision have no cause. This is so first of all because such would be impossible in a world which is causally determined through and through, and secondly because it could not then be rational and suited to the real situation which calls for it. Hence it would be unmotivated, and could be made neither by an I nor by a non-I. It would not, accordingly, be a decision of the given person, and the action stemming from it would not be that person's own deed. The person could not at all be held responsible for it. If we still wish to maintain that the acting human being is, and can be, responsible for his own, and only for his own deeds, then we have to admit at the same time that these deeds have, in their way, to be causally induced. Therefore, two matters have to be explained: 1) what it means for a deed or decision to be one's 'own'; 2) how their being indubitably causally conditioned accords with the agent's being responsible for them.

Ad 1. A deliberate decision and action can pass for a given person's 'own' only when they spring forth directly from the I-centre of that person, have their authentic origin in it, and when this I-centre commands and directs the execution of the action emanating from it, therefore the action can be accepted as one's 'own' not when the I-centre merely has some personal interest at stake, but when it holds whithin itself the decisive impact over the total course of the evolving action. This can come about in two different ways. In the first case the I accepts only what takes place within its own psyche, in the sphere of its personal being (of its being thus and so [*Sosein*]), or what encroaches into this sphere from without and which the I accepts only out of necessity, as it were, because it cannot do otherwise. Here, however, approval is granted to some mode of behaviour, without the I actually assimilating it or making it its own. In the second case, however, the I draws the decision out of himself, out of his own deliberation which is unswayed by extraneous reasons, and proceeds to engage in the endeavour of acting. Complete unconditionality by external motives and reasons thereby comprises the optimum situation in which a volitional decision is made, and in which an action undertaken by a personal I is performed in the strict sense as the given person's own action or deed. Various restrictions of the sphere of personal being and of personal life are however possible, within which a human being could nonetheless perform actions that are his 'own' in the absolute sense. In other words: a human being cannot always undertake his 'own' acts and strictly his 'own' actions and decisions in all his life-endeavours and spheres of being. The sphere of one's 'own' acts and endeavours expands or contracts depending on the life-situation and on the person's development. A situation can (but need not) exist in which a human being (despite his being a person) no longer desposes over *any* sphere of his own decisions and deeds, and is consequently totally unfree, whereby everything in his life is imposed from without. And even when the I sets itself in opposition to this, or attempts to oppose it, it is completely powerless or helpless; everything runs its course without the possibility of its being influenced by the I. This is also the limit, at which a human being is no longer responsible for anything that happens in him or to [*mit*] him, or for anything that he appears to do or to sustain. A multiplicity of spheres of a human being's own decisions and deeds, spheres of widely varying structure and scope, lies between the one extreme at which the sphere of one's own decisions and actions stretches out as far as possible, and the opposite extreme at which it shrinks to nullity (but where the type of 'own-ness' [*Eigensein*] is still subject to various modifications).

There is a correlative multiplicity of various possible modes or types of responsibility or, better, of accountability. That is to say, this accountability can in any given case be either unconditioned and total, or, on the other hand, conditioned and restricted or shared in various ways in accordance with the various possible ways in which a given decision or action is a human being's 'own'.

I shall presently describe in greater detail several cases of these different variants of accountability and of the ownness of deeds. I should like, however, to underscore the dissimilarity of the conception of the 'freedom' (i.e. of the ownness of the decisions and deeds) of a human being developed here from that of the customary treatment of the problem of freedom and its possibility. For the most part, one subscribes either to the view which completely denies man's freedom, since it is excluded by a radically conceived determinism of the real world, or, at the opposite extreme, to the view that a human being is endowed with total, unconditioned freedom. Cases which lie, so to speak, in between these conceptions are not considered at all; nor is what is primarily at issue here taken into consideration, namely, that decisions and deeds are one's *own*. That the point of view adopted by me is possible should naturally not be advanced as an unfounded hypothesis, but must be grounded in both the nature of a human being and the structure of the real world. I shall try to show later that here lies an essential ontic fundament of responsibility. For the time being, however, it is in order to point out the variants of conditioned or shared accountability of a human being, which lie between the limiting cases which have been cited.

One such case of accountability occurs most prominently wherever an action rests on a decision reached in conjunction with others. The nature or, more aptly, the kind of action then involved requires that it follow from a decision made in consensus with other people who belong to the same community. A ship begins to sink; its rescue can succeed only if all the people (not just the crew) on board cooperate. Ordinarily, there is a ship's commander who gives all the necessary orders, but he can do so only because everyone else, the members of the crew and the passengers, recognize him as captain. This recognition is already a joint act of those present on board. But the captain might be stupid or ill and consequently issue entirely unreasonable or ill-advised orders. He might then be removed through mutiny. This mutiny is once again a joint decision and deed: without electing a new captain, for which there is no time, all those present on board (crew and passengers) begin the rescue action together. This joint rescue action consists of a wide variety of modes of conduct, which must all be coordinated, and in the coordination of which there is a high degree of instinctive communication and cooperation. The undertaking along with the execution of the rescue action, the growing coordination of actions with the passing of time as well as the gradually evolving new hierarchy within the initially amorphous mass of people – all this leads to the 'own' deed of the entire community, a community which is authentic as a result of having arisen in this way. But this character of being an 'own' deed rests on this community's individual fellow-members' *own* decisions and actions, which come about only after the decisions and deeds of the remaining members have been taken into consideration. The 'ownness' of an individual decision bears here the character of participation in a common willing and doing: everyone does what he does by himself, but he adapts his behaviour to that of others. He helps others and, reciprocally, receives help from them; they help each other. And for this very reason the responsibility of the community is also shared and divided in a certain sense among its individual members, who in their own domain are only 'co-responsible' but for this reason are indeed responsible in the special manner of a restricted, conditioned, and shared responsibility. But it is the community as a whole, as a new subject, which is responsible in the full sense. On the other hand, the responsibility of the individual fellow-members holds in force only insofar as their participation in the rescue operation actually has its last ground in their own self, even though this operation is handled under a continual reckoning with the decisions and actions of others; but in no case is it simply forced upon anyone by the others.

We have in the final analysis an essentially different sort of case of a conditioned or joint own decision or action in every instance of the own decision of a concrete human being, a human being who is fully developed in his personal being, who indeed is not all mind, but a being anchored in its body, all of those actions are ontically founded in this body and are co-determined by it in the progress of their occurrence. On the other hand, in the majority of cases these actions reach out beyond the purely corporeal, and do so essentially, in their nature. We are therefore concerned here with acts which are not purely bodily in a genuine sense, such as, for example, breathing or digesting, but which preserve their mental nature: for example creative thinking, the act of admiring and recognizing another's heroism, and the like, although these acts are co-determined by bodily processes as to the course of their occurrence and their various characteristic traits.[7] For as long as we live, we always have a part in the vital processes going on in our body. These processes, in turn, are always co-conditioned by the processes of consciousness, by psychic processes, by purely mental acts. Often the body suffers or ails on their account or, on the contrary, blossoms thanks to them. To be sure, it is not easy to clarify objectively and determine with rigour and precision this being reciprocally conditioned. But both pathological physiology and psychopathology can instruct us about various noteworthy facts regarding this relation. Daily experience alone supplies us with many examples which distinctly attest to this. The acting human being who makes decisions realizes fully which of these two factors has played a more significant, or even a decisive, role in arriving at his decision or in the performance of his deed. There are cases, for example, in which both factors, the body and the psyche or mind, effect an act of love in original unity, so that what is bodily is thereby only an expression and outlet for an authentic, psychical, mental love, and this love is only a completion of the bodily yearning for unification with the partner. Both of these factors, whose heterogeneity is barely noticeable in the human being as a whole, work together, as it were, in a unity. Consequently, the act of love is performed by the personal I wholly centrally, and however much it is thereby conditioned by its body, it is nonetheless driven by it in the same direction, impelled by the love impulse. We can say: the act is the whole human being's *own* act, and especially that of the personal I. Obviously, we should not thereby forget the role of the partner. If everything proceeds well and happily, then this act is something that belongs to the loving pair itself as its own. The peculiar 'we', as the subject of the act and of the subsequent acts and actions superimposed on it, is thereby constituted in the experience of both lovers. The character of ownness of the doing and acting of the partners in this case differs from, for example, the ownness of the act in which a scholar decides suddenly to work on some particular theoretical problem because he has an insight that the solution to this problem must be obtained before the solutions to other important problems can be reached. For the scholar as a mental I this decision comprises his *own* act, even though this resolve could not come about without the existence of his body and the physiological processes occurring in it, processes about which the scholar knows nothing at the given moment. Of course, this act is neither causally unconditioned nor is it unmotivated by the theoretical situation in the respective science, but this does not deprive it of its character of being strictly the scholar's own deed. The act, so characterized, can be performed by him even when the exhaustion of the body is counter-productive or when treatment of the given problem could for various reasons be personally ill-advised or downright dangerous for him.

If under these conditions he still comes to a decisive resolve and carries through the treatment of the problem, then his act is all the more independent of the conditions and thereby acquires even more the character of being the scholar's own act and – what hangs together with this – the scholar thereby bears full responsibility for his act and can assume this responsibility in full awareness.

Let us return, however, to the previous example, which we shall now modify essentially. In this modified case a man can sense a violent desire for sexual union with some woman, and in such a way that he senses it distinctly as a bodily desire, in which his psyche or mind has no positive share whatsoever. He simply does not love the given woman, nor does he believe that this desire and its eventual satisfaction can be judged by him as morally positive. The desire is overpowering, however, and finally leads to his succumbing to it, despite all resistance by his personal I, and culminates in the sexual act. Let us add that there is an absence of any motive, such as that the woman really loves him and would be deeply unhappy if this union were not to be realized, so that the man would have talked himself into it for the sake of her happiness, and would thus have made her happy. No. He simply yields to the power of his bodily drive, although he knows very well that his personal I condemns it. He does it anyway, and indeed – should we not admit it? – he does it after all *himself*, although when doing it, he 'forgets himself', as we say. Can he then say to himself: "I did not do it; it is not my very own deed. Only my body did it."? Certainly, he is not merely present at the time; it is not as if he allows it to happen entirely without his participation. It is in every case 'his', his own deed, in a two-fold manner: firstly, he succumbs to his lust; secondly, he commits the sexual act, which, even though bodily, is not after all strictly bodily to the extent that an assenting behaviour of the personal I is thereby altogether missing. To be sure, both the submission and the conscious witnessing of the I is passive. That, however, which was called the 'assent' of the I is no longer purely passive. There is involved, as Husserl might have said, an active passivity. And it depends precisely on the fact that that whole complicated process is after all the personal I's own behaviour, although not as strictly its own as it would be if the I were resolutely present in the situation cited. As long as everything runs its course in such a way that it could still be interrupted at the last moment owing to a decisive intervention by the personal I, but this intervention does not happen, to that extent this behaviour is the man's own doing, even though it is, in its character of ownness, a very modified, weakened deed. What happens with, and in, the woman is her own doing, unless it is, for example, a matter of her being brutally raped. A human being's behaviour is not his own doing only if *everything* is compulsory, and not consented to in any way. Wherever there is still a trace of acquiescence and a possibility of intervention on the part of the personal I, there is also present responsibility for what happens on the part of the agent, however modified this responsibility might be. On the other hand, wherever everything is forced and there is no possibility of assent and of interrupting the course of events, there also the responsibility of the given human being vanishes. Any talk of an 'agent' is then also out of place. The various forms of 'own' behaviour indicated here entail different variants of responsibility: full and unconditioned responsibility and its various restricted, shared, weakened modalities. All these are cases that are accounted for in criminal law and investigated in great detail in the study of criminal conduct. The highest degree of responsibility occurs where the deed is undertaken and accomplished in full awareness with intent and with premeditation by the personal I. And there is no responsibility whatever wherever a human being's conduct is entirely forced and takes place without any trace of the I's assent, possibly with a complete absence of cognizant awareness.

But what does it mean that the agent is 'responsible' for the deed and its outcome? It means: 1) that the agent becomes 'culpable' as a result of effecting a negatively-valued factual state by performing a deed which, in its consequence, is negative, 'bad', 'evil', and that means that he himself becomes 'blemished' through his misconduct or transgression, becomes encumbered with a negative value; and if he realizes a positively-valued factual state, thereby accomplishing a 'good' deed, he secures merit and thereby a positive value; 2) that ensuant to accomplishing the deed and the realization of some positive or negative value the agent faces the requirement of redressing the inflicted harms or wrongs, in the sense of meting out justice, and of making reparation for, as well as effacing the negative value of, his deed through the positively-valued act of remorse; 3) that this demand upon the agent places on him the obligation of complying with it. That this obligation burdens him is just the reverse side of his being responsible for his deed. If he does not fulfill it, then he charges himself with a new offense and is on that account indeed responsible for a second time. On the other hand, if he has secured merit for himself thanks to his deed, then no obligation grows out of it for him, but only the entitlement to recognition. But it becomes incumbent on other people to reward him for his good deed or at least to acknowledge its positive value. If this does not happen, then an injustice has been committed, and whoever was supposed to offer this recognition is responsible for it.

IV

Assuming Responsibility

Sometimes the agent also assumes responsibility for his deed and its outcome. This means, first of all, that he acknowledges that he has burdened himself through his offense. In the case where he had done something to someone, he discerns the other's right to reparation as well-founded, and effects the act of recognizing the obligation of recompense that weighs upon him. As a result of these acts he begins to take steps which are supposed to bring about reparation and expiation for his deed. The assumption of responsibility by the agent comes into relief especially clearly when the result of his deed consists of the realization of some positive value which is questioned by other people, or is taken by them for a negative value, which the agent has not to efface, but rather to assert and defend. In this case, assuming responsibility takes on the form of the agent's standing up for this value and also for the justification of his deed. The assuming of responsibility enables him to willingly take upon himself all the suffering dealt him in the conflict over the value defended by him.

If someone is responsible for a deed, then the duty of assuming responsibility for it weighs upon him. If he does not assume it, then he charges himself with a new blame for which he is responsible. But the assuming of responsibility and compliance with the requirements directed at the agent which follow therefrom, as well as the fulfillment of what is demanded from him, relieve him of his blame and his responsibility becomes thereby debilitated or annulled.

V

Responsible Action

In the preceding we treated of that responsibility which holds sway after the completion of an action. But how is it with the problem of a responsibility which is just emerging in the course of acting?

How does the action run its course where it has been undertaken from the outset with a view toward (or having taken account of) a specific responsibility that will result from it?

We can act without worrying at all that we can become, or be, 'responsible' for our action. We simply immerse ourselves in the acting, and through it aim to bring something to realization. Someone acting in such a manner incurs the responsibility for this action, for acting in this way regardless of anything. One may steer all one's actions in such a direction that something bad or something good can result from them and in such a way that the former is to be avoided and the latter promoted. In all this, one still reckons with the fact that, possible inflicted harms aside, blame can also be assigned, or merit awarded, to the agent himself. One can act in such a way, that at every step one asks oneself whether one's action is justified. The agent must maintain in his purview the values to be realized or rejected in the process, for not only the course of his action depends on the range of this purview, but also his accountability for it. Various possibilities then open up. Paying attention to these values can be more or less clear, or obscured to the point of having these values outlined in their quality only dimly and indistinctly. It is, above all, of the greatest importance that a distinct connection emerge between the possible values and the nature of the unfolding action or of the action about to develop, along with the circumstances under which it is to develop. It can happen that precisely this connection is not transparent and, even worse, that one has no time to devote to the grasping of this connection. A peculiar uncertainty therefore enters into the whole process, since the agent cannot surrender himself fully to the acting itself, but is at the same time preoccupied with becoming aware of the dangers (of the threatening negative values), or he feels at least that he ought to concern himself with this; he consequently performs the individual steps of the action with a kind of uncertainty and lack of precision. It is for this very reason that the accountability of his doing and acting is constrained within narrower limits. It may occur that neither the respective values nor their connection to the impending action are grasped, but the agent can no longer interrupt the action already begun, and feels increasingly pressured to carry it on, to a possibly bad conclusion. If he then resigns, and allows to happen whatever will happen, then he acts irresponsibly, but for this very reason he becomes responsible for acting in this way. Even in a situation such as this, his conduct, on which the degree of his responsibility depends, can be various. He can deny any responsibility, so as to declare himself in some sense not responsible; or he can admit inwardly that he is acting badly, and be ready to take on the onus of responsibility for his action and irresponsible behaviour and to willingly acknowledge the consequences of his conduct. Finally, he can simply despair and accept it all.

Responsible action takes on a special form and threatens the agent with a responsibility which is all the more weighty when he aspires to realize a value opposed by other people who consider it evil, or when the pervading legal situation forbids the realization of this value. Yet the agent strives not only toward its realization but at the same time stands behind it and underscores its worthiness. His action consists of struggling for the realization of the value. He is then condemned by his opponents even more heavily, and encumbered by them with a still greater responsibility; and he himself not only opposes this, but also hopes that justice will be accorded him and that he will be liberated from the burden of negative responsibility, so to speak: his merit will be acknowledged.He finds his support in the clear grasp of both the value-quality of the final outcome of his actions and the worthiness of the given value; on the other hand he finds it also in his own courage, which helps him to struggle alone against other people and to willingly accept the unjust punishment that will be dealt him after the success of his action. He need not in all this become aware of the opposition between the evil of the (unjust) punishment befalling him and the positive value of the true heroism which is due him for his deeply responsible action. But his action is genuinely responsible and unfalsified in its high moral value only when, having acquired this awareness, he struggles not with a view toward a reward for his heroism, but rather with an awareness of the authentic worthiness of the value which he aims to realize. This whole process concludes tragically if it finally turns out that the act of grasping the value for which he fought has led him astray after all, and he is wrong. A very complicated situation then arises, and it is difficult to decide justly for which positive or negative value he is finally responsible. But what remains beyond question is that even then he is responsible to a high degree for his conduct, and for this reason the value due him for heroically abiding by his ideal and for the tenacity of his struggle is not denied him.

These diverse kinds of responsible actions disclose that the agent must be endowed in a particular manner with respect to both his ontic, categorical structure and his character traits. Thus not only responsibility itself, but also responsible action, which proceeds in this way or that, must, in order to be able to occur at all, have determinate ontic foundations. The discovery of these foundations is precisely the task which now lies before us.

VI

Value as Ontic Fundament of Responsibility

Various positive and negative values are bound up essentially with responsibility and with the demands for reparation and deliverance from responsibility which derive from it. The sense and possibility of responsibility, especially of bearing responsibility, are first determined by the existence of these values, by their mutual existential interconnections, by the possibility of their concretization in real objects and factual matters and by the requirements issuing from the material aspect of these values. It is therefore first of all necessary to bring into view the kinds of positive or negative values that come into question. Briefly, they are values of the following types:

A. 1. The positive or negative value of the outcome brought forth by the agent's deed.
2. The positive or negative value of the deed leading to that outcome.
3. The positive or negative value of the agent's volition, i.e. of his decision and intention.
4. The positive or negative value which accrues to the agent as a consequence of performing his deed, and for his overall conduct.

B. 1. The value of what is realized in the reparation, and which makes amends for, or 'equalizes', the harm (injustice) inflicted on someone.
2. The value of the mode of behaviour, especially e.g. of the remorse, which annuls or makes amends for the negative value of the misconduct burdening the agent.
3. The value of the reward or recognition which is commensurate with the value of the possible merit.

There are generative existential relations, if I may put it so, among the positive or negative values of group A: the value of the outcome generates the realization of the value of the deed and, as a further consequence, the value of the agent.[8] The value of the reparation or of the act of remorse frequently elicits some new act from whomever was the target of the agent's action, namely an act of forgiveness ('pardon'). This act is in itself positively valuable. The absence of this act where it ought to occur is in itself negatively valuable, and indeed, in a moral sense; it stems from a character trait of a human being which we may call obstinacy or callousness. At the same time there are interconnections of determination among values: the material aspect of the value of the outcome determines of itself the material aspect of the value of the deed, while the latter determines for its part the material aspect of the value of the agent. On the other hand, the values of group B somehow exercise certain functions of de-realisation [*Entrealisierungsfunktionen*] relative to the positive or negative values of group A. The value of reparation, or of what it brings to realization, annuls the negative value of the harm or of the injustice done. And the value of the agent's remorse annuls the negative value of the evil deed, etc.

The value of justice stands above all these values with their existential and material interconnections. It can be realized by fulfilling the demands which are imposed upon the agent by the responsibility he bears.[9] We can also say that justice sets up the demand for all those 'equalizations' which are supposed to come about between the negative values effected through the evil deed and the positive values realized owing to the reparation required by responsibility.

If there were no positive or negative values, nor interconnections of being and determination which obtain among them, there could be no authentic responsibility whatever, nor any fulfillment of the requirements posed by it.

This principle discloses the first outlook on the ontic foundations of responsibility. The existence of values and of the interconnections obtaining among them is the first condition for the possibility of both the idea of responsibility and of the meaningfulness of the requirement directed at the agent that he assume responsibility for his deed and fulfill its requisites. This is also the condition for the possibility of the agent's being burdened by responsibility for his deed, and for his being able to be freed of this burden. Here finally lies the last ground for calling someone to account, and therefore for conferring on this process its ultimate justification. Even responsible action would be without sense or purpose if in it we were not to reckon with values, were not to take into account their existence or possible annihilation. All situations relating to responsibility that we have differentiated and the possibility of their realization in a concrete instance would lose their legitimate sense if values did not exist in any way.

Indeed, for this reason important theoretical problems arise for the general ontology of values, which cannot be solved in an arbitrary manner if responsibility is not to lose its sense, and the requirements posed by it are not to lose their justification. To begin with we have to explain what kind of positive and negative values in general come into question in regard to the various specific kinds of actions. Essential correlations between human modes of conduct and positive or negative values are undoubtedly at issue here. The most important, however, are the existential value problems: questions concerning the existence of values and their modes of being, questions which go to the essence of responsibility and its realization.

Perhaps we can best call to mind what it is that we require of responsibility in this matter if we consider those theories of value which actually deny the existence of responsibility. In the final analysis there are three such sceptical theories: the theory of the so-called 'subjectivity' of values, the theory of values as of social origin and the theory of value 'relativity' which includes the theory of values as historically dependent.

All these theories are of course ambiguous in various ways, and they do not threaten the sense and reality of responsibility in all their significations. Their common background consists of the dualistic conception of the world on the one hand, and a sensualistically tinted empiricism, on the other. I cannot treat here of all of these interpretations of value and of their link with responsibility.[10] I therefore confine myself to a discussion of a few select conceptions.

The psychologistic conception of values, according to which they are supposed to be something psychical or, more precisely, something having the character of consciousness, though it has been predominant for a long time, is today no longer in force. The view is still quite widely disseminated, however, that values are supposed to be 'subjective' in the sense that they do not really appertain to various kinds of objects (to things, works of art, people, modes of conduct, e.g. moral acts, logical formations such as theories), but are merely certain illusions or fictions for individuals who, for a variety of reasons, ascribe them to various objectivities so as to raise the semblance of their actually appertaining to these objectivities. This comes about, according to the given conception, predominantly as a result of certain human feelings or aspirations or, finally, from certain utilitarian motives. At best, there are allowed certain phenomenal apearance-characters to emerge on the respective objects, but *sine fundamento in re*. As soon as these reasons or motives fall by the wayside, as ought to be the case, for example, in an act of cognition, then the respective objectivities turn out to be completely free of those illusory characters, to be strictly value-neutral, i.e. 'objective', in their existence and qualitative determination. Values do not exist at all in genuine being and qualitative determination. They are in every case, as one says, merely 'subjective', at most illusions on the part of people who have the correlative experiences. Here we set aside further arguments for a 'subjectivistic' theory of values so understood.[11] For, only the consequences of this theory with respect to responsibility are important for our principal theme. Clearly, if none of the enumerated values were to appertain to the respective objectivities and modes of conduct, then there would be no responsibility for anything. It would then be completely irrelevant how one acts and what one occasions through this action. Neither the perpetration of a deed (even where it is fully informed) nor its outcome would as yet provide grounds for bearing responsibility for it. There would also be no justification for calling someone to account if the deed did not occasion something *good* or *bad*. All criminal conduct or recognition of merit would be entirely meaningless. Of course, someone who is ignorant of the true situation might be inclined to assume responsibility for his deed and possibly even attempt to undertake reparation. But he would then be subject to a remarkable illusion which would issue in conduct which was purposeless and senseless.

Those who would wish to deny values on the basis of a subjectivistic orientation attempt to save responsibility, as well as the process of being called to account, and to defend the legitimacy of this process, by reducing values to socially or politically instituted requirements (commands), or to entire legal systems embodied in different forms of social organization, requirements and legal systems which are directed at the individual and burden him with various 'obligations'. In the case of a failure to fulfill or comply with the given requirements, it is the legal system which allows for the person involved to be called to account.

Many such social requirements and legal systems have in fact been set up; the individual has been supposed to submit to them in accordance with their sense; and he has frequently been unable to contradict them, even where he happens to consider them unfounded. But now there are two possibilities: either the given requirements are substantively[12] grounded, sensible and purposeful, in which case they presuppose the effectiveness and the existence of the respective values, an existence which is immanent to the objectivities involved – whereby the reduction of values to social decisions fails; or this reduction simply signifies that there are *no* objective values *at all* existing *cum fundamento in re* and independently of social decisions.[13] In the latter case, these social or state regulations and requirements are in the first place willful decrees which are devoid of any substantive grounding; such is the case even if one were to assert that they are issued only 'for the good' of the rulers, dictators or ruling classes. Even if this 'good' were tantamount to usefulness or sensual pleasure, it could not lead to a refutation of *all* objectively existing values, since one must then grant some effective value to at least this usefulness or sensual pleasure. It is precisely for this reason that the *general* subjectivistic conception of values is untenable. But the possibility has thus been created of acknowledging the meaningfulness and reality of responsibility in at least *one* case, namely when the outcome which results from the personal deed of some person possesses a positive or negative utility- or pleasure-value. If, on the other hand, there were cases of responsibility where the outcome would possess a moral value, or some other value different from a utility-value, then these would be rendered impossible by a denial of all values other than utility-values. Thus if one wants justly to maintain the sense and value of being responsible also in these cases, which are ordinarily treated at the very beginning, then one must abandon not only the general subjectivistic theory of value, but also the one-sidedly utilitarian one. In favour of this view there is the further fact that the conscious bearing of responsibility, as well as its assumption and all conduct ensuing from it, also possesses in itself some positive (or perhaps, in the case of a failure, negative) value, and it would be completely mistaken to regard this as a utility- or pleasure-value. Acting in a responsible manner, or conscientiously fulfilling the requisites imposed by responsibility, is often to the agent's extreme disadvantage, but then the authentic value (i.e., the moral value) of reparation, of remorse, etc. is actually increased and is not at all diminished through the lack of usefulness of this mode of conduct. In a theory of value, therefore, both utilitarianism and hedonism are in conflict with the meaningfulness and reality of responsibility.

Utilitarianism threatens the possibility of authentic responsibility for still another reason: it very frequently leads to relativism in a theory of value. For the cutting edge of a utilitarian theory of value is directed not only specifically against moral and aesthetic values. At bottom its tendency goes much further, indeed by emphasizing that utility-values are, as one says, only 'relative'. What represents usefulness, and hence a value, for one man need not also be useful and valuable for another man. And translated into the historical mode this assertion states: everything which is useful in some historical epoch might be useless in another epoch. And in a natural utilitarian generalization, this reads as follows: all values have a merely 'historical validity', but since the historical world continually changes, all values have a validity restricted to only some historical epoch and necessarily lose it in another epoch.

This relativism in value-theory can be interpreted in various ways. It frequently takes a form in which it again falls into conflict with the postulate of responsibility. One then argues: if something, without itself changing, is experienced at one time as good (beautiful, useful,etc.) and at another time as bad (ugly, harmful, etc.), this must imply that that thing is in itself neither good nor bad, neither beautiful nor ugly, but is devoid of any such values altogether. And if at one time it is found to be 'beautiful', and at another 'ugly', then it in fact only *appears* to be so. All values are in consequence only a 'subjective' semblance; a value is not something which really and effectively appertains, and can appertain, to some object. In this way relativism in value theory is transformed into a sceptical subjectivism, the acceptance of which implies that there can be no authentic responsibility for anything.

Not every value-relativism, however, is of this kind. And so one must seek an alternative interpretation of the relativistic conception of values, in which authentic responsibility would still be possible, despite the concession that some values really are 'relative' in some sense other than the one outlined above. Besides this we still have to consider whether the moral values, which are primarily at issue in situations involving responsibility, ought to be counted among relative values at all.[14] To this end we shall isolate two interpretations of the relativity of values which come under consideration for the existence and meaningfulness of responsibility. Something is 'relative' in a certain sense, if it appertains only to an object in some system consisting of at least a pair of objects. It finds its sufficient, and perhaps also necessary, foundation [*Fundierung*] only in this system, or in all the objects belonging to the same, and not in some randomly selected member of this system. Thus for example we rightly say that hay is nourishing, and thus useful, for a horse but not for a dog. Likewise, meat is nourishing for a dog, but not for a horse. Therefore neither hay nor meat are 'nutritive' (more generally, 'useful') of themselves alone, but are so only in relation to objects of a determinate domain, which can utilize them as nourishment. But then this 'being nutritious for something', is nonetheless no fiction or illusion for the animals in question, but a wholly real and effective qualification of the appropriate means of nourishment, without which the corresponding animal could not live at all (if it were not replaced by some other equivalent means). For this animal it therefore signifies the highest real value, whereas for another animal this same means of nourishment is no nourishment at all, and precisely for this reason has no utility-value whatever for it. To take away hay, oats and other nutritive means from a horse is bad. And whoever would do so would be *responsible* for it, just as he would be if he were aimlessly to slaughter these animals. The existence of a value which is relative in this sense thereby comprises a sufficient condition for finding someone guilty of destroying such a value, i.e. for holding him responsible for such destruction, just as it is a sufficient condition for treating as meritorious the generation of such foodstuffs for particular animals. Naturally, it is thereby presupposed that the very life of the given animals is itself somehow valuable. Now this value too can perhaps be relative in the same sense, but it need not be. This changes nothing in the authentic existence of relative values so understood.

A value of something is relative in a second, related sense if it exists for only a determinate finite domain of objectivities, and not for all objectivites in general. This is in fact the case for all those values, which, as values, have their sufficient foundation and thereby also their existence only within some system, but which are not 'relational'[15], as in the previous instance. For example, a moral wrong can be inflicted on a human being by forbidding him, or depriving him of, his freedom of thought and the expression of his convictions, but a horse or a dog cannot be harmed in this way, since this freedom is not at all accessible to them as a value. But this harm inflicted on a human being does not thereby become either 'relational' in the previous sense, nor somehow illusory or non-existent. A moral wrong is done to someone with such an action, and precisely for this reason the doer is responsible for it and can also be called to account, since the given person has had an established and primordial right to a certain value taken away from him, a value which necessarily belongs to him as a man, even disregarding the fact that deprivation of freedom itself signifies a negative value for a human being.

One should not reply to the above by saying that freedom of thought and expression or the freedom of conscience were not always regarded as values, and that the recognition of these values is a 'historical product' of a particular human culture (of the European spirit, of this or that social class, or of the liberalism of the 19th century, etc.). This historical change in the treatment of freedom as a value cannot of course be denied. Yet, by pointing to this change, one at bottom wants to say that this value does not at all exist in itself. The *having been recognized* or the *cognition* or, finally, the *appearing* of the value is unjustifiably identified with its *existence* and with its sufficient *foundation* in an object or in a system of objects. Naturally, one can be in error when ascribing a value to someone, or when failing to credit him with it. An analogous error is possible in the cognition of the physical properties of a determinate material thing. Yet in neither case does it follow from this fact that the given value, or this property, cannot exist in other instances. Indeed, where one has to do with something autonomous, and in particular with something real, it is always possible that errors will be committed in cognizing it, and that only after extensive efforts will one reach the knowledge that a determinate value or property really appertains to some object. The fact that in some epochs personal freedom of thought and belief were not considered to be fundamental human values, or that perhaps historical times will again arrive in which the valuableness of freedom will be denied, in no way proves that it is a fiction or a delusion of certain people, or that it is not a negative moral value to wrest this value from man; it proves only that human cognition is imperfect in this regard and that, at most, further researches on the essence of freedom, and of human nature, are called for. This is all the more necessary – as history teaches – as the danger grows that the conception of freedom as a value may become distorted, falsified or violated through extra-cognitive considerations and forces. The actual existence of these values is not dependent on this historically conditioned transformation of conceptions of them and on a refusal to acknowledge them. In other words: the fact that specific values (such as freedom for man) are restricted in their accessibility and attainability to a certain group or species should not be confused with the historically variable recognition of these values, and this varying acknowledgement should not be used as an argument for the fact that these values do not exist at all but are merely a phantom or a chimera for certain people. Whoever considers values to be historically conditioned, mad delusions of mankind (mad, since, after all, frequently one gives up one's life for them!) must nonetheless come to grips with the fact that precisely for this reason he denies the possibility of any responsibility, and as a consequence must relinquish the demand that human beings assume responsibility.

In all this, of course, one still needs to determine somewhat more precisely what talk about the existence of positive (or negative) values should mean. One can have two things in mind. In the first place something like 'justice', 'freedom', 'remorse', 'mercy', 'generosity', 'honesty', etc. and at the other end, e.g., 'obstinacy', 'cruelty', 'hatred', 'stupidity', etc. is held to exist as value or disvalue *as an idea;* i.e. there exist *ideal value qualities* which allow of concretization only in an individual case and thereby make possible valuable individual objects. In the second place, however, this concretization and individualization in the individual case is held actually to obtain in fact, and to have the sufficient condition of its existence in the individual object (thing, conduct, event). In both cases one ordinarily speaks about the 'existence of values' and in both significations this 'existence of values' comes into question for making responsibility possible. In the first sense we are concerned with the indispensable condition for the possibility and meaningfulness of responsibility in general; in the second case, on the other hand, it is a matter of an individual case, whose correlative factors do in fact contain individual concretizations of these ideal value-qualities, owing to which responsibility first comes about in fact.

With this, I believe I have demonstrated the first ontic fundament of responsibility. But there are still other such fundaments, which need to be discussed next.

VII

Responsibility and the Identity of its Subject

In performing a deed which leads to the realization of a positive or negative value, we *become* responsible for this deed. But we *remain* responsible for it even *after* its performance, so long, at least, as we have not been in reality vindicated, or freed, of this responsibility; and just so long, too, can one be called to account. The bearing of responsibility ceases after the vindication, and being called to account loses its sense and would then be unjustified. However, until this happens the agent is burdened by an obligation of restitution and of relieving himself of the blame which oppresses him. A responsibility which would exist only at the moment of completing the deed would be somehow senseless: it could not then exercise a function which is essential to it, that of being the source and ground of the restitution which is to be realized in the future. Even though it emerged out of happenings in the real world and is borne by a real human being it seems to continue to exist and somehow to hover over the course of events. It lasts through a definite time span – between its genesis and annulment – but is as if lifted out of the stream of processes and newly emerging events which continue to develop. It does not change during this time as long as no steps have been undertaken toward its discharge. The force with which the agent experiences the burden oppressing him can indeed vary in the course of time. The agent can get used to it. Or, conversely, it can become increasingly oppressive, even unbearable. Yet, at the very moment the deed is performed, this responsibility is unequivocally determined by the nature and value of this deed, as well as by the nature and value of the outcome and by the attitude of the agent toward his own deed and toward what is accomplished by it, and it depends on these, and only these, factors. Since these factors can no longer be changed once they have arisen, so also the responsibility, in the given individual case, remains unaltered in its sense and essence. To be sure, at the moment of the performance of the deed and emergence of its outcome it has become a real fact, but it seems to transcend reality and to retain its ideal validity, if we may put it so, unaltered precisely because it neither vanishes nor changes in its sense. What can change is the way in which it is cognized and understood by the agent himself and by other people. Sometimes a long time may pass before the agent becomes aware of it and understands its full sense; it may also be concealed from other people for a long time and not be rightly cognized by them even when they have discovered it. But all this changes nothing in the least in the content of the responsibility; it continues to exist until some day the agent himself decides to dispose of it through restitution or through remorse, or until the day arrives when he is called to account and justice confronts him. This remarkable nature of responsibility presupposes several things with respect to the agent himself on the one hand, and on the other hand with respect to the imbalance in the state of values which has been brought about by the agent's deed.

In order for the agent to be able to bear responsibility and also to rid himself of it, his identity, especially the identity of his personal being, must persist, despite all transformations which may meanwhile occur in him, and it must be maintained for as long as it takes him to get rid of the responsibility. It may have to be maintained – and this is the peculiar thing – even after his death. This may appear paradoxical, but is explicable through the unchangeable existence and sense of responsibility until its resolution (or annulment). The same holds as regards being-called-to-account, since this too may extend beyond the agent's eventual death. For this reason, legal proceedings in which he can be convicted or absolved of responsibility, can be conducted even after his death. Justice must be accorded him in either case.

This matter presents us with difficult tasks. On one side we have to clarify the essence of the identity of an object which changes in time, in particular of a human being. On another side we also have to discover the conditions for the possibility of a person's maintaining this identity. Both lead to fundamental and important problems which are at the same time difficult to solve, problems which cannot be treated here.[16] We shall have to content ourselves with a few remarks pointing to the dangers threatening the bearing of responsibility and being-called-to-account which stem from a failure to sustain the identity of the agent.

Every human being is a corporeal and psychic being whose personal 'I' is engaged in a special way whenever he is engaged responsibly. Not only do ever new physical and physiological processes take place in the body itself, but at the same time new cells are continually formed, while other cells waste away and, as they are decomposed, are expelled from the body. Besides this, an exchange of material constantly takes place between the body and its surroundings. Along with all this, however, their reigns – as theoretical biologists such as von Bertalanffy have pointed out – a dynamic equilibrium or steady state in the body, so that, as a many-celled being, it remains over a given period of time one and the same whole. At the same time it appears that there are certain perturbation limits of this equilibrium within the bounds of which these disturbances can be made reversible, but the overstepping of which ends with the body's death. As far as I know, neither these limits nor the ultimate grounds for the possibility of maintaining this dynamic equilibrium have been clarified in general[17], especially where the human body, which is relatively speaking the most familiar, comes specifically into question. Aside from that, between the moment of conception (the moment of fertilization of the egg) and death there is a characteristic regulated developmental process of growth, maturation and aging up until the disintegration or decomposition of the whole – however variously this process may shape itself in an individual instance. And finally it should be mentioned that there is the continuity of being which is the *sine qua non* of the body's self-sameness and oneness. 'Continuity of being' means that during the existence of the body there is no interruption in the being of the body as a whole. However, in view of the fact that there is a continual exchange of material in the body, as well as a generation and dissolution of billions of cells, it is not easy to demonstrate this continuity. Perhaps it could be shown that in the course of this entire flux of material and cell exchange certain bodily organs (e.g. the central nervous system or the regulatory system of the glands of inner secretion) are, after all, identically sustained in uninterrupted being, which would ensure the identity of the body even in the presence of other exchangeable organs.

In order to resolve this question one would either have to carry out experimental research or have at one's disposal a general ontological theory of the human organism. For the time being we are in possession of neither. But one can now give a negative criterion: if within the span of time between birth and death there is a phase in which *no* part of the body in question exists, then the body from the time before this interruption of being is not identical with the body after this break, even if other circumstances were to speak in favour of such identity.

The identity of the body of a human being, or of a person, appears to be indeed indispensable, but not sufficient, for the identity of that person, whereas the maintenance of this identity is necessary for the bearing of responsibility as well as for being called-to-account. There are, however, certain pathological facts, the so-called 'dissociations of consciousness' or of the I, which would seem to endanger both. These dissociations appear in various modes; there are two different limiting cases which are of particular interest to us. The first involves a break in the memory or recall of earlier events or experiences from the time prior to the onset of the break. Secondly, the dissociation can consist in the simultaneous (and phenomenal) presence of, so to speak, two I- and disposition-centres in the given person which are in conflict with each other. It is then uncertain at any given moment which I-centre predominates and carries out the respective deed for which it is to be held responsible. What is at issue in the first case is the way in which the break in memory occurs: whether absolutely, so that whoever is afflicted by it knows absolutely nothing, after the loss of memory, of the life before the break and can recall nothing when someone recounts to him the facts of his earlier life; or only relatively and restrictedly, whereby the afflicted person has not forgotten everything of his earlier life, and where his lapse is only temporary. If it is an absolute memory break and if, moreover, a significant shift in the character of the given human being sets in, then of course the metaphysical non-identity of the afflicted person has not yet thereby been demonstrated. But if the above actually did take place, then the second person, living after the performance of the deed would not be responsible for the first person, living in the period before the break in memory. But also if this second person, following a complete loss of memory, would not possess any direct knowledge about the 'first' person and his deeds or experiences, and would not thereby feel in any way as the first person, it would be apropos to ask if he could still be responsible or called to account even despite the fact that the identity of his body could be exhibited. The burden of responsibility continues to rest on the first person, and therefore he should be called to account (just as this would be possible even after his death), but he should not be punished, since every punishment would befall not him, but the 'second' person, even though the latter is hardly responsible in this case. Pragmatically one would probably say: if the second person cannot in any way recall the deeds of the first, then it is likely that the 'first' person was not in possession of his faculties at the instant of action, and is thus not responsible for his deed.

The strict identity of the acting person is therefore the second ontic foundation of responsibility, as well as the foundation of the bearing of responsibility and of being justifiably called to account.

VIII

The Substantial Structure of a Person and Responsibility

Testimony of the authentic identity of a person in the course of his life which is founded on consciousness and memory appears to be unsatisfactory, just as the identity of his body is insufficient toward this end. This identity must be much more deeply anchored in the essence or structure of a person. The way in which this essence is conceived turns out to be of special importance for a theory of responsibility, since not every answer to this question is satisfactory for the possibility of bearing responsibility. So, for example, in the second half of the 19th century the widely held view was that a person is nothing other than what was later called the stream of consciousness, whereby here and there in some cases (for example, in the work of Wundt) its cohesiveness was additionally emphasized. This held for all psychologists or philosophers of the time, who, like for example Brentano, identified consciousness with the psychical (with the so-called 'psychic phenomena'). This was because such thinkers considered themselves responsible scientists only when they took no step in their conceptions beyond the sphere of experiences (in the sense of empiricism). Until the times of William James or Bergson, and, later, Husserl and the Gestalt-psychologists, individual experiences were thereby conceived as self-sufficient wholes of elements and complexes, in themselves invariant, so that a person came to be resolved into a concatenation of so-called 'presentations' [*Vorstellungen*]. The identity of the acting person which is indispensable for responsibility is then not present, and it would be unintelligible how under these conditions one could still pose the requirement of accountability for actions which are executed. We would then be lacking any ultimate agent as well as someone who would be responsible for the given deeds.

A somewhat different conception of the person emerges when the person is identified with the unity of the stream of consciousness.[18] This unity is also frequently called the 'I'. Or, put differently: the unitary [*einheitliche*] stream of consciousness and the I, so understood, are supposed to be the same. A separate problem is how the unitariness of the stream of consciousness can be securely grounded even though there are many regularly repeating interruptions in the continuity of the flux of experiences (as for example in sleep). It is however questionable whether this problem is solvable strictly on the terrain of pure consciousness.[19] Husserl indicated how the continuous transition from one experience to the next occurs with the aid of retention and protention. For longer time intervals, the availability of recall is certainly not without significance, but already various difficulties emerge with regard to the question of how recollections are possible in general, and how it is to be established that after lengthy periods of sleep one feels oneself as the same human being, without the necessity of thereby appealing to transcendent objects and processes. None of the solutions to these problems on the basis of pure experiences suffice for grounding the possibility of responsibility and of responsible action. One cannot, after all, say that it is the unitary stream of consciousness which is responsible for the deeds actualized in the occurrence of single experiences. The personal I is indispensable as the originary source of volitional decisions and for the performance of responsible actions, and likewise its identity is indispensable throughout the whole duration of bearing responsibility.

One can ask, however, why it should necessarily be a *personal* I. Why should the pure ego of the original, transcendental consciousness not fully suffice for responsibility? The identity of this ego is indeed maintained in the flow of consciousness and comprises accordingly the ultimate foundation for the unitariness of this flow. It is also the source of every deliberate decision, thus there accrues to it the responsibility for its modes of action and deeds. Is a personal I, a person, then really needed for this purpose? According to Husserl, both the person and his existential centre [*Seinszentrum*], the personal I, is a transcendent object constituted in determinate sequences of pure experiences, an object which precisely for this reason reaches beyond the absolutely immanent transcendental consciousness and its ego. This ego is, again according to Husserl, relative in its essence and being with respect to particular manifolds of experiences constituting it. Is it necessary to reach to this personal being, which first has to be constituted, in order to make responsibility possible, and thereby penetrate into the realm of being of the real world? Or indeed is it *permissible* to do so, with a view to this end? Does one not relinquish in this way precisely that factor which is really the proper bearer of decision and action, – and of the bearing of responsibility – i.e. the pure ego? In contrast to this pure ego, according to Husserl, the personal I is supposed to be a constituted, somehow secondary, formation, which cannot be an authentic bearer and agent of action, since, among other things, it is only constituted *in* acting.

But, does the personal I, as a constituted formation of the conscious life of the pure ego, really lose its capacity to function as an executor of acts and subject of action? Is this personal I somehow a different and second ego, in comparison to the 'pure' ego about which all transcendentally oriented philosophers speak, Husserl included? And is there between them some difference in the locus of origin [*Ursprünglichkeit*] of the decisions and actions undertaken? It seems that such is not in the least the case. Pathological phenomena of dissociation aside, there do not exist in *one* human being two different original egos. The alleged differences in locus of origin and in the centrality within the stream of consciousness and within the being of the person, seem to be altogether contradictory to the essence of the ego. There can be *only* the *one*, indeed ultimately original and originary [*quellenhafte*] ego. The 'pure' ego must be identical, in its ego-like structure and in its role in the human being, with the 'personal' I. Both the pure ego and the personal I can be equally correctly considered as the axis of every action and responsibility. But, as I have tried to show elsewhere[20], the 'pure' ego is merely an *abstraction* – which is, to be sure, methodologically not unfounded – from the concrete personal essence of a human being, and it can be neither existentially independent of the psyche of a human being, and in particular of one whose personality is shaped this way or that in the course of life, nor existentially self-sufficient in relation to it. The isolation [*Hervorhebung*] of the 'pure' experiences, which unfold to form the stream of consciousness, together with their identical act source, the pure ego, from out of the full existential domain of a human being is merely the result of a methodically irreproachable procedure, the so-called 'transcendental reduction', which must be carried out for the purposes of a theory of knowledge free of fundamental errors. It demarcates that which is immanently accessible to cognition, and therewith existentially indubitable, within the full existential and qualitatively determinate composition [*Seins- und Soseinsbestand*] of a human being. It does not, however, change anything of the real, essential relations between the 'pure' (or, better: 'purified') ego and the psyche or person of a human being, and on closer examination it should not do so. Husserl, as we know, goes much farther as regards this point, and believes that the 'reduction' is capable of separating out pure consciousness (more accurately, the pure stream of consciousness) and the pure ego as a certain metaphysical residuum, with which the real human being, and specifically his psyche or person, is to be contrasted. The human being and his psyche are then existentially relative in their being with respect to a determinate manifold of experiences and to the pure ego. Husserl thus recognizes an essential distinction in mode of being between these two existential spheres, and insists that the pure ego is ontically dependent on neither the person nor the psyche of a human being, and so could exist even if the person did not exist, whereas the person (and the human being as a whole) could not exist without the pure ego and the correlative pure experiences.

However this matter is to be settled (and I would not here want to resolve it with some simple *credo*, since to decide it in a responsible manner would require extensive analysis), I must emphasize that one cannot restrict oneself to the pure ego and to pure experiences when considering either the bearing, or assuming, of responsibility. For, first of all, the deed for which the agent is to be responsible must be a real action in the real world; it must also be performed by a real human being with a defined character. The mere experiencing of this action, as something not truly accomplished *realiter*, would not at all suffice for the bearing of responsibility. Responsibility arises for the agent only out of the reality of the deed. And a pure ego devoid of any characteristic features, of the sort which Husserl at first set forth[21], could realize neither the deed nor the bearing of responsibility for it in a manner stemming from, as well as motivated and determined by, the character of a person. The carrying out of the deed itself is subject to a two-fold condition: to the real circumstances in which it takes place and perhaps to the equally real causes in the world; on the other hand to the nature of the person as an acting subject, as this is developed at the moment of the deed, whereby his body is naturally not without influence on the course of the deed. The human being must be characterised by, for example, particular discretion and care if he is to act responsibly. He must frequently possess great moral courage and fortitude when assuming responsibility where it is dangerous to defend the values for which he struggles or to openly admit his culpability, and – if it should come to that – willingly to accept the consequences of his deed. He must often display inner strength and perseverance in bearing responsibility. He must first of all have the skill clearly to grasp positive and negative values, and have a sensitive conscience in order to be able to recognize clearly before himself the possibly negative value of an action already begun, which was for him deceptively worthy. He must also have the strength to overcome his own inclinations or desires and to oppose enticements or temptations. All these are real properties or capacities which form the character of his person and which are displayed or expressed in his modes of behaviour and experiences, but which are not reducible to, or identifiable with, these experiences. If he lacks any of these varied character traits then both his action and the way in which he assumes responsibility in fact run their course entirely differently, and he becomes encumbered with serious, perhaps oppressive, guilt. None of this would be realizable for a pure ego.

If we concede all this, then we have to insist that in determining the conditions for the possibility of responsibility we transcend the sphere of pure consciousness and of the pure ego and include in our considerations the person along with his total character. All theories which reduce the person to manifolds of pure experiences are insufficient for the clarification of the ontic foundations of responsibility. Fulfillment of the requisites of responsibility is possible only insofar as a human being, in particular his mind and his person, is regarded as a real object persisting in time[22], an object which has a special, characteristic form. The agent, as an acting person, must additionally have a special form which makes acting in the real world possible for him, and which makes possible the specific modes of conduct involved in assuming and bearing responsibility. This is a wide theme for complicated considerations which cannot be further developed here, though we must point to the tasks of responsibility as one indispensable factor in the entire problem-context of responsibility. Firstly, however, let us go into greater detail concerning one feature of the structure of a person who is capable of being responsible.

IX

Freedom and Responsibility

A person who is to bear responsibility for his deed must, as we have already established, be *free* in his decisions and deeds. According to our earlier considerations this means nothing other than that the given conduct is his *own* deed. But this in turn means that the deed follows from the person's initiative and at the moment of its being undertaken and in the course of its performance it is at least *independent* of any factual matters which do not include the person in his immediate environment, factual matters which could in principle exert an influence on the person's decision and on the implementation of the deed. This presupposes, on the one hand, a definite formal structure of the person, and on the other, a particular structure of the real world in which the person lives and acts. Both issues now need to be clarified.

In order to be 'independent' of the surrounding world in his decisions and in the actions issuing from them, the person must, above all, contain a centre of action, which enables him to take initiative and at the same time to have defence mechanisms which prevent his being disturbed in his acting. But he must also be sensitive to outside intrusions, insofar as his responsibility springs from a determinate form of his living together with the surrounding reality, and particularly with other people. The person must therefore be open and receptive in his behaviour and in his so-being, and at the same time protected and insensitive in other respects. His behaviour in acting and reacting, if it is to relieve him of the responsibility which burdens him, must also be 'rational', i.e., it must lead to the appropriate goal. The person must be capable of finding, and disposing over, the means which make possible the attainment of this goal. The person's openness must allow him not only to receive stimuli and affectations from outside but also to cognize them, to understand them. His being sheltered, and likewise his being open, therefore, do not have to be fortuitous, but must frequently be of a highly complicated kind which becomes transformed in the course of life, enabling him to adapt to the changing situations and not only not to submit to action in his interplay with the real world, but also to act responsibly and to assume responsibility for his action.

In other words: the acting person (a whole which together with the body forms a unity) must, as I have put it elsewhere[23], consist of a relatively isolated system, and indeed a system of a very special kind, which is impossible for dead things and which also cannot be realized in all living beings. The task of exactly working out the general form of such a system, which is furthermore subject to various modifications, has not been discerned thus far, and it has also not been surmised that here lies the key to the solution of the so-called problem of freedom.

It cannot of course be denied that many concrete factual states have been empirically discovered and investigated, so that a quite rich stock of factual material has actually been accumulated, but for various reasons this still did not lead to an understanding of the gradually evolving problem. On the one hand this was due to the fact that one treated the human being either purely materialistically as *'l'homme machine'*, which is also partially the case in current cybernetics, or as a whole composed of two heterogeneous, and also somehow disjoint, factors – body and psyche (consciousness) – a whole, in which at best an ultimately mysterious 'psycho-physical parallelism' governs. But then – in order not to pursue an 'irresponsible metaphysics' this psyche was reinterpreted as a flow of 'experiences', of 'psychic phenomena'. For this reason one could never consider the human being as an original unity, a whole. Those on the other hand, who were at all inclined to speak of 'systems' in the physical world, rather than to decompose the world into mere events which in some inexplicable way occur juxtaposed in an orderly manner, managed to distinguish only between, so-called 'open' and 'closed' systems. Closed systems were in fact regarded as an ideal limiting case, which could never be fully realized in actuality except, perhaps, in the case of the whole real, material world itself. 'Open' systems in contrast were frequently treated as if they were 'open' *from all sides*, i.e. nowhere 'shielded', 'delimited', 'isolated', so that they would then have to decompose into mere events, which would extend in all directions and vanish into the infinite manifold of the world-process. These 'open' systems were therefore once again something like a merely conceptually formed ideal. If however an 'open' system is to be able to sustain itself effectively within the real world for a time, as something identically the same, then it should not be universally open but must, at least in some respects, be bounded off from the surrounding world and partially isolated or, better, shielded from it. In the experimental practice of physical research one has striven always somehow to demarcate the investigated system in reality and to isolate it with respect to appropriately chosen aspects, hence to build isolators, screening devices, into the concrete research situation so that the phenomenon, or process, to be investigated could proceed, and consequently be observed, without being disturbed in its nature and purity. No experiment at all would be possible without these practical mechanisms. But the general concept of a relatively (partially) open, and likewise of a partially shielded, isolated, system was not arrived at even on the basis of these countless, practically realized cases.[24] So the organism, and subsequently the human being, could also not be conceived and considered under this aspect.[25] This was the case in particular because the human body was treated as a mere special case of a material mass, 'linked' to 'consciousness' in some mysterious way.

The acquisition of so many valuable results with reference to the human body was possible in empirical investigation only because one worried very little about the concept of an open system and always used artificial barriers by means of properly adjusted isolators or screening devices, and only afterwards were the processes and factual states made possible by this arrangement forced conceptually into an 'open system' schema. Still, the understanding that a human being as person is such a very complicated, partially isolated, system of a higher order, hierarchically built up out of many lower systems, has heretofore not dawned on the consciousness of anthropology and its sub-disciplines of psychology, anatomy, and human physiology. Today, therefore, we possess only scant information on the structure of a human being as a partially isolated system. We have to restrict ourselves here to indicating several of the main features of such systems.

First of all the conception of an organism as it has developed in theoretical biology thanks to the studies of von Bertalanffy is not wholly satisfactory. The main emphasis is laid there on the so-called dynamic equilibrium which governs within the organism and makes possible its continued existence. However, it has not been adequately shown how this equilibrium is possible for even a short interval of time. It is [seen as being] maintained merely due to an accidental setting together and arrangement of the organism and its environment, or through relatively constant mechanisms and organs within the organism itself which protect it from destruction by alien factors, isolate it from at least some external affects, and thereby make possible the relative constancy of the life processes. The condition for the existence of such an 'organismic' system inheres in the fact that there is possible not only access into its interior by external processes and an intercourse with the outside world, thus that it remain 'open', but also that it have so-called 'protective walls' which shield it partially from the outside world and therefore isolate it relatively. Empirical research into the structure and function of organisms and into the multifarious processes occurring in them indicates that every organism is in fact, and must be, such a 'relatively isolated' system.[26] A multi-cellular organism (although it appears that this also holds for a one-celled organism) is a relatively isolated system of a very high order, and as such contains in itself very numerous, likewise relatively isolated, systems of lower and lower levels, which are hierarchically ordered and variously situated within the organism, and are at the same time both partially interconnected and also partially segregated, as a consequence of which they can exercise the specific functions which are characteristic to them relatively undisturbed. An appropriate entirely peculiar division of labour develops among the various systems, which allows very diverse functions or processes to take place simultaneously. At the same time it becomes feasible for them all to interlink into a totality of functions, the life-process of the organism. Since, however, these subsystems are at the same time open, this also makes possible their reciprocal influence, and thereby their collaboration.

In order to illumine this, let us take as an example the systematic structure of some higher organism, e.g. of a mammal or of a man. We take as our point of departure the fundamental idea that the execution of *two* basic functions belongs to the essence of an organism: to sustain its life and to make possible the preservation of the species, i.e. to have progeny. The following hierarchically ordered parts and their subsystems can then be exhibited in the organism:

A. *The Sustenance System*

I. The Basic Skeletal and Motor Systems:
Partial Systems:
1. skeletal system
2. muscular system
3. the skin (also as an outer protective mechanism)

II. System of Material Exchange:
Partial Systems:
1. system of gas exchange
   a) blood and the haemogenous system
   b) the circulatory system
      α) the heart
      β) the arterial system
      γ) the venous system
   c) lungs and the respiratory system
2. system of nourishment (fluid and solid substances)
   a) system of motive limbs
   b) prehensile apparatus (work)
   c) oral cavity
      α) palate
      β) teeth
      γ) salivary glands, etc.
   d) esophagus
   e) stomach
   f) intestinal system
   g) pancreas
   h) liver
   i) kidneys
3. excretory system
   a) bladder
   b) ureter
   c) large intestine
   d) perspiratory glands in the skin

III. Regulatory System:
Partial Systems: 1. nervous system
a) central nervous system
α) brains
β) spinal system
b) system of peripheral nerves (the sympathetic systems)
2. system of inner secretion
a) pituitary gland
b) adrenal gland
3. blood as the body's warmth regulators, warmth regulators in general, perspiratory glands
4. defensive system
a) production of antibodies
b) phagocytes (white corpuscles)
c) expulsion of foreign bodies
d) closure mechanisms (capilary constriction)

IV. Information System:
Partial Systems: 1. system of external senses and links with the central organ:
a) sight
b) hearing
c) tactile and temperature apparati
d) olfactory organs
e) gustatory system
2. system of 'deep sensations' [*Empfindungen*] (highly complex)
3. threshold-of-consciousness system (in the brain)
a) cortex
b) thalamus
c) *substantia reticularis*
4. system of storage and transmission of information
a) memory
b) language

B. *The Reproductive System*
1. sexual organs
2. sex glands
3. cyetic system

As we see, each of these systems, outside of the ultimately lowest systems (elements), is superordinate with respect to lower systems, which work together and make possible the function of the immediately higher system. At the same time each of these systems is distinguished by being located in some sack, in some covering (e.g. pericardium, pleura, hard and soft meninx, and the like), which segregates it from other systems and which simultaneously exercises the same function in every system: on the one hand it protects the system from certain strictly defined kinds of influence to be found outside the system, and always in response only to a certain degree of intensity of influences and to a determinate kind of impress exerted by them; on the other hand, however, it permits certain special kinds of outside influences to encroach into the interior of the system, and it allows certain processes taking place in its interior to pass outside into certain other systems of the body. At the same time, this covering allows certain select substances to penetrate into the system, as well as allowing these or other substances to leave the system. The covering is like a sieve which is differently permeable in one direction than in another. Consequently, the interior of the system exhibits a chemical composition different from its surroundings in the same organism. The function of the covering of the system leads everywhere to the same kind of effect, although great differences in detail obtain in this regard among particular systems: there occurs everywhere a definite *selection* of influences affecting the system or of substances getting into it, as well as a selection of forces and substances leaving the system. In consequence of the heterogeneity of the functions of the systems which are subordinated to the organism as a whole, there comes about within the organism a peculiar collaboration of all these functions, out of which that dynamic equilibrium in the total functioning of the organism that Ludwig von Bertalanffy speaks about first emerges. As long as the dynamism of this equilibrium is maintained within certain unsurpassable limits or as long as it comes to a restoration of equilibrium, after some impinging disturbance, due to the appropriate protective mechanisms – the given organism remains alive. It appears, however, that there are certain natural aging processes of the organism. This leads to the equilibrium becoming increasingly more labile and increasingly more difficult to restore, until finally it comes to non-equilibrium, and death ensues.

Let us give some examples to support this conception of the organism. I confine myself here to examples relating to the structure of the human body.

The whole body is surrounded by a well-defined enclosure – for man this is the skin, for the majority of mammals – the hide. It separates the body from the external world and exercises various functions in the life-process; it is composed of many layers, into which are built a great number of different organs. Determinate functions accrue to it precisely because it forms the boundary between the body and the external world. It discloses many small apertures; at bottom, it is something like a dense net, which participates in the consumption of oxygen by the body and in the expulsion of CO_2. Death results if it is burned over a large surface, since the assimilation of oxygen through the skin is severely hindered. Small quantities of water are also allowed to pass through the skin into the interior of the body, although it is for the most part kept out. On the other hand, perspiration gets out through orifices in the skin. Water and various chemical substances leave the organism through the skin with perspiration. No sooner are the walls of the capillary vessels located in the skin damaged, then the skin becomes suffused with blood, but this is not let through provided the quantity of blood is not too large. But if the skin is cut, blood flows out through the incurred incision. If the flow of blood is not counteracted, then it comes to a 'blood drainage' of the organism. In warm-blooded animals the skin plays a certain, though not overly significant, role in thermal regulation.[27] Fat and muscle both contribute as constituents of the so-called 'outer casing' of the body, which exercises the function of its thermal isolation from outside temperatures. In this respect the sense of the relative isolation of body systems from the external world perhaps manifests itself best in the changes of skin temperature and the changes of body warmth bound up with these.

The digestive system, especially the stomach and intestines, is another instance of a subordinate, relatively shielded system within the body. Thanks to its walls it withholds nutritive substances from the remaining parts of the body and makes it possible for the initial digestive processes to proceed, for the most part without interference from the other processes occurring in the body[28]; at the same time, however, due to mechanisms built into the walls of the small intestine, it makes possible a selective migration, so to speak, of certain chemical products of digestion, through these walls into the blood, and therewith into other parts of the body, where, through the mediation of other chemical reactions, they are utilized for the synthesis of chemical compounds necessary for the life-processes of the organism. The abdominal cavity, where the greater part of the digestive system is located, is separated from the thorax by a membrane (diaphragm), and this membrane, in turn, makes possible the in principle undisturbed progress of digestive processes, on the one hand, and the functions of the lungs and heart, on the other, although that is not tantamount to saying that the membrane is absolutely dense and impermeable. The heart, with the veins entering and arteries leaving it, and the lungs are once again separated from each other by appropriately constructed membranes (pericardium, pleura), which make possible the undisturbed progress of the processes occurring in their interiors. The latter should not be taken to mean that these processes occur wholly independently of each other. For without the mechanical work of the heart, blood could not flow into the proper parts of the lungs and chemical processes in the red corpuscles could not be carried out there, and without this chemical 'cleansing' of the blood and supply of oxygen to the red corpuscles, the heart could not, in turn, realize its mechanical work. All this is made possible only because both these systems are not absolutely closed off from each other, but are partially open and partially shielded. There are paths between them along which the mentioned dependencies may flow. There are partial systems in the body which at least at first glance are superordinate to other systems, as, for example, the entire nerve apparatus which, along with the processes occurring in it (electrical currents, chemical processes?), governs many other systems in that it supplies them (for example, the heart) with impulses appropriate to their functions and also regulates them appropriately. At the same time, this system is highly segregated and shielded from the remaining parts of the body by membranes (e.g. meninges) and even bones (skull), although it must itself be provided with oxygen (and other substances). Thus, it depends on blood circulation for its vitality and functions, and especially on the functioning of the heart and lungs, the functioning of which it itself sets in motion and regulates. In this way they sustain a mutual equilibrium and it may be a point of contention as to which of them is subordinate to the other. Yet the relative isolation of both systems from each other is maintained and is indispensable to their regular functioning. If some hole opens up in the cerebral artery, then to begin with a certain part of the brain becomes dysfunctional due to the bleeding and is then destroyed, should the organism not succeed in draining off the blood. The heart can also come to a standstill because of this, and death follow. The glands, perhaps the entire system of glands of inner secretion, also seem to play a superordinate role with respect to other systems, in that particular discharges exert an overwhelming influence on the functioning of many systems. Each of these glands is encapsuled in a casing and is to a high degree independent in the production of special chemical compounds, but in spite of this the glands are subject to certain outside influences leading to the emission into the field of the organism of the highly specific chemical compounds which are produced, whereby tremendous alterations in the processes of many body-systems are sometimes induced (phenomena of allergy, etc.).

Of special interest to us is the very complicated system, consisting of many apparently segregated parts, which I have called here the information system. There are the different sense organs composed of many specifically and variously structured nerve cells, the ends of which are, as we say, 'sensitive' [*empfindlich*]. Their functioning is very peculiar and, in the final analysis, still continues to be very mysterious. Although they are all shielded by membranes, they are subject to various outside affectations such as electromagnetic waves or chemical processes, and are also partially susceptible to purely mechanical processes which affect their boundaries and elicit peculiar chemical, and perhaps also electrical, transformations in these cells. These transformations are not however restricted to the nerve ends, but are transported along the path of the nervous system itself all the way to the central parts of the system (the brain), and evoke new processes there. Remarkably, it does not end there; something entirely heterogeneous appears, a qualitative formation which one ordinarily calls a 'sensation', and inseparably with it also a cognizance [*Wissen*] of this 'sensation'. It is localized in a definite manner, either at some definite place on the body, for example on the skin, when we touch something with our finger, or in the interior, or, finally, completely outside our body, but never in the brain, despite the oft repeated assertions by physiologists and physiological psychologists. In a state of wakefulness we constantly have such 'sensations', and indeed in immense quantities which on the one hand show the things appearing to us in their various states and processes, and, on the other hand, also reveal to ourselves our body in different postures [*Lagen*] and behavioural modes. In having them, we possess a certain stock of bits of information about the world surrounding us and about ourselves. It appears to be correct that we receive this information owing to a completely definite system of mechanisms located in our body, closely interconnected with the central nervous system and the peripheral nerves. I have already said that this system of mechanisms which provides us with information is bounded and enclosed in a casing on the one hand, but is 'open' and therefore stands in close relations to various other systems of the body, on the other. It will presently turn out that it is, or must be, 'open' and 'screened' (isolated) in a very special way. Henri Bergson already pointed out that a human being always has only a certain definite *selection* of sensations (out of all those he might have, were he not constrained by the peculiarities of his sense organs and also by his central nervous system). For example, only a quite restricted part of the spectrum of electromagnetic waves (or photons) can set off photochemical reactions in the eye which are accompanied by the phenomena of light and colour, whereas no such phenomena occur outside of this region of waves. Perhaps there are corresponding chemical processes in the eye also for other wavelengths. But they are somehow mute or blind, and therefore procure for us no information. One could say that the eye is structured in such a way that it is isolated or shielded from the outside world in this respect. To other wavelengths it is 'open', and supplies us with the respective information. It is likewise insensitive to any of those physical processes which provide us with sounds or noises, i.e. the eye is appropriately shielded from them. In contrast, the ear is open for precisely these processes, and with the aid of other parts of the central nervous system provides us with sound phenomena. Every sense organ is a partial open system which is attuned to a *special selection* of outside processes and at the same time also shielded in other respects. But there is still another selection of a different kind which can be met with in these sense organs, namely the so-called threshold of sensitivity of the respective organ. The process impingeing on the organ must achieve a certain (minimum) intensity before a sensation (e.g. a light-or colour-appearance) can come about at all. If by contrast the light intensity is for example too high, and the eye is not artificially shielded, then it is damaged and no longer provides us with any sensations.

A very complicated empirical problem is what role the different kinds of selection play in the life of the organism. It would be premature and risky to want to solve this problem merely along the lines of a utility-conception or, as Bergson has done, to say that the phenomena reaching the organism always 'mirror' man's possible action. But it can be said without any great danger that not only is what the sieve of these sense organs allows through, but also what it blocks out, important for the life of the animal (and, in particular, to a much higher degree for human beings). If all the 'information' (phenomenal data) corresponding to the totality of processes that impinge on the body over a given time interval were to reach the human being, then such a tumult would arise that he would not be capable of grasping them altogether, leaving aside the question of whether the data would then be at all differentiated. For our problem it is important primarily that the sieve of sense organs blocks and keeps away from the human being a certain mass of data. Of decisive significance for our main problem is also the fact that a human being possesses only a very limited number of variously attuned sense organs that are not adapted to all the modalities of the processes which are continually impinging on, and perhaps even penetrating, his body (we do not 'hear' Hertz waves, or cosmic rays, or radioactive waves). I shall speak about this presently. First, however, certain details still have to be filled in about the sub-systems of the information system of the human body.

A special informational organ, probably a very complicated partial network of the nervous system, furnishes the human being with a wealth of data in the form of so-called 'deep sensations' (muscle and joint sensations, sexual sensations, pains etc.). They inform the human being about the normal and anomalous processes in the interior of his body, about the state of the individual organs and limbs (for example, about the position and movement of the limbs), so that the human being continually feels his body from within, and thereby feels, as we say, this way or that, for example 'exhausted' or 'fresh'. A new, noteworthy selection is thereby carried out once again, a selection from all the possible data which could reach us, but do not in fact do so. Of the 'normal' processes in our body, we (luckily) experience nothing at all, for example, of the diverse chemical digestive processes. In contrast, we are informed in a flash about other processes, for example about sexual arousal. We are made aware of the movements of our hands and feet through manifold muscle sensations, but these sensations are normally so fleeting and peripheral that we ordinarily know little about them; they do not interfere in any way for example in our mental work or in conversation with our friends (although, there, once more, various muscular sensations run their course in our palate and lips). Not until something out of the ordinary comes up (a pain resulting from the improper placement of the foot) do 'sensations' swarm to the foreground of our consciousness and begin to distract us. If muscular sensations in our fingers were to thrust themselves upon us during a piano recital so as to make us somehow attentive to them, then we would be unable to continue playing. But if we did not possess these sensations at all (for example following a cocaine injection), then playing would again be quite impossible for us.

Fleeting 'sensations' that flow by enable us to have purposive control of our limbs. Generally, however, they must be very muffled and carefully selected with respect to their degree of attenuation in order not to attract our attention but merely to facilitate for us the guidance of movement. In this role they are an essential factor of the bodily movements which form a whole, and they perform their subordinate, auxiliary function within this whole. This function serves also to point out the very close relation between the functions of an information system of this kind and the mechanical functions of the system of bodily movements. On the other hand, it can be easily shown that anatomically these functions belong to two different systems which are partially isolated from each other.

In the schema of the structure of the human body out of relatively isolated systems as presented above, a particular sub-system has been singled out within the information system which I have called the threshold of consciousness [*Bewußtseinspforte*] (as a special constituent part within the brain). To begin with, this is only a conceptual hypothesis which is brought in because one seeks a bodily factor as a *pendant* to the most radical transformation which occurs in human beings, the transformation from the absence of consciousness to an aware, 'wakeful' state, to a being conscious, to a 'being-in-possession-of-one's-senses'. Pathological cases (such as for example a cerebral haemorrhage) aside, absence of consciousness is a normal state of man in deep, dreamless sleep. As far as I know, it has not yet been explained on what this state of sleep depends. It can depend either on a special state of certain organs in the brain, for example on some particular inhibition [*Vergiftung*], or conversely on a process of de-inhibition [*Entgiftung*], through a complete 'setting-out-of-action' of the nervous system, or it can depend on there being some specific organ, as it were, in the central nervous system (cerebral cortex, *thalamus, substantia reticularis*?) which makes possible man's wakefulness (his conscious living) or entails an absence of consciousness following a change in its functioning. The whole information system is set out of action, even though for example the sense organs remain intact (and can even be exposed to outside affectations), and even though all the remaining vital processes like breathing, digesting, etc., continue in their course. Access to wakefulness or consciousness is opened and after a while closed, just as if someone were closing a gate and then opening it. The fact that often dreamless sleep sets in of itself after a period of time, and then also passes of itself, indicates that we are dealing with a primordial life-phenomenon which is deeply anchored in the structure of the human (animal) body. What brings it about appears to be unexplained. Nevertheless, we encounter here an ultimate fact which essentially distinguishes animals, and in particular human beings, from other organismic beings, a fact which could not obtain without some organic basis.

Our stream of consciousness does not, however, contain only those experiences which relate to current states of our body and of the outside world, but also so-called recollections (or, more generally: the 'retaining-in-mind' of facts which belong in the past or future). It is universally accepted that in the first case there are specific mechanisms in the brain that enable us to have access to past facts in the form of recollections. It has not been completely clarified on what these mechanisms depend. Their occurrence is inferred, since after certain instances of brain damage (aphasias) memories in general, or memories of a particular kind, are lost. Amazingly, in the normal (intact) state of these brain mechanisms it is not the collective past of a man's life that is accessible to him in the form of recollections, but always only *selected*, individual recollections or the – to a certain degree potential – awareness of what is retained in memory. Attempts have been made to explain by means of the so-called association theory why at any given moment just these rather than other recollections are awakened, as if the experiences present precisely now (perceptions, feelings, and the like) 'awaken' the respective recollection, or allow it to arise at all. But is the corresponding system of the brain thereby set in motion? Does something change in the process taking place in it; or, does everything proceed without anything happening in the nervous system? Physiologists would certainly subscribe to the first alternative. But to do so is to concede that the corresponding part of the brain is somehow segregated, isolated from our consciousness if an awakening of the recollection is not achieved, and that this isolation is somehow terminated when the recollection is actualized. In this case also, one is presumably dealing with some relatively isolated subsystem of the central nervous system, whose structure and function leads to a selection of recollections. The majority of what is past and retained in memory is normally not allowed to pass into the state of actual consciousness, and only singular, once experienced facts are brought 'to recollection'.

I set aside here the question of how things are with facts to come in the future – whether they can be foreseen or only presumed and thereby expected, whether one should speak at all about facts obtaining in the future – since these questions are still very obscure. It would be very important, however, to tackle these problems also, since the attitude toward what will become fact in the future is especially important for responsible acting. One has to carefully reckon with what will ensue from one's action. But perhaps everything rests on correct and sufficiently many-sided inferences from facts established in the present.[29]

The stream of consciousness is constituted in its elements as an entirely specific factor in the essence of man, owing to the whole system of information and in particular to the 'threshold of consciousness', it is a stream which along with its constituent parts and functions is especially tightly integrated into the system of the body. As a pure occurrence it has the form of a process and is therefore not a 'system'. As such, the stream of consciousness needs an ontic foundation, and finds it in fact in the body on the one hand and in the human psyche on the other. It is, so to speak, a surface of contact between the body and the psyche of man. On the one hand it consists of data, conveyed to the ego by means of the bodily information system, about bodily happenings and properties, and further about the properties and processes of external things. On the other hand it contains from time to time manifestations and modes of appearance of changes in the psyche, and of its properties. It genuinely belongs to the essence of the psyche to be conscious, to have experiences, but its manifestations must also pass the threshold of consciousness. But the psyche itself is, in its properties as well as in the transformations occurring in it, nothing specifically 'consciousness-like'; it is itself not experience, but it expresses itself in experiences. And not everything that happens in the psyche must at once, or in general, attain to awareness. It seems that only acts of thought are consciousness-like, or consciously performed. Perhaps it is also the same with acts of the will, especially with volitional decisions.[30] These are in both cases modes of behaviour, or better put, 'deeds' of the ego, which is the organizational centre of the human psyche and which 'embodies' and 'represents' [*vertritt*] it. It is whatever 'speaks' on behalf of the human psyche, performs various acts, assumes responsibilities, enters into obligations, etc. All this cannot happen unconsciously. The ego draws its power for this from the powers and capacities of the psyche, and finds support for its deeds in its body. An ego 'without a psyche' is impossible; at bottom, this would be a self-contradictory concept. There are various [moments] in the psyche, however, both from the realm of occurrences (for example an emerging love or some other emotion[31], internal collapse, despair, dawning hope, etc.) as well as from the domain of character traits (like malice, inner weakness, valour, intelligence, etc.) which do not always reach awareness and hence belong to that which the ego does not know of itself. Indeed the ego must first become intimate with what is happening in its psyche. The psyche can sometimes close itself off to the ego as regards some of its states; the latter must then overcome a certain recalcitrance in order to unveil what is concealed in the former. Also, sometimes the ego cannot control the psyche, even though it seeks to dominate over it. The psyche then turns out to be 'intractable' [*widerspenstig*], just as the body sometimes does. The ego learns from both body and psyche only whatever crosses the threshold of consciousness. In other words it seems that with respect to the ego, the psyche forms a system just as relatively isolated as the body, which is partially open and partially closed relative to the ego, and that the psyche is therefore also not accessible or open to the stream of consciousness throughout its domain. The ego can attempt to 'unlock' what is closed off in its psyche. Just as any isolation of a system can be broken through, given the proper circumstances and adequate pressure, so it is also with the barriers which sometimes separate the psyche from the ego and from consciousness. Besides, it is possible that the systems of the human being, who frequently changes and consciously transforms and develops himself in the course of life, are not all rigid, unchangeable formations, but can also undergo change, and indeed in the sense that their isolation factors are altered, or that the places which were initially shielded later open up, and conversely. This is already indicated by the fact that the isolators can be broken through, given an appropriate intensity of impinging forces. This can lead to a breakdown of the whole system; in other cases, the breach can be closed up again and the infiltrating factor repulsed by appropriate elements, so that everything returns to equilibrium once again.[32] It appears that such situations occur in both the corporeal and mental life of human beings. If certain realms of the psyche are for the time being closed off from the ego, so that no knowledge of them reaches it nor is it directly influenced by them, then during that time the ego is independent in its mode of behaviour from the respective region of the psyche's being and from any changes in it. For as long as that is the case, the ego is free in its decisions and deeds from the corresponding happenings in its own psyche.

It is a particularly difficult problem whether what happens in the psyche can *directly* affect the body (and conversely) i.e., without the mediation of the ego and of consciousness; to what extent, that is to say, is the psyche open or closed off (isolated) from the body? The facts which Sigmund Freud pointed out seem to indicate that there are in fact cases in consequence of which some psychic state (which belongs to the 'unconscious') affects the body directly in such a way that it falls ill. There alos seem to be enough instances in everyday, normal life, in which some arousal (e. g. of an erotic nature) or fright first evokes a change in our body that is imparted to us as a sensation, so that we first learn in this way that something happened in our psyche. This whole region, which apparently holds concealed a wide cariety of facts, would have to be submitted to more precise investigation before we could arrive at clear and certain insights. I mention it, however, since through further investigations we could clarify to what extent the psyche can be treated as a system which is relatively isolated from the body. If this conception could be upheld, then the human being would consist of the following elements: the body (system A and B), the ego with the stream of experiences (C) and the psyche (D).

One more fact needs to be pointed out by way of closing this consideration of human nature. We know that the aggregate nervous system resolves into various subsystems: in particular, into the brain and the countless branched out peripheral nerves or into the vegetative and animal system. If some nerve end of the animal system is oroused by some factor, an impulse is sent out from there to the nerve centre. Only then does a change occur in the brain, after which, if it reaches and crosses the threshold of consciousness, there emerges a sensory phenomenon or the undergoing of a sensation. This path from the periphery to the centre is traversed with a finite speed, so that some time passes before the sensation emerges. This time may be very brief[33], but it is still quite long from a physical or, better yet, microphysical point of view. The ego or the human being can react at all only after first having suffered the respective sensation, and a certain time elapses again from the undergoing of the sensations to the onset of the reaction. In this short time between the attack on the given sub-system and the moment at which a responsive action can begin, or at which the human being acts under the influence of this stimulus, the human being can act independently of the stimulus already assaulting him. There exist much longer time spans, in which the human being is independent of external happenings in his behaviour, where he is isolated or shielded from outside influences by the mechanisms mentioned above. It is also within these limits that he can act 'freely'

The conception of man as a relatively isolated system which is constructed out of a number of subsystems therefore opens up the possibility that the human being realizes actions which are his *own*, actions which are *independent* of the external world, however much this acting is, within the human being himself, causally conditioned. Both the domains and time intervals in which this occurs do not depend only on the systemic structure of man, but also on the particular individual history of the given human being and on the circumstances in which he finds himself in the world at any given time. To be sure, this completely general characterization tells us nothing at all about which and about which kinds of actions can in general be 'freely' exercised by the human being. Only a very detailed investigation could furnish us with an answer to this question. But at the moment we are only concerned with the *fundamental* possibility of man's *own*, 'free' actions, man as a mental and bodily being. This possibility is excluded in a universally deterministic world in which there could be *no* relatively isolated system *whatever*. But since man, as a bodily and mental being which is at the same time 'centred in the ego' and conscious, appears to be a higher order system in which there resides a hierarchy of relatively isolated systems both within the human body on the one hand, and within the psyche on the other; and since both of these systems have their expression and exert their effects within pure consciousness and in the modes of behaviour (acts) of the pure ego, by which volitional decisions are undertaken, then still further questions arise, such as the extent to which this ego is, or can be, free and independent in its volitional decisions from the processes and properties of its body on one side, and from its psyche on the other. What conditions do these various sub-systems have to satisfy in order for these decisions to be really possible as the (personal) ego's 'own' deeds?

It is obvious that also these questions can be answered only after carrying out far more extensive investigations into the general structure of the systemic make-up of the human being. We would thereby have to examine further what kind of actions and decisions of the will are involved here. It is to be expected that the answer to this question can come out differently for the different kinds of action. But all these are problems which can be attacked only when one has first acknowledged the conception of human nature outlined above. If one rejects it, then it becomes at least doubtful whether one can speak at all meaningfully about responsibility.

X

The Causal Structure of the World

The problem of the possibility of free action of a person bearing responsibility is not yet thereby solved, however. For there remains the second half of the total problem-context, namely, is the causal structure of the real world such that relatively isolated systems are at all possible within it? This is an even more difficult problem than the question concerning the fundamental structure of man. We have to restrict ourselves here to the most salient remarks.[34]

To begin with, if the real world were to form the kind of causal system which emerges from the conception of Laplace, and in the last analysis from all of modern natural science and philosophy, then, as has been frequently ascertained, there would be no free decision of the will possible in this world, nor any free human (and animal) action. For this conception includes the assertion that *all* events in the real world (thus, also volitional decisions) together form one *single* system of causal relations, in which, as effects, they are uniquely and necessarily determined by their causes. I call this conception 'radical determinism'. If one admits that every decision of the will comprises an event in the world, then it is impossible to consider it as not having a cause. Therefore a positive solution of the problem of freedom can be expected only when 'freedom' is not identified with having no cause, but rather when it is conceived as the agent's 'independence' from external factors, and when it is at the same time demonstrated that radical determinism is untenable. I have attempted to give this demonstration in the just cited volume on the causal problem. Here I have to be satisfied with a few indications.

The fundamental presuppositions of radical determinism are of a two-fold kind. On the one side it is accepted without discussion that every cause is prior to its effect. In principle, this is held to be self-evident by all the natural scientists to this day. The second presupposition is often expressed in the form of the proposition that in the real world 'everything is linked [*verbunden*] with everything else'. I prefer to formulate this in the form of the assertion that all events in the real world form *one* system of causal relations. It can be stated even more exactly, but thoroughly in accord with Laplace's conception: if one forms two world-profiles [*Weltschnitte*] of *simultaneous* events, of which one is antecedent to the other, then the events of the first world-profile are causally linked with those of the second. The later profile (or the events in it?) is uniquely and completely, directly or indirectly, determined by the first. If, says Laplace, one had an 'equation' of some determinate world-profile (state of the world), then all earlier or later world-profiles would be calculable.

In practice, as human beings who are always limited in the cognition of the world, we do not know such equations. Only an omniscient God could foresee the whole future on the basis of one state of the world. We must always constrain ourselves to calculating a *section* of such a state of the world. But the unity and cohesiveness of the world consists, it seems, not only of the succession of such world-profiles, but also of *one* present. How, therefore, does it stand with all events and the things at their basis which exist in *one* and *the same* present? Are these also linked by mutual causal relations? If this were to be affirmed, then one would have to abandon the assertion that always only those events stand in a causal relation, of which one as cause is antecedent to the other as effect. If, on the other hand, one maintains this assertion, then there are *no* causal relations *whatever* between events of the *same* present. But then how is their relation to each other to be understood? Are they fully independent of each other in every respect, and do they comprise infinitely many loose (unlinked) events or things, which are segregated from and in no way condition each other? If one denies this, then only two possibilities remain. In the first case, there would be no multiplicity of events (or things) at all in the state of the world, but it would consist of *one* internally unified whole which would be wholly unchangeable in this present and would first change abruptly, as a whole, in the transition from one present to the immediately succeeding one. Consistently, both the cause and effect would always be *one* total state of the real world. It would then make no sense to ask for *single* strictly *delimited* causes and effects in the world, as natural science (and especially physics, as well as the sciences of animate nature) constantly does. If, meanwhile, one wanted to maintain the multiplicity of the events occurring in *one* present, then the wholeness of the world, its unity, would be lost, or it would have to remain unintelligible, at least until it has been shown wherein its inner connectedness consists or in what it is grounded. So one arrives at the conception that there is a multiplicity of events (or things) in a state of the world, but that there also obtains some other principle of the cohesiveness of the world-state, or of the mutual compatibility of all its elements. This principle could be a causal connection in which cause and effect are *simultaneous*, or a completely different existential connection between simultaneously existing elements of the world, or finally both the one and the other. This, therefore, needs to be investigated.

The Laplacian conception of the causal order in the real world and of its structure in general is therefore not at all as clear and self-evident as might appear at first glance and as it has been held to be (for 200 years) by philosophers of nature and natural scientists. Twentieth century physics has altered this conception only by interpreting the world-profile of simultaneous events not in the sense of a certain ‘plane’, but in the sense of the surface of a cone.[35] But then the same question still remains regarding the connectedness or lack of connectedness of the events taking place in *one* 'conically' understood simultaneity.

In place of radical determinism in the sense of Laplace, and of indeterminism, which are mutually contradictory and both very unsatisfactory, I propose a third conception. According to it this world would consist of an immense multiplicity of partially open, and at the same time partially isolated ('shielded'), systems, which despite their mutual partial segregation and shieldedness are 'interlinked' through causal relations. In various systems of a world so structured there are then on the one hand factual states which are simultaneous[36] but at the same time existentially independent, and on the other hand also factual states which are causally interdependent existentially. The former correspond to those aspects of two or more systems whose respective states are mutually and simultaneously shielded. Other factual states are either members of a causal connection in which cause and effect are *simultaneous*, and then belong to one and the same (simple) system or to two different subsystems of *one* composite system, the 'open' sides of which make possible the contemporaneousness of the cause and its effect; or they comprise the components of a causal connection in which the cause is antecedent to its effect; in the latter case they always belong to two different systems in which either the respective open places make possible[37] the genesis of the causal connection or there occurs a break in the isolation of the system. Should such a break take place, then it is a process which has its beginnings in some other system. It changes at the breakthrough point and, as thus transformed, penetrates into the interior of the infiltrated system. Here, either immediately or after a time, there occurs an intersection of this process with another process in the same system. This intersection is an event which must have some cause. In this case it is composed of two events which comprise the beginnings of the intersecting process and take place in the two participating systems (in case the process crosses through the boundary of the system at an open place, or in case it takes place in the interior of the second system, and on the boundary at the infiltrated point).

The direct causal, existential connection is thus understood in this case as a relation the first member of which (the cause) takes place antecedently to the second member (the effect). The occurrence of each of these processes is, taken each for itself, *not* a sufficient (though it is a necessary) condition for the intersection event's taking place at the conclusion of each. In this way two processes also link together two systems. But it would be premature to assert that because of this both these systems become *one* system of a higher level. For this interaction might be the one and only event which links them. This does not appear sufficient for the formation of a higher system out of two systems. It must be conceded that the fortunes of the first system, into which a process from another system penetrates, depend at least in part on certain antecedent factual states of the second system.

The systems existing in the world can be simple or composed out of several also relatively isolated systems. The composition of the system can be either hierarchical or consist of equi-ordinate systems which partially condition each other. In such a superordinate system, for example, two processes can at first develop independently in two sub-systems. At some instant they both break through the walls of their systems or pass through the open places in their boundaries and enter the domain of the super-system which comprehends them both where they intersect. The intersection event is then the effect of the initial events of both these processes, which together form the most immediate, even though not the direct, cause of this effect; but both are situated within the super-system. Cause and effect then both lie in the same super-system comprehending the sub-systems, although the effect has its most immediate composite cause in two sub-systems different from the super-system itself. Both those processes at first take place simultaneously and independently in the two sub-systems. Their beginnings were naturally caused by some other, perhaps earlier, events which might in turn be situated in different systems. The causation of these events and their mutual causal independence do not exclude each other. At the same time they are also causally independent of the processes and events unfolding outside of the two sub-systems, but which still always remain within the same super-system. Finally, also as far as their intersection event is concerned, they are independent of the processes and events which occur completely outside of the respective super-system and from which they are shielded. Concurrently with all this, there must exist in the interior of the given super-system a number of sub-system walls which are adapted to definite processes and are to a certain degree impermeable so as to make possible this independent progress of several processes in *one* super-system. The effect is causally independent of the super-system's environment to the extent that the aggregate of the initial events of the processes intersecting within the super-system and thereby leading to this effect lies in the interior of the super-system. It can also be that several of the initial events lie partially in the interior and partially outside of the super-system. Together they all form the composite cause of the effect taking place in the system, which effect stems from the intersection of the respective processes. This effect is then in part causally dependent on the environment of the super-system, but is partially independent of it. As we can see, various complicated situations can emerge in the causal conditionedness [*Bedingtheit*] of an event. There is not even excluded the case that the causation of an event within the interior of a super-system lies entirely outside its domain, as, for example, when two processes break into the super-system and intersect in its interior, but which themselves have their initial events and perhaps their causes *outside* of the given super-system. There are likewise cases for which the 'inner' conditionality is more decisive than the 'outer' conditionality, or conversely, although *both* factors are indispensable to the genesis of the effect; the kind of effect resonates to either the one or the other factor of the cause. In particular, the magnitude of this 'inner' conditionality is decisive for whether the effect and the process resulting causally from the interaction of several processes represents (as we have expressed it previously) the super-system's (e.g., the human being's) '*own*' deed or, conversely, whether it is conditioned by external factors to such an extent that it indeed unfolds in the interior of the given super-system but is already wholly 'forced' and 'alien'.

Of course, the possibility of the causal structure of a world built up of many hierarchically or equi-ordinately existing systems that we have just sketched needs to be demonstrated in deeper-reaching ontological considerations.[38] But this is a very extensive investigation, whose first beginnings and directions of research have been barely indicated here. This conception should therefore be neither presupposed nor considered as worked out. What has been outlined, however, should open up a vista onto a certain problem which is to point to the possibility of 'free' decision and action in a world which is causally ordered in this manner. The novelty of this conception depends, among other things, on its allowing various degrees and modes of 'freedom' and 'non-freedom' (all the way up to full non-freedom) in contrast to the traditonal conception according to which there can be either absolutely free or absolutely unfree decisions and actions.

Naturally, after a purely ontological working out of this possible causal structure of the world, an empirical or metaphysical investigation of the facts must be carried out which is to demonstrate the factual structure of the real world in this respect.

XI

The Temporality of the World and Responsibility

Responsibility, and the fulfillment of the requirements which are imposed by it on the agent, is interwined with time in a three-fold manner: 1) through the agent's *remaining* responsible after accomplishing the deed; 2) through the remaining valid of the values which are created or destroyed by the agent's deed and for the destruction of which he is responsible; 3) through the connection of all these actions with the causal order of the world, which on its side presupposes the temporal structure of the world. Thus, the possibility and meaningfulness of responsibility depends on the kind of temporal structure the world has, or wherein it rests. Various conceptions of time have been submitted for discussion throughout the history of European philosophy. There are some among them which make it impossible to speak meaningfully about responsibility, and some which make its realization possible. They thereby stand to each other in various conflicting positions.

Thus there is the Kantian conception of time as an *a priori* form of intuition, which shows itself to be a form of the world of appearances in the course of our cognizing the objects of the real world experientially and thereby itself comes to be grasped as a form. With Kant the world of appearances is contrasted to the world of things in themselves. But the Kantian conception allows two different interpretations; first, an *agnostic* interpretation according to which these things are *unknowable* [*unerkennbar*] with respect to temporality or spatiality and categorical structure, and indeed either in general for every arbitrary subject of cognition or merely for us humans, who have to make use of *a priori* forms of intuition and categories when cognizing; secondly, an *ontic* interpretation, according to which the real world of things in themselves is altogether *atemporal*.

The so-called 'realistic' conception of time is set in opposition to the Kantian conception; according to the former the real world and the things and processes in it, as they are in themselves, are temporal, without it thereby being stated how time itself is to be conceived.

If the Kantian conception in its ontic interpretation were correct, then neither the bearing nor assuming of responsibility, nor, finally, the fulfillment of the demands posed by it would be possible. Responsibility could exist, and be shorn off through the fulfillment of its demands, only in the *world of experience*. But then one could not justly speak of *moral* responsibility, which in a metaphysical sense burdens human beings in reality and imposes on them an actually existing culpability. And, in fact, it would be equally inadequate to the merely phenomenal character of time as well as to the purely phenomenal character of the categories, especially causality. This, then, also compelled Kant himself to an essential revision of his standpoint as soon as he attacked the problems of freedom and morality. I do not wish to go further into this here. I restrict myself to the assertion that a *merely phenomenal*, appearance-like responsibility could not possess a moral value in the authentic sense, nor would it be capable of really burdening the agent and imposing on him the obligation of vindicating himself. Moral values and their realization require something more, so to speak, than a mere appearance-actuality. Thus responsibility and the realization of its demands can become actual and sensible only with an authentic, not merely appearance-like, reality of the temporality of the world and of what happens in it.[39]

Yet responsibility would not be possible in every conception of the temporal structure of the real world. Once again there are conflicting views in this regard. In every conception of time there is a distinction made between past, present and future which carries over to that which belongs in the present, in the past and in the future, i.e. to that which is, which was and which will be. St. Augustine was of the opinion that only that which belongs to the present exists, while that which belongs to the past and the future does not exist at all; the first, because it once was but no longer obtains and the second, because it is still to be, but has not yet set in. Their 'no longer' and their 'not yet' is decisive for their non-being in the present. For this reason, past being is strictly speaking no being at all. But St. Augustine says at the same time that this 'past-being' is only tantamount to 'being-represented-as-past' and 'future-being' is tantamount to 'being-represented-as-future'. In the first case it is recalled, in the second it is expected. In other words there are the phenomena of that which belongs to the past and future but there is no 'that which belongs to the past' itself or 'that which belongs to the future' itself, for 'passing' means as much as 'ceasing to be'. 'To be past' therefore, means something more, and something far more radical, than merely 'to be no longer present or available for someone'. As 'recalled' it remains there to consciousness and as such it is still *quasi*-present, but in itself it no longer exists in the true sense. One argues analogously in relation to 'that which belongs to the future'.

The 'present' in the sense of a 'now-being' or of 'that which belongs to the now' can thereby be understood in various ways. For the most part the 'now' is understood as a so-called 'time-point', as a punctual limit, as a place within the time continuum. 'Now being' is tantamount to 'coming-into-being' and thereby, indeed, at the same moment concomitantly 'going-out-of-being', vanishing. The now-being is temporal, but without extension. There is no duration of that which belongs to the now, and in fact there is no 'duration' (at all), since 'to endure' means, to begin with, 'to exist longer than in one now'. But this is in fact excluded by the radical conception of a 'punctual' now, since the 'enduring' of something presupposes that what endures somehow maintains itself within being over a span of time as *something identical*. And this 'span of time' signifies first of all a temporal phase which radically transcends *one* now. As soon as 'passing away' means as much as 'stepping-out-of-being', vanishing, annihilation, the possibility of remaining identical over more than one present is excluded. Strictly speaking there are then neither things as objects persisting in time nor processes which unfold in some temporal phase. There are only momentary events which are set into being punctually and at once vanish. For this conception of what exists in time, duration is tantamount to 'stepping-into-time' and 'vanishing-out-of-time' ever anew, in a multiplicity of now-moments. For this reason some '*creatio continua*', an ever new creation, was demanded of God for the real world, since every created world immediately vanishes. There are then infinitely many, ever new worlds, and their manifold thus has the force of a continuum. In view of this conception there is no human being who would remain the same to be responsible for his action, nor any action, nor the bearing of responsibility, nor, finally, its remission through the fulfillment of its demands. In order for continually unfolding processes and things, as objects persisting in time, to be possible, one must concede that besides 'now-stepping-into-being' and 'now-stepping-out-of-being' there is also 'what has been' or 'what belongs to the past' which would remain *identical* in correlation with what belongs to the now, even though it continues to exist in some other mode of being.

The agent is responsible for his deed and its outcome only when they have become reality. They then belong to the past. But if there is no past deed (no 'what has been done') in any sense, then nothing remains for which the agent could be held accountable. But then also the values which are realized or destroyed through the deed, like their realization or destruction, cease to be. To the extent that one has a recollection of the performed deed and its negative consequences, one can in fact assume responsibility, or call someone to account for them, since the recollection determines the direction of how the inflicted harm should be redressed. Without this recollection both the attempt at restitution and the reparation would be without an object. But if nothing existing were to correspond to what is recollected, then there would be no way to distinguish it from something merely imagined, and the right to call someone to account for something non-existent would be unfounded – would, indeed, be an injustice.

Thus the meaningfulness and realization of responsibility in all the various aspects distinguished here would seem to require some other account of the essential nature of time and of temporal being and, in particular, of real being. But it is not easy to grasp this essential nature of time positively and in a way that would satisfy the postulates set by responsibility. On the one hand one cannot permit an obliteration of the differences among being-in-the-present, past-being and future-being. One should not therefore identify being-in-time with the being-present-of-everything, as if the mode of being of the past were the same as the mode of being of the present. On the other hand, one should not interpret being-in-the-future in the sense of being-in-the-present. The no-longer and the not-yet must somehow be retained, and at the same time the coordination of these three forms of time and being must follow accordingly. Strangely enough, the succession of past, present and future would not be correct when understood ontically, no matter how inclined one would be to so order the factual matters contained in these three sections of time (if we may be allowed to employ such an expression here). For the second member, i.e. the present, has a noteworthy existential priority over against the other two members of this succession. One should not say: first, something must be in the past, then it will be in the present, and only then will it be future. One of course rightly says: the year 1900 precedes the year 1901, and the latter precedes the year 1902, if in fact we are living in the year 1900. But in order for something to be capable of being 'past', it must first be 'present' in some now, in order to be 'past' in another subsequent now. Hence, it is so to speak anchored in the present in a two-fold manner; in that present in which it 'now' is, and later was, and in that now in which it has already become 'past' or, more accurately, in some continuity of further 'nows' which make it ever more past, and further removed from each continually new now. One can also not say in an analogous sense that something must first be future in order to be capable of becoming 'present'. It, likewise, draws its being-in-the-future from the current present. Taken for itself alone it *is not yet*, and indeed it *is not* in the same sense in which the word 'is' corresponds to being-in- the-present (in the now). Being-future is also different from being-past, and indeed as being, as a way of being. What belongs to the future does not differ primarily from what belongs to the past by its different position with respect to the now, i.e. by what comprises its *relative aspect* in relation to the now, which is naturally a fact, but is different from what belongs to the past above all in its *mode of being*. When something is transformed from what belongs to the now into what belongs to the past it loses something of its mode of being which was immanently contained in it when it was still something that belonged to the now and not to the past. Both that which belongs to the present and also that into which it has been transformed in coming to belong to the past are likewise 'real', i.e., are both above all *existentially autonomous*. Each is in itself such as it is wholly independently of whether it is experienced or cognized by anyone. Passing away cannot deprive what is real of its existential character.[40] However, in the transformation from what belongs to the present into what belongs to the past it loses something of the mode of being which it has in the now. For what is presently real in the now is *in actu* (as was said in the Middle Ages). It *is* with a completeness and a plentitude of determinations and in a fulfillment of its being, which confer on it both effectiveness and activity

[*Effektivität und auch Aktivität*]. But it loses all this in precisely that now in which it is attained.[41]

What belongs to the past no longer has this '*in actu esse*'. But one can so to speak trace in its being past, that this '*in actu esse*' did exist in some determinate now. Something which was *never real* but merely imagined, expected or hoped for, cannot be stamped with this peculiar '*in actu esse*'. The existential moment of what belongs to the past, which, owing to its essence, is not and cannot be contained in the mode of being of what belongs to the future is not the '*in actu esse*', but an '*in actu fuisse*' with a distinct reference to that determinate now in which it was not yet past, but was rather now actual. What belongs to the future is not *in actu*, has not attained to a plenitude or fullness of being and endowment, leaving aside the fact that its being expected or hoped for is indeed what characterizes it as non-present or as not yet fulfilled. But what belongs to the future must have a foothold in the *in actu esse* of current reality; it must draw from it its capacity to pass over, at some definite moment in time, into the plenitude of an *in actu esse*. The potentiality of its attaining to *in actu* which in an essential way characterizes the mode of being of what belongs to the future is grounded in some existent *in actu* for as long as this transition does not happen. This potentiality characterizes what belongs to the future as something which, at some definite moment in time (in some determinate present), passes over into the actuality or effectiveness of being and thereby acquires the *in actu esse* in this present, in order to lose it at the very same moment in favour of an *in actu fuisse*, though never by regaining the potentiality that it had as something that belonged to the future. What once attained to effectiveness and plenitude of being and endowment in some now can never vanish or be dislodged from the past. What is expected or hoped for cannot be realized, and thereby also cannot be what in an authentic sense belongs to the future, when there are factual states which have become real in some now which exclude it from the world that has come about in that now. In other words: something's being what belongs to the future is determined from out of some present and the real factual matters contained in it; what is real is not determined from out of what belongs to the future. What belongs to the future is existentially founded in what now belongs to the present and is determined in its endowment by the latter.[42]

It is in this transformation of existential characters that there resides the characteristic mode of existence of temporal, real being. Thus, both what is of the past and what is of the future differ essentially in their mode of being from something that exists in some now; but one should not say that either does not exist at all. The present conception of the mode of being of what is of the past and of what is of the future differs essentially from St. Augustine's, which simply identifies what is past with something recalled and what is future with something expected, whereby they become equated with absolute non-being as soon as they find themselves outside the field of illumination of recollection or expectation. The existential foundation of what is of the past in the corresponding present does not consist in its being recalled by someone or inferred from other facts, possibly through an appeal to causal connections. However much recalling or inferring are means to the *discovery* of what is 'truly' [*wirklich*] of the past, hence, of what actually was in some once bygone now, they would lose all truth-value if what is of the past were to be merely somehow intentionally projected or created, if it were not *encounterable* in its own peculiar *in actu fuisse*, as something which in its own being [*Eigensein*], as well as in its endowment, is existentially independent of being recalled or inferred.[43]

An agent can be held responsible for a deed performed by him, and for its outcome, and consequently also be rightly called to account, only if we are allowed to speak of what is of the past and what is of the future in the sense here indicated; and only when one has indubitably demonstrated to him that the deed with which he is charged was in the strict sense actual in some bygone now, hence that this deed has the character of an *in actu fuisse*, should he be sentenced (if, of course, all the already discussed conditions have been fulfilled).

We recall this here, since the role of values for responsibility compels us also to go into their place in a temporally structured, real world. Can it be maintained that values also display that special mode of being which is characteristic of real objectivities existing in time? It would be difficult simply to consider values, and particularly moral values, as particular real objects. Are they at all situated in time and are they subject to the transformations in mode of being described above? I have already mentioned earlier, in a cursory way, that matters stand somewhat differently here and indeed in such a way that there arises the appearance of values hovering over the occurrences unfolding in time. And yet, one does not speak without reason about the 'realization' or 'destruction' of values. It is, in fact, for precisely such outcomes that the agent is responsible. In responsible acting the intent with which some action is undertaken appears to be directed at creating values, or at least at avoiding the destruction of particular values. In certain cases the action is directly geared toward realizing some values at the expense of destroying others.[44] It is precisely in those cases in which this intent is exercised by the agent's ego, and therefore in which the realization or destruction of some value does *not* come about *accidentally*, that the agent is responsible for the outcome. We must therefore insist that it is indeed such value-realizing or value-destroying deeds that are involved in the case of responsibility. And the values then involved appear to be altogether drawn into and entangled in the course of the real occurrences in the world. For this reason the being in time of values is at issue when realizing or destroying them. After all, the agent is called to account at an instant in which the values destroyed or created by him no longer exist.

But how is the 'destruction' or 'realization' of values achieved? Let us assume that a great and valuable work of art is deliberately destroyed. In the last war this was done with the intent of devastating the culture of some nation. And how did this happen? Museums were blown up or burned, i.e. the physical fundaments of the works of art were destroyed. Savonarola also was burned, presumably on account of the negative moral or religious values which he was supposed to have realized through his deeds; it later turned out that they were, to the contrary, authentic (positive) moral values. Yet here neither the positive nor the negative values themselves are somehow directly destroyed, but rather the body of the human being who incorporated them into his life. Values of whatever kind are always values *of something* or *in something*, or, put differently, values which are founded *in* something. They find their necessary and sufficient foundation in that of which they are the values, a foundation which enables them not only to emerge on this object but also to be somehow embodied in it, to attain to a concrete embodiment in which they subsist for as long as this object retains unchangeably the qualitative determinants which found these values. If those determinants change or vanish entirely from the existential scope of this object, then they lose their particular concreteness. The object loses its value like some picture whose colours have lost their tone under the affect of light. If the existential fundament of values is completely destroyed, shattered or burned, then the concrete value is also destroyed in the sense of having been robbed of its being in a concretion which is made possible by the fundament, and then it is discernible only as something ideal or essential. Thus the agent is responsible for destroying or creating this existential fundament of a concretization of values, a fundament that is either real or itself founded in what is real.[45] That is to say, speaking more precisely, he is called to account for the destruction or creation of some real objectivity *qua* ontic fundament for some definite value which has been made concrete. If both the destruction (or creation) and the concretized value were not to remain in an *in actu fuisse* mode of being but were to vanish altogether, then there would also no longer be any factual ground for the calling to account. And what is of particular significance here is that the past concretization of some value loses none of the validity or rank of the value in question owing to the *in actu fuisse* of this concretization.

The circle of problems and of possible solutions which stand in connection with the problem of responsibility in its various forms and contexts is hereby closed. They seem to me to be the most important problems to come into question in this connection, although I would not wish to state that they have been entirely exhausted. The thesis which I should want to defend affirms only that the essence of responsibility in its various forms and contexts not only points to the questions discussed here, but at the same time also demands definite answers. But should it turn out in further investigations that these questionsmust be answered otherwise, then the danger would arise that the generally accepted postulates for responsible acting, for assuming responsibility and for the right to call to account would have to be put in question. Yet, perhaps the further course of the analysis could show that in order to be better able to ground the meaningfulness and possibility of the realization of responsibility, not the solutions to the problems given here would have to be improved but rather their linguistic formulations.

Notes

[1] I shall not concern myself here with 'accountability' as a possible human character trait.

[2] If by chance a cat crosses the street in front of a car and the driver applies the brakes sharply, resulting in an accident, it is the driver, and not the cat who is responsible for the accident, even though the cat causes it. The cat is too dumb to scrutinize the situation and assess the significance of its behaviour.

[3] A two year old child who causes a car accident is not responsible for it, but rather his parents, who did not prevent the child from running into the street.

[4] One can ask if cases cannot occur here in which the person is also responsible for such passive tolerance of the pressure exerted on him. However, this would not be the case until the person would by himself recognize this enduring (of pressure) or if there were opportunity to oppose this pressure, but the person, either for lack of courage or fortitude, would rather bear it than assume the risk of conflict. But then the person would be responsible not for this enduring itself but for his acquiescence [*Anerkennung*] or for his cowardice.

[5] That *several* possibilities (and not just one) can exist is an ontological fact which follows from the structure of the world, which we shall still have to go into in the following.

[6] Nicolai Hartmann (see, *Ethik*, 3rd edition, Berlin, W. de Gruyter, 1949, p. 639) has pointed out the dissimilarity between "freedom of the will" and "freedom of action".

[7] I touch here on a point in which the various conceptions of a human being – materialistic, dualistic, spiritualistic – are engaged in a still unresolved controversy. Its resolution would naturally also benefit the solution of the problem of responsibility. Still, the special character of the conditioned or shared 'ownness' of the deed or resolute decision can be descriptively determined independently of which of these conceptions of man will gain the upper hand. A description of this character is all I wish to provide.

[8] But it can also be the case that the agent's action in itself possesses a positive or negative value, independently of the value of the result, for example when it is accomplished in a particularly responsible way. For example, it can be morally 'good' if the agent strives to realize some value despite being fully aware of impending personal dangers.

[9] The problem of what it means for certain values to 'annul' or 'equalize' (counterbalance) other values, or to 'elicit' them, is a particularly difficult one, which, as far as I know, has never been treated or solved. Nevertheless, this peculiar relation between values, or its

meaningfulness and possibility, is everywhere tacitly presupposed. Without it no justice would be possible at all, and its sense would be unintelligible.

10 I partially clarified the ambiguity of the concepts of objectivity and subjectivity in "Betrachtungen zum Problem der Objektivität", *Zeitschrift für philosophische Forschung*, XXI, 1967. See also my article, "Quelques remarques sur le problème de la relativité des valeurs", *Actes du IIIe Congrès des Sociétés de Philosophie de langue française*, Brusells-Louvain, 2–5 Septembre 1947, Paris 1947. [A translation of the Polish version of this essay is contained in this volume, p.119. Tr.]

11 I consider this view to be fundamentally false, without however denying that sometimes this kind of illusion does, or can, come about.

12 And not merely by a dictate of power [*Machtspruch*].

13 Besides, it is entirely unintelligible how such requirements, dictates or legal systems could of themselves create any values. What is ordered or demanded is not somehow 'better' because it is ordered or demanded, nor is a failure to fulfill it somehow 'bad' because it has not been fulfilled, as something demanded. Hence, we cannot say that fulfilling what is demanded is 'better' for the individual because he gains something by it, or that by not fulfilling it he is 'punished', therefore receives something bad. For, what is demanded does not on this account become in any way 'more valuable' than its opposite. But this faulty argumentation also indeed presupposes what it was designed to do away with, i.e. the acknowledgement that in certain instances positive or negative values do exist.

14 I am inclined to deny this. See the already mentioned article "Quelques remarques sur le problème de la relativité des valeurs".

15 Nicolai Hartmann introduced the word 'relational', in his *Ethik*, for the kind of values that utility-values are.

16 In ch. XIV of my book *Der Streit um die Existenz der Welt* I tried to elaborate the formal problems of the identity of an object enduring in time, as well as the question of the necessary formal conditions for sustaining identity in the sense of 'remaining the same'.

17 The latest surgical advances indicate what cannot be exchanged in the human body.

18 This identification is, surprisingly, still present in Scheler's *Der Formalismus in der Ethik und die materiale Wertethik* (1919, 3rd ed. 1927). (English trans.: *Formalism in Ethics and Non-Formal Ethics of Values*, trans. Manfred S. Frings and Roger L. Funk, Evanston, Northwestern U. P., 1973.)

19 I tried to provide a solution in the *Streit*, vol. II, 2.

20 Compare, *Streit*, vol. II, 2, ch. XVI.

21 Later, as we know, beginning with the *Formale und transzendentale Logik*, Husserl accorded so-called 'habitualities' to the pure ego, without however showing that these habitualities belong to the absolute sphere of transcendental consciousness, rather than to the real sphere of the constituted world. But this has to be demonstrated if the conception of habitualities is not to come into conflict with the theory of the 'transcendental reduction'. Besides, none of these habitualities was investigated in detail by Husserl. Therefore, we cannot say whether they are at all applicable to a consideration of responsibility, or can contribute anything to its possibility.

22 I have tried to exhibit the form of an individual object persisting in time in the *Streit*, vol. II,1, pp. 59–173. These are extensive analyses which cannot be developed here.

23 *Streit*, I, § 13, p. 90 ff.

24 I first pointed out the idea of a 'relatively isolated system' at an international forum in connection with the problem of causality in my paper "Quelques remarques sur la relation de causalité", which was read at the International Congress of Philosophy in Rome, 1946. The full text of this paper was also published in *Studia philosophica. Commentarii Societatis philosophicae Polonorum*, (III, 1947). Von Bertalanffy, in "An Outline of General Systems Theory" in the *British Journal for the Philosophy of Science*, vols. 1,2, and K.E.

Rothschuh (*Theorie des Organismus*, 1957) have, among others, taken up the concept of a system from the side of biology; but they define a system in a different way, without placing stress on the necessity of a partial isolation of the system.

[25] Von Bertalanffy speaks about 'open systems' in vol. I of his *Theoretische Biologie*, where he also considers the so-called dynamic equilibrium or steady state of such systems. By the system's "openness" he understands only its allowing exchange of material with the surrounding world, whereas my concern is primarily with the possibility of a penetration of causal processes through the boundaries of the system. He does not notice thereby that these systems must have mechanisms which necessarily lead to their partial shielding and segregation, and which on the shielded sides do not allow, at least for a time, any transit of causal relations from the outside to the inside, or they at least essentially weaken their impact.

[26] Obviously I am no biologist, and I only appeal to certain results of the research of natural science. I believe, however, that as a philosopher I am entitled to draw on them without being reproached with so-called 'scientism'. For, as a philosopher, I wish to show here only that certain requirements need to be set up with respect to the essence of responsibility in its diverse variants, the fulfillment of which comprises the conditions for its possibility. A definite structural make-up of the human being, who as bearer of responsibility must be free, belongs, among others, to these conditions. The factor within the human being itself which makes this freedom possible is indeed a structure of a special kind. And I only ask natural science whether this structure can be demonstrated from its side. Natural science also helps me to describe this structure more accurately. The principal features of this structure are however derived by me from the idea of a living organism, and natural science facilitates for me the analysis of this idea. Should it turn out that the results of natural science are true, then for me this would only imply that my ontological efforts are not purely mental constructions (as one may certainly be inclined to maintain), but are *cum fundamento in re*, and open for me the path to metaphysical considerations.

[27] Extraordinarily complicated interconnections among various processes obtain there, in which the interplay between various systems of the body finds its expression. See, for example, B. Landois u. R. Rosemann, *Lehrbuch der Physiologie des Menschen*, I, p. 331 ff. (on "warmth-economy").

[28] The individual parts of the digestive system are also separated from each other by closure mechanisms (sphincters), for example the stomach from the duodenum. Various phases of the digestive process proceed without disturbance owing to this, after which the sphincter opens and part of the chyle is propogated further.

[29] Yet is it possible to posit beyond any doubt that there are no 'presentiments', no givenness at all, of what will come in the future?

[30] 'Perhaps', since it is questionable whether decisions are not sometimes made in the psyche before a conscious decision is made.

[31] Emotions are in a wide sense states [*Zuständlichkeiten*] and modes of activeness [*Aktivitätsweisen*] of the psyche, which are not in themselves 'experiences'. M. Geiger rightly speaks about "the consciousness of emotions'. See *Münchener Philosophische Abhandlungen*, Leipzig 1911.

[32] It is so, for example, when bacteria invade the body, but are then destroyed by antibodies.

[33] "The speed of transmission within the animal system is quite large (60–125 m/sec. = 216–450 km/hr.) and represents a speed record for vital happenings in general" (See, Landois u. R. Rosemann, *Lehrbuch der Physiologie des Menschen*, II, p. 649). The so-called 'reaction times' in fact vary widely depending on circumstances, but generally fall within the limits of 150–400 m/sec., which comprehends very diverse components, so that only a fraction of these times is attributable to processes in the nervous system.

[34] I hope to succeed in publishing the next volume of my *Streit* under the title *Über die kausale*

Struktur der realen Welt. It was basically written in the years 1950–54, but it needs to be supplemented by a confrontation of its results with those of contemporary natural science, which I have not managed to do thus far. (This work was published, in its incomplete form, by Niemeyer, Tübingen in 1974.–Tr.)

35 I do not take account here of the change in the theory of causation which was effected as a consequence of Heisenberg's Uncertainty Principle and in the sense of Bohr's conception of complementarity. These changes are frequently interpreted in the sense of relinquishing the causal relation in the microphysical world. I cannot go into this in greater detail here.

36 The systemic structure of the world does not depend on whether this 'simultaneity' is understood classically, so to speak, or *à la* Einstein.

37 We cannot make a thorough study here of the further difficult problem concerning the conditions that these 'open' sides of the system would have to satisfy before it can come to this. We must also relinquish treatment of the problem regarding which non-causal existential connections can, or must, obtain in the world in order to ensure the cohesiveness of the world (or the state of the world). In connection with this, see *Streit*, vol. II.

38 Likewise, the concept of cause must be determined differently than is ordinarily done. See the already mentioned treatise in *Studia philosophica* or *Streit*, vol. I.

39 Nothing at all could be stated about the authentic reality of responsibility from the point of view of the agnostic interpretation of the Kantian conception.

40 N. Hartmann has also asserted this in an article on temporal being.

41 I must emphasize that I cannot approve the conception of a now as a point boundary between past and future, as a position in the time *continuum*. I have carried out a critique of this conception in my paper "Man and Time" which was read at the Descartes Congress in Paris, in 1937 [and is translated above]. However, a positive elucidation of now-being requires more extensive investigations than are here possible. Besides, the whole matter has no further significance for our discussion.

42 It is of course possible that something that belongs to the future is existentially founded in some other future thing, but this only means that the latter precedes the former and must first be present before that founding relation to the succeeding future something can be established.

43 If this were not so, then it would make no sense to say that we recalled something *falsely* or that we forgot it altogether and only afterward called it back to memory. The court procedure aiming at establishing by means of witnesses' testimony whether the accused in fact perpetrated the deed with which he is charged would then be meaningless.

44 As we know, Max Scheler bases his doctrine of moral values on the fact that in the case of some conflict of being between values, the higher values ought to be preferred and realized, even when this involves the danger of destroying certain other positive, but lower, values. If this preferring is adapted to rank differences obtaining among values, then the deed based on the preferred value is morally positively valuable, and it is morally bad in the contrary case. Here I do not wish to resolve the question as to whether it is in such and only such cases that morally good or bad deeds are involved. Let it only be pointed out that even Scheler, who considers values to be ideal objectivities, speaks about the realization and destruction of values. Even if we had to concede that following Scheler it is only 'goods' and not values which are here at issue, this does not dispel the problem troubling us as to whether and in what sense goods, along with the value-moments attaching to them, can be 'realized' or 'destroyed'.

45 Beside the concretized values there are also the *ideal value entities* [*Wertwesenheiten*] as well as the general *ideas of values* [*Ideen der Werte*]. These latter are outside of the real world. In this world, only the values concretized on individual objects correspond to them, values which, owing to the changes occurring in their existential fundaments, are drawn into the temporal course [*Zeitverlauf*] of reality. It must, however, be remarked that both the

founding of value-concretizations in individual objects and the sense of this 'concretization' need to be further investigated and clarified. In the article "What we do not know about Values" contained in my book *Erlebnis, Kunstwerk und Wert. Vorträge zur Ästhetik 1937–1967*, Tübingen, Niemeyer, 1969 (originally published in Polish (Kraków, 1966) translated in this volume) I have pointed out the difficulties that stand in our way.

Remarks on the Relativity of Values*

The old problem of the relativity of values depends on a number of theoretical attitudes and commitments which as a rule remain hidden beneath the plane of analysis. In striving for a deeper treatment of this problem, we have to proceed carefully, and attempt to unveil the obscurities and ambiguities in the proposed solutions to the attendant problems, solutions which are quite frequently accepted without a detailed and conscientious discussion.

There are three auxiliary problems that are important in connection with the problem of relativity. First, what is the sense of 'relativity'? Secondly, what are the differences between the particular kinds or types of values, assuming that a multiplicity of values is to be admitted at all? Thirdly, should the problem of the relativity of values be treated quite generally, hence for all values, or should it be formulated separately for each kind of values?

I

One usually speaks about the relativity of something, and in particular about the relativity of values, in a variety of significations which ordinarily are not sharply delimited. Though repeated attempts have been made to differentiate these significations,[1] they have never in fact been properly distinguished in a rigorous and unequivocal fashion, nor have they been precisely formulated. First of all, then, another effort has to be made to determine them rigorously.

* This article is a slightly expanded translation of the author's paper entitled "Quelques remarques sur le problème de la relativité des valeurs", which was supposed to be read in Brussels on Sept. 5, 1947, at a session of the III. Congress of the French Philosophical Societies.

The French original was printed in *Actes du III Congrés des Societés de Philosophie de Langue Française, Bruxelles-Louvain, 2–6 Septembre, 1947,* Paris, 1947. It appeared in Polish in *Przegląd Filozoficzny*, 1948, pp. 82–94. (This is a new translation, based on the version of the article that appeared in Ingarden's *Studia z estetyki*, III and differs both in style and substantive particulars from the translation by Guido Küng and E.M. Swiderski which appeared in the *Journal of the British Society for Phenomenology*, vol. 6 No. 2, May 1975, pp. 102–108. I wish to acknowledge my gratitude to this earlier version. Tr.)

(1) The first signification of the relativity of a value has a quite distinct epistemological colouring, along with on ontic sense which is bound up with this epistemological tinge. We say that a given value (e.g., the beauty of some painting or woman) is relative because we cherish the belief that we perceive a beautiful painting, whereas in actuality we are mistaken in ascribing to it a value (here, the value of beauty). We are deluded by a peculiar kind of deception when a painting or a woman seems beautiful to us, or when we find a given dish 'tasty'. In actuality, as some would try to convince us, these are properties that 'do not exist', that do not accrue to those objects to which we ascribe them, but in which we believe we have perceived them. It is, of course, not a matter of occasionally erring or falling victim to a deception when assessing a value, or when assessing objects as to their value, that is at issue; but rather the claim that every instance of assessment or apprehension of the value of something, or of objects in their value, is deceptive. That is to say, a peculiar deceptive phenomenon is produced in every case, and it is indeed this phenomenon of something which passes for actual and inherent in the very object with which we comport, but which is really a mere semblance, that makes up the value itself. It matters little whether we have here an error of purely intellectual assessment (an evaluative *judgment*) or a concrete delusion which occurs in a more or less sensory apprehension. The situation may vary in different cases. At any rate, the more concrete and intuitive the phenomenon in which a value manifests itself to us, the more strongly are we ordinarily convinced of the intrinsically inherent presence of this value in the given object. Also, the possible degrees of error or deception which occur in individual cases are of little importance here. It is therefore all the same whether we are absolutely (completely) mistaken, in which case we attribute to the object something that is 'really' wholly alien to it (according to those who subscribe to the relativity of values), or whether there exists to some degree in the object a basis for such attribution. This has no decisive significance for the sense of relativity which I am here trying to explicate.

(2) We speak of the relativity of values (of the beauty of a painting, of the high-mindedness of a person, and the like) in an entirely different sense when we in fact have in mind that one and the same thing or person has 'its' value altered in accordance with an alteration in the surrounding circumstances, circumstances which do not imply a change due to this alternation in the very object that 'has' the given value. For example, a particular portrait by Raphael no longer has that same high value of specific uniqueness or 'exceptionality' as soon as another portrait appears, say by Rembrandt, which, though completely different, performs the same artistic function as the former. Another example is the

automobile which has lost its value (or, at least, has had this value diminished considerably) as a means of extraordinarily fast and comfortable transportation since the advent of modern aircraft, faster and more comfortable than the car, even though cars have meanwhile undergone marked technical improvement, and have become faster and more comfortable than they were at the turn of the century. Therefore, not only have cars not become 'worse' in themselves, but have even improved, and yet they have since 'dropped in value' because quite independently of their vicissitudes some other more valuable objects have come into being, objects which do not, owing to their inception and existence, elicit any real change in automobiles.

This change of value without any real concomitant change of the object possessing it, and even the very possibility of such change, is perhaps the paradigm phenomenon for the world of values. The value of the object exists, or at least can exist here, 'objectively' ('truly') and does not at all depend on our cognition or some behaviour or other on our part (which can remain entirely the same in the two cases represented, while the value nevertheless undergoes change); rather, it depends on the circumstances in which the valuable object finds itself. What we frequently have in mind in speaking about the 'relativity' of values lies in this alteration of the value of an object in the light of the appearance of other values, in some sense by comparison with the latter. It is not as if the value itself were to depend on some sort of superiority of one object in comparison with another, nor is it a matter of comparing these objects so as to have the value emerge only after having made the comparison; it is simply that the value of an object is sensitive, as it were, to the very appearance in the world of some other value, without this other valuable object exerting any effect whatever on the first object. That is what we have in view when we speak about the relativity of values in sense (2). It is not, by the way, unrelated to the meaning employed earlier (1), though it does differ from it completely.

(3) A still different meaning of 'relativity' is involved when a certain thing or person has value *for* something or someone other than the valuable object. For example, a certain vegetation is nourishing for animals of one species, but is toxic (or harmful in some other way) for animals of another species. The value contains here in itself, in its essence or, if you will, in its sense a singular 'relativity' or, to put it better (after N. Hartmann) a 'relationality'. One could also say: every value of something has its own qualitative determination, which can be quite diverse in different instances. There is contained in the very sense of 'nourishment', 'harmfulness', 'usefulness', and the like, a more or less unequivocal reference to something other than what is 'nourishing' or 'harmful', namely, to that *for which* nourishment is 'nourishing' or 'harmful'.

(4) The value does not yet become 'relative' in either of the first two distinguished meanings through its relationality alone (wherever the latter appears). The value is not, therefore, a certain kind of illusory phenomenon due solely to its relationality, but can be, in spite of this, something 'objective', something that exists and effectively determines the thing which 'has' this kind of value. But in any event, the given thing 'possesses' the value insofar as it itself bears a certain relation to some other thing (that thing precisely, *for* which it is 'nourishing' or 'harmful'); it does not possess it as an isolated real entity, existing for itself, without any connection or relation to anything else whatsoever. This relation needs to be distinguished from the relationality of the *quality* of the value. Value in its currently considered meaning is not therefore 'relative' because it appears due to the occurrence of a certain relation between the thing whose value it is and some other thing, but solely because its very quality is relational. A value is thus 'relative' in a different sense, if what we have in mind is that the basis of its coming about is the occurrence of a certain relation between the thing in which the given value appears and some other thing. W. Tatarkiewicz speaks of the relativity of values in this and only this sense, regarding all other meanings of relativity as outright conceptual confusion. A value which is 'relative' in this sense can, but at the same time need not, be a value whose qualitative determination is 'relational'.

It has to be emphasized that when values with a relational qualitative determination are in question, the relations which obtain between the valuable thing and that thing for which it is valuable can be of two fundamentally dissimilar types. They are either relations which we establish through the comparison of objects, and between which there are at the same time no real interactions, as, e. g., when we compare two works of art and on this basis state that one is 'deeper' than the other, or that it is more coherently composed, and the like. Or, to the contrary: they are relations which depend on the occurrence of certain real processes that evoke real changes in both members. For example, a certain food is nourishing if and only if by working on a particular organism it evokes changes in that organism that are conducive to its life. In this connection we need to distinguish two variants of 'relative' values in the currently discussed sense: a) those for whose appearance in the object the occurrence of a purely comparative relation is sufficient and b) those that exist to the extent that definite real interactions and processes occur between the valuable object and the one for which it is of value. Values such as 'nourishing', 'useful', 'comfortable' and the like, cannot therefore be counted among the so-called 'relative features', like 'left-right', 'bigger-smaller', 'better-worse' and so on, not to mention that it is highly doubtful that the value of something be a 'feature' of that whose value it is.

(5) The 'relativity' of the value of something is frequently spoken of in the sense that the value is something existentially derivative as far as its mode of being is concerned, something which in its mode of being is deprived of that autonomy and actuality of existence that characterizes, at least in some cases, the thing itself which possesses the value. One thereby holds the opinion that the value does not exist somehow in and through itself, like the thing which comprises its existential basis and which determines it. The sense, however, of that peculiar mode of being is not clearly specified, but is contrasted to the 'reality' of that which is not 'relative' in its being. At any rate, in holding this position one maintains that value is independent in its existence neither of the existence of the thing that 'possesses' it, nor of the existence of other real things which co-exist with the former. In particular, it is not independent of the conscious subject, who, as we sometimes put it, 'creates' or 'produces' the value of the thing through an act of consciousness or by its manner of behaving towards a particular thing (or, more generally, object) which subsequently 'acquires' the value.
We ought to distinguish here two possible cases:

1) the existence of a value is determined and brought forth only by certain objects (by the one that has the value and by others from its surroundings), or,
2) the value is determined and elicited in its existence and attributes by the human subject, and sometimes even by a whole human community.

Without attempting to determine more precisely the mode of existence of the values in each of the cases distinguished here – and it seems that the modes of existence of values can yet differ considerably amongst each other, depending on the type of value in question in a given case – we can assert that the existence of values is not the result or consequence of the fact that the human subject cognizes the object which has the value. The existence of a value, even in a case where we could agree that it is the product of human consciousness or of a way of behaving, is independent of the actuality and essence of cognition. Acts 'creating' value (assuming that something of the sort exists at all) are of a kind entirely different from that of cognitive acts, and are at the same time dependent on the cognition of the thing possessing value. The fact of ascribing a value to a certain thing is not in this case an error or delusion, but is itself conditioned by the objective cognition of the thing having the value, and by the cognition of the value itself in its qualitative determination.

(6) It seems that we should distinguish one more variant of the 'relativity' of values which is commonly confused (in part) with 'relativity' in the

epistemological sense (1) and (in part) with the relational 'relativity' (3) of values. At issue in this variant are values that are accessible only to some appropriately qualified subjects, but not to all possible subjects.

A subject who wants to acquire an apprehension of this kind of value, and wants to be able to comport with it (to behave toward it in this way or that) has to fulfill well-defined conditions, which in principle are not accessible to all subjects indiscriminately. Consequently, many philosophers, from the various epistemological points of view they have come to hold, are inclined to believe that these values are 'relative', and even 'relational'; for practically speaking they exist solely for (are given only to) subjects of a special kind. Because it is accepted that something exists as absolute and objective only if in cognition it is given equally to all, the belief follows that values accessible only to some people are nothing but a strange and unsettling illusion. They are conjured up, the account goes, by certain modalities of our cognition or by those variants of our conscious experiences through which we comport with particular objects of the concrete world surrounding us. But from the fact that a certain value is given only to subjects of a particular kind it does not really follow at all that the value does not exist in itself as a special qualification of the thing that has it, nor that it is something relational in the sense already discussed.

For example, the beauty of a musical work is something perceptible only to a hearer who knows how to listen, a listener who understands the given composition and is capable of a proper emotional response to its qualities. The emotion of which this response consists opens up for us a vista onto the loveliness of the composition, shimmering in all its aesthetically valent qualities, and allows the subject to grasp it directly. Beauty, aesthetic charm, a specific ensemble of aesthetically valent qualities, etc. – all these are various kinds of special qualities which are what they are in themselves, and are at the same time in no way relational, with respect to anyone or anything. One could say that because they do not themselves refer to anything else, they are self-enclosed and self-sufficient. Perhaps they are not anything essentially so actual as real things are, but by the same token they are not merely a deceptive illusion of something else, for they do not pass themselves off for something other than what they are, i.e. certain special qualities or ensembles of qualities. Whoever knows how to reach them will find them; whoever is insensitive and blind will pass them by indifferently, as it were, and for him they do not exist. But because their existence is not indeed 'existence for' someone or something, the circumstance that someone does not encounter them in the surrounding world accessible to him in no way disturbs their absoluteness (non-relationality) and objectivity.

II

It is quite possible that there are still other meanings of the relativity of values.[2] However, the distinctions made here will suffice for the subsequent discussions. First of all, they let us realize that at least some of the meanings of relativity make it plain why in practical life we employ the same word to designate 'relativity' in different senses. That is to say, there are certain kinships and interconnections among the distinguished instances of 'relativity', which, in the case of an imprecise specification of their meanings, lead to a coalescence of their conceptions into a single one. It is also possible that the various 'modes of relativity' can appear simultaneously in one and the same value or type of values, though this is not at all necessary; one could also reckon with the opposite possibility – that in some values or types of values they will appear singly, or even not at all. It is understood that each of these relativities has its contrary, and these oppositions differ amongst each other commensurately with the differences amongst the relativities themselves. The following methodological index should be drawn from this state of affairs: posing the problem of the relativity of values requires its formulation in at least six (different) ways.

(1) Is value merely an illusion resulting from our faulty manner of cognizing it or the thing that 'has' it, or, to the contrary, is it a certain peculiar and 'true' quality or 'essence' which is found as intrinsically inherent in various aspects of the world surrounding us?

(2) Is value a special qualification of certain objects which is subject to changes depending on the circumstances in which the valuable objects exist, circumstances which do not evoke any other changes in these objects themselves? Or, on the contrary, is value a certain constant qualification of certain objects which is inert to the circumstances in which the valuable object is found, and in particular immune to the appearance of any other values in the existential environment of the given object, which is also independent of anything other than the properties of the object which 'has' the respective value?

(3) Is the value of an object given to us in direct comportment with the object a 'relational' quality appearing in or on this object, as a result of which it is a value for some other object – or is it, on the contrary, an 'absolute' ('non-relational') quality, hence one that does not display any qualitative reference to anything else at all?

(4) Is value something that appears in or on the valuable object because a certain definite relation obtains between this object and some other definite object, and is the value univocally specified by this relation, or,

on the contrary, is it conditioned in its existence and qualitative determination only by the properties of the object which 'has' it?

(5) What is the mode of existence of the value of something? Is its existence 'relative' in some sense, and if so, in which? Thus, e.g., does the value of something exist as derived from something else? Does its existence depend not only on the very object which has it, but also on other objects, and in particular on the existence and behaviour of a human subject who apprehends the value or the object possessing it? Or perhaps, finally, is the existence of a value existentially heteronomous, like the existence of purely intentional objects? Or, to the contrary, is the existence of the value of something the same as the existence of that which possesses it? In particular, if the thing which has the value exists in the mode of reality, does the value of the thing then exist in the real mode? Or, finally, is the existence of value (as many in the history of philosophy have tried to maintain) 'absolute', more perfect than the existence of things in the mode of reality?[3]

(6) Is the value of something of such a nature, in its essence, that it has to be accessible and knowable *in concreto* for all possible subjects, or, on the contrary, only for a subject who is capable of apprehending it (the value, as well as the object possessing it, in those of its qualifications that are relevant to the value) and is therefore endowed with some special faculties?

III

Having set out all these problems, we realize that it is impossible to solve them if the concept of value is taken quite generally and left in that vagueness with which it is most frequently employed. We need first to define it rigorously and at the same time to answer the question as to whether we are dealing with the same kind of values in every case, or, what is more likely, whether we need to differentiate various types or kinds of values. If we were to agree that values differ from each other generically, the problem of their eventual 'relativity' would then have to be restricted and solved for each particular kind in turn, the investigations in each of these cases being carried out independently of the solutions acquired in the remaining ones. Without this limitation, the problem remains too indeterminate. And it is not at all obvious that the solution of the queries raised above for one type of values would be binding for values of other types. On the contrary, one could expect that for values of different types the matter of their 'relativity' will turn out entirely differently. But in such an event, the problem of differentiating the fundamental types of values, and the exact definition of each of them, becomes all the more urgent.

The performance of this task is very difficult in the present (1947) state of inquiry into values, since thus far the very principle for the partition of values remains unknown to us. Therefore, we can today do no more than point to certain groups of values with which we are empirically familiar, on the basis of our contact with them, without being able to define them rigorously. Let us do so, however, in order to bring into relief the problem itself, and at least sketch certain likely possibilities for its solution.

a) It seems there exists, for example, a particular group of values which I shall call 'vital'; for example, the value of nourishment for a particular animal, or the value of the efficacy of various organs (eye, ear, etc.) for the animals of a given species, or finally the values of various kinds of inorganic tools that are useful to living beings, or at least serve for the creation of objects that are useful to them. Here, it seems to me, belongs a special class of values, those of an economic type, having particular importance (at least in certain cases) in everyday living.

Are vital values, or their specific variants, 'relative' in any of the senses differentiated above, or are they 'absolute'?

We cannot say with complete certainty prior to a detailed examination of all the variants of this type of values.

It may, however, prove useful to articulate certain probable conjectures on the subject. We can tentatively submit: it seems that all vital values are 'relational', but are at the same time objective qualifications of the objects in which they appear, insofar as these objects remain in definite, real relations with other appropriately paired objects. It seems also that these are qualifications which change in accordance with the kind of object that makes up the second member of the relation between the things which constitute the existential foundation of the values. But at the same time, at least some of them are always constant, immutable to changes in surrounding circumstances (and are in this sense 'absolute') for any pair of objects constituting the foundation of the interaction out of the occurrence of which the given value issues.

As far as the mode of existence of vital values is concerned, this is a very difficult problem to solve and it cannot even be crudely sketched here. From one side it is however probable that vital values exist at least in the sense that they can elicit changes in certain real things, things which constitute a necessary condition for the existence of such values. From another side it is also probable that these values exist in a manner very different from that of the existence of the real things which constitute their existential foundation.

From the fact that vital values are (probably) 'relational' it does not at all follow that every value in general possesses this same type of relativity, assuming, naturally, that values are to be admitted which are not vital in any sense.

Are vital values accessible to, and knowable by, all possible subjects (do they even have to be so accessible), or do they necessitate special conditions on the part of the subject in order to be knowable or accessible only to the extent of enabling him to comport with them in concrete living and purposeful behaviour? Here, again, is a question which is too specialized and difficult to be able to solve here. But what we know from biology, for example, on the subject of ecological conditions for the life of particular animals, what appears likely on the basis of Uexküll's researches on the so-called 'environment' [*Umwelt*] of animals, what we know, finally, from our own human experiences of changing conditions that accompany the relocation of people from one social setting to another – all this suggests that we should come to grips with the possibility that specific vital values or types of values are only accessible in their full qualitative determination to suitably qualified subjects. The lack of these qualifications does not testify to the non-existence (illusoriness) of the corresponding vital values; rather, to the contrary, this lack frequently ends catastrophically for the unsuitably qualified individual and confirms thereby the existence of that which the inappropriately qualified individual does not detect among the data that is given to him in his experience.

These remarks, however, do no more than open up certain perspectives on the problem which should be followed up in detail.

b) There exists, it would appear, a special group of cultural values. Aesthetic values such as beauty and ugliness, for example, belong here, as do the cognitive values of truth and falsehood, and so on.

All aesthetic values, or at least the fundamental ones, seem to be non-relational (which cannot be said of 'artistic' values – to be distinguished from aesthetic ones). They are not anything 'for' someone or something, but exist as special qualifications of certain well-composed and well-harmonized objects. These qualifications stem from a singular concordance of qualities of a wholly distinct type, qualities that are immanent to aesthetic objects and that depend on nothing other than the properties of the qualitative and formal endowment of these very objects. In this sense, aesthetic values do not appear to be 'variable', do not appear to be susceptible to changes that are extraneous to the aesthetic object, and their variation occurs only with the onset of changes in the aesthetic objects themselves. At the same time, however, it seems to be true that aesthetic values do not exist after the manner of real objects, that they are probably qualifications or a peculiar superstructure of purely intentional objects, having, at most, their existential foundation in certain real objects. Moreover, it seems that they are not perceptible to everyone, but only to subjects who fulfill quite special and not all too frequently realized conditions as regards their perceptive and emotional capabilities.

c) To take one more example, let us for a moment address 'moral' ('ethical') values. Are we to concede that they are 'relative' values in one sense or another?

It is difficult to answer this question, since despite all research on the subject of moral values it has not yet been adequately clarified whether they form an entirely distinct group of values differing specifically from other groups, or whether, to the contrary, they are to be assigned to one of the other groups, for example to vital values. If, however, they do form an entirely distinct group, then the problem of their eventual relativity in the senses differentiated above has to be posed completely separately. Most important of the questions to crop up here is, naturally, the question as to whether every 'moral' value is merely a curious and distressing illusion created by our manner of living through experiences, and possibly by our cognition, or rather an actual qualification of certain human deeds and actions, or of human will, or, finally, of the person who is a subject responsible for consciously performed deeds. The argument sometimes brought to bear here in favour of the 'relativity' of moral values – that the same human deeds are in different periods and cultures regarded at one time as 'good' and 'noble', and at another time as 'bad' and 'ignoble' – does not, despite appearances, attest to the relativity of their value in the sense of illusoriness. It merely testifies in favour of the fact that there is error or deception in certain cases of conflicting valuations. To show that a given deed evaluated differently on distinct occasions is neither 'good' nor 'bad' but rather morally irrelevant requires separate proof: the incompatibility of the two evaluations does not suffice, though it admits the possibility of the moral neutrality of the deed. All the remaining problems that we could raise, based on the distinctions we have introduced here, do not have the importance, it seems to me, of the problem singled out. But this problem is itself tightly interconnected with the problem concerning the mode of existence of moral values, and with the problem of whether moral values are relational or not. The solution of the problem of how to effect a demarcation between moral values and vital values (especially utilitarian ones), depends, among other things, on the answer to the question discussed above. We would make a significant advance in value theory if we succeeded in providing a well-founded answer to these questions. At this moment we can only make conjectures of one sort or another, which we could not properly substantiate.

With this I conclude my remarks on the 'relativity' of values, well aware that these remarks can only contribute to a slightly more precise articulation of the set of problems associated with the whole issue.

Notes

1 Of those attempts known to me, the most important undertaken in this direction belongs to Władysław Tatarkiewicz (cf. *O bezwzględności dobra* (On the Absoluteness of Good), Warsaw, 1919), but even here numerous doubts and reservations arise regarding particulars. Thus, with all due respect to his effort, I beg to differ with him on various points. It is impossible to discuss these issues here.

2 This matter obviously requires further analysis, which cannot be carried out here.

3 We have to remember, however, that this whole discussion concerns values *in individuo*, as I shall put it, that is to say the values of particular, individual things and not of something that would be in some sense 'general', non-concrete.

What we do not know about Values*

Interest in various problems concerning values has grown considerably in the post–war years. Some progress even appears to have been made in this direction. Nonetheless, there has been little success in finding satisfactory answers to a series of important questions and in overcoming difficulties encountered by value theory. Great effort is being expended in the treatment of various special problems, mainly within particular realms of values, whereas fundamental, general problems lie fallow. We are in jeopardy of losing sight of their importance for more specialized research, and of the fact that the latter can be stifled as a result, or at least deprived of a deeper foundation. Thus, it will perhaps prove useful to focus attention on several fundamental questions in the general theory of value, in order to make it more forcefully clear to ourselves that these remain unsolved, and ask ourselves why this continues to be so.

I must at once emphasize here, as I point to a number of difficulties and gaps in our knowledge of values, that I am not at all driven by the tendency to deny the existence of values. I am also far removed from the skeptical superciliousness with which values are often treated; the frequently surfacing attempts to 'reduce' values to certain subjective modes of human behaviour or even to the behaviour of entire human communities are likewise alien to me – as if values themselves did not exist and there were only certain deceptions or illusions having their source either in individual attitudes and needs or in those disseminated by certain communities. On the contrary, my purpose is to become conversant with the difficulties encountered by value theory in order to seek the ways and means of removing them, and of attaining a genuine basis for a well-founded recognition [*Anerkennung*] of the existence of values as determinations of objects of a special kind. Even if in some cases they were to be concomitantly conditioned in their existence by the individual who would be related to the object having the value, they would still have some sort of essential foundation for their existence and qualitative endowment in the object which they characterize.

The following are the problems to which I wish to devote some attention here:

* A paper read at an academic session of the Cracow Division of the Polish Philosophical Society on January 18, 1964, and subsequently in June, 1965 at the Universities of Belgrade and Sarajevo.

(1) On what basis are we to distinguish the fundamental types of values and the realms of values that are correlated with these?
(2) What is the formal structure of a value and its relation to what 'possesses' the value (to the 'bearer' of the value)?
(3) In what way do values exist, insofar as they exist at all?
(4) What is the basis for the differences between values in regard to their 'rank', and is it possible to establish a general hierarchy amongst them?
(5) Are there 'autonomous' values?
(6) What is the status of the so-called 'objectivity' of values?[1]

Ad (1). It nowadays no longer seems doubtful that we need to distinguish a number of realms of values which differ so much from each other that it is not possible to reduce them all to some single category. This insight also appears to be one of the invaluable achievements of modern value theory, since a great many errors stemmed from trying to solve various problems for *all* possible values at once. But is everything set in order with this distinction alone?

Following trends which have appeared in the phenomenological literature and elsewhere, we can distinguish the following domains of valucs:

a) vital values, to which utilitarian and pleasure values are closely related;
b) cultural values, in particular
   1. cognitive,
   2. aesthetic and
   3. social values (customs);
c) moral values (in the narrower, more precise sense of the word).

Many variants of values are distinguished and contrasted to each other within these particular realms of values; efforts are made to give their more specific definitions, and finally also to describe the specific values appearing in individual cases. In the process of making all these distinctions one at least has the feeling of committing no error when, for example, a certain aesthetic value is contrasted with some moral value. There do occur cases, however (not too infrequently, I might add), where in juxtaposing two different values we cannot reach a decision concerning the difference between them and whether one of them should really be deemed an aesthetic value and the other a moral one.

We then face the question how we are to decide on this difference. What is the proper *basis* for distinguishing values of one type (for example, aesthetic) from those of another (for example moral)? To this question we either receive no answer at all, or an answer which does not seem sufficiently clear or adequately grounded. For we do not have at our disposal any satisfactory general definitions of particular value types, and we do not have them because thus far no clear and unequivocally determined *principle* has been established for *dividing* values in general into their particular genera and species. The acquisition of such a principle is hindered, among other things, by the quite widespread (and probably correct) conviction that the decisive moment in respect of which specific values are distinguished from each other, and values of one basic type are distinguished from those of another basic type, is their *qualitative* determination.[2] Values would then have to be subdivided into genera and species in accordance with these qualities. But the source of the difficulty lies precisely here. When we juxtapose different qualities, or objects endowed with different qualities, in direct intuition, we do indeed succeed in ordering them according to their qualitative kinship (the similar ones together, the dissimilar ones into different groups). Yet, when we are faced with articulating this result conceptually and stating what it is that kindred qualities have 'in common', what it is that decides their kinship, we find ourselves in a great quandary. For as we well know, it is not possible to define qualities conceptually, and it is especially impossible to specify that non-self-sufficient or dependent moment which determines the kinship of two different values and which, after all, somehow participates in these qualities. But we should not only know how to wrest this non-self-sufficient qualitative moment intuitively out of the qualitative endowment of differing values, but also be able at least to name it unequivocally, having conceded that it is impossible to define it conceptually.[3] For how could we, without being able to do so, provide this principle for dividing values into their basic kinds?

The difficulty is further compounded by the fact that those values belonging to a group which has been delimited (even if only provisionally), in turn also differ from each other quite markedly in their qualitative endowment. In the group of aesthetic values, for example, it is not only the value of 'beauty' that appears throughout (as has been often erroneously claimed); beside beauty there appear also, say, charm or grace (*la grâce*), nobleness or sublimity, also the value of the pretty, which is much more akin to beauty; but even beauty itself still appears in a wide variety of qualitative modalities. The beauty of ancient Romanesque architecture is different from that of purely French Gothic. It is no different in the domain of moral values, where we find not only the 'good', but also, for example, accountability, justice, self-sacrificing devotion, bravery, high-mindedness, etc. Moreover, in *every* realm of values we encounter opposites. Opposite beauty there is ugliness, opposite good we have evil, opposite bravery is cowardice (especially in civic life), opposite the value of the forgiveness of evil, vengeance or vindictiveness, etc. In such cases it is not at all as if negative values were simply the *absence* of the corresponding positive value. On the contrary, these are all values which are positively determined in their quality, each in its own peculiar manner. In view of the blatant contrariety of the qualitative determinations of these values, how are we still to find that moment that is 'common', as we ordinarily say, to all moral values?

It is certainly possible, at least in particular instances, to state a number of conditions under which, in concrete situations, there appear values of one kind or another, say, moral values, conditions which do not simultaneously obtain, or at least need not obtain, where for example aesthetic values appear. There has been more than one attempt to set forth such conditions, and indeed conditions which, according to some philosophers, have to be fulfilled by the object having the given value. It was claimed, for example, that the condition for the appearance of moral values (both positive and negative) is the freedom of the human being who is to realize them. This is, *nota bene*, a necessary but not sufficient condition. The deeds of a person who is deprived of freedom (free choice) can be beneficial and bring well-being to others or, on the contrary, they can be extremely harmful, but they are in either case neutral in a moral respect. In the same way, the mental health of a man, which allows him to assume responsibility for his deeds, is only a necessary condition of the moral value of human deeds. An insane person cannot commit any morally commendable or deplorable deed, even if he were to act in accordance with ethical laws. But mental health alone is not enough for effecting morally worthy deeds.

Even if, in a particular case, we were successful in setting forth the complete set of such conditions, we would still not acquire in this way an understanding or explanation of the peculiar nature of the values in question. Along this path we could at best circumscribe the range of values of the given kind. This would of course be a valuable result in the exploration of values, but the attempt to 'reduce', as we are apt to say, the qualities of moral values, for example, to the set of conditions for their appearance is not theoretically satisfactory, and is, moreover, an error.[4] For these conditions do not make up the quality of the value stipulated by them, nor do they determine this quality.

The disclosure and establishment of these conditions can only be accomplished if we already have in intuition that specific quality which we are interested in elucidating. Conversely, familiarity with even the complete set of these conditions cannot of itself provide us with the possibly missing intuition, nor even aid us in its acquisition. The modes of intuitive cognition are also varied. Even if that cognition is given in full clarity, what is thereby given is not yet for that reason alone thematically grasped in its qualitative distinctness and so distinguished from among all other qualities as to be always capable of faultless identification. But so long as this full awareness has not been achieved, we cannot be certain that our intuitive contact with the respective objectivity, with the quality which lies at the basis of the cognition, is a genuine intuition that instructs us unerringly about what is given in it. Yet even if we have already succeeded in attaining this genuine intuition, the fact that some quality or aggregate of qualities is *given* effectively still does not suffice to enable us to *say* clearly and unequivocally what this peculiarly qualified something is.

Some will tell us: Obviously, the quality which determines a value or a value-type is a certain abstract moment that characterizes it; it makes up its nature, or its genus. I have no intention of challenging this statement, but it does not explain or single out that abstract moment in its constitutive determination, it does not specify the qualitative endowment of a value. But knowing this would appear to be necessary for distinguishing the basic genera of values in a satisfactory manner.

Numerous attempts have been made to define the individual types of values by appeal to the attitude of the recipient or creator of the particular kind of value. So, for example, we are accustomed to saying that aesthetic values are those values which become manifest in an aesthetic attitude, or which evoke that sort of attitude in the recipient.[5] Aesthetic values are sometimes characterized by so-called 'disinterested enjoyment or appeal' [*das interessenlose Gefallen*]. This disinterestedness is supposed to distinguish them from the engagement or commitment which is supposed to be operative in relation to utilitarian values (to which, as we know, moral values are sometimes 'reduced').

Recourse to the attitudes or activities of the recipients of certain values can be helpful to us in delineating the range of cases in which values of a particular kind appear, but it cannot replace for us the immediate cognition and conceptual apprehension of the very values which are in question in a particular instance. Moreover: searching out those characteristic attitudes or activities of the recipient of values can only be accomplished successfully when we have at least already managed to attain to an intuitive cognition of the qualitative determination of the given values. For after all, out of the many different mental attitudes and activities we have to select just those that come into play in the case of receiving precisely the value at issue. Thus this procedure is not always fruitful where we have not yet managed to acquire knowledge of the qualitative determination of the value.

It still happens, especially in Poland, that the value and its quality are *identified* with the attitude in which we discover them, or with the experiences, in particular with so-called 'enjoyment' [*Gefallen*], that occur in us in that attitude.[6] This view is quite outmoded, and it is impossible to set forth once again all the arguments against it. It will perhaps suffice to point out, as has often been done, that 'enjoyment' (or 'pleasure' of one sort or another) is a certain state or behaviour of a person who is contemplating, for example, some painting or work of architecture, a behaviour which runs through its characteristic course and passes rather quickly. And we have as many instances of 'enjoyment' as the number of times we comport with a particular work of art, and the same holds for as many people who do likewise. The gentle beauty of Vermeer's painting, on the other hand, is one and the same, and always attaches to this painting irrespective of how many people view it, or when and how many times they do so. So no matter how difficult it may be to give an account of the quality of this beauty, it is at any rate something different from the experiences or mental attitudes of the observer. And we need to make an effort to come to grips with the nature of that peculiarly qualitative stamp of the given painting and its dissimilarity from, say, the serene beauty of Raphael's portraits.

Some philosophers maintain that no value is amenable to conceptual determination, that value is not definable.[7] But this would be true only if every value were determined in its matter [*Materie*] by a simple, original quality. This may perhaps hold as regards some values, but it can surely not be demonstrably asserted of all values. For if that were the case, it would be impossible to form groups of kindred values, or to compare values of the same basic sort as to their so-called 'rank', but that we can form such groupings and make such comparisons is after all indisputable. And this in turn attests to the fact that in at least some cases simpler qualitative moments are distinguishable in the qualitative endowment itself (in the matter) of the value. One can also give an account of the fact that some of those moments play the role of characterizing a genus or species, whereas others are moments that differentiate the lowest variants within a species or even certain strictly individual values. It is obviously not so with all values; where this does occur, however, we are not dealing with some qualitative 'hodge-podge', as I shall put it, in which these distinctive moments would be simply arbitrarily juxtaposed, separable parts within the whole. On the contrary, investigations have thus far shown that such is certainly not the case. Those qualitative moments which can be distinguished are merely so-called 'abstract' moments, that is to say, mutually or only one-sidedly dependent. If they turn out to be *one-sidedly* dependent, two different cases can occur: A may be one-sidedly dependent either in an unequivocal or in an ambiguous manner. In the first case, A must always appear, within the framework of a single whole, together with a moment B which is strictly determined in its matter (with B and only with B); in the second case, on the other hand, A can appear together with any B_n from a determinate set of moments B which differ amongst themselves, but it must always appear together with some one of them within the framework of the same whole. In the first case, B is a moment which complements the matter of this whole.* In the second case, A is a generic moment for many kindred wholes: whilst it is ambiguously dependent with respect to B, each B_n is univocally dependent with respect to A. The individual B_n then comprise the differentiating moments for the variants of the genus A. Such generic** moments should therefore be sought in the matter of a value which is not absolutely simple. The abstract generic moments of the value-matter can serve as the principle for grouping values into distinct types. It still remains an open issue in all this as to what can serve as a principle for the division of *all* values into basic classes. Perhaps we shall manage to return to this question. We should not forget, however, that values may exist whose matter is so peculiar, original and unrepeatable, that they cannot be ordered into any group or class of values.

Ad (2). The instant, however, that the problem of the partition of values into basic types begins to emerge in this fashion, we have to realize that we are thereby entering a new domain of problems concerning values. That is to say, the problem of their *form* surfaces.

There are many unclarified problems here. That this is so is best shown by the fact that there are many incompatible views on the subject. We also make a variety of statements about values in our everyday comportment with them which in a way suggest certain tacit assumptions concerning their form. We utter various judgments about values which ascribe to them a diversity of characteristic features or properties or determine their nature in such a way as to treat them as if they were *objects* of a particular sort. To be sure, no one will claim that beauty, say, or a good is a *thing* in the way that a tree or a rock is.[8] Yet, values are treated as if they were the subjects of properties which endure in time. No one, on the other hand, would be inclined to maintain that a value is for example a process and indeed not even when it is the value of something which has in *concreto* the form of a process unfolding in time (for example a musical composition). Even in general value theory we often express ourselves as if values were objects, attributing to them traits of one sort or another, etc. On the other hand this appears to contradict the fact that a value is never something that exists for itself, but is always the value *of something*. Irrespective of its type, be it a utility-value, such as, e.g., the value of an efficient motor, or the moral value of some person or deed, or the value of

* In the German version the phrase "the matter of this whole" is replaced by "the A, and forms a whole with it". Tr.

** In the German 'generic' is replaced here by 'differentiating'. Tr.

a particular work of art, there always exists something, (or some *thing*) which 'possesses' the given value. And there is no value whatever which would exist without that something of which it is a value. When some machine is taken completely apart, and there is no more machine, its value also ceases to exist as a result.[9] For this very reason value is always non-self-sufficient (dependent) relative to the object to which it 'accrues', if it accrues to it at all. It is therefore never a self-sufficiently existing object, and as such it can also, strictly speaking, never be an object in the sense of being a subject of properties.[10]

We might conclude from the above that the value of something is a *characteristic feature* or *property* of that something. And this, in turn, appears to accord with our frequently saying of a particular object, which possesses, say, the value of beauty, that it is 'beautiful', or 'good', etc.

But this conception is not entirely devoid of dangers.[11] If values were properties of valuable objects, we would have to deny to many objects the capacity for possessing values. Physical things, for example, can and do have only physical properties, for example, this or that shape, density, or thermal or electrical conductivity. But something like the nutritiousness or beauty of vegetation or the style or elegance of the shape of a dish (say, a porcelain plate) cannot be found among the physical properties of these things. Consequently, some philosophers propose that the purely 'substantive' [*sachliche*] properties of a thing be distinguished from value as a quite special kind of determination.[12] It is debatable, however, whether we should concede that value is a *special* property of a thing, or whether we should altogether abandon considering it as a property of something at all.

We could attempt to articulate the first option along two different paths. We would then say that value is indeed a property of the valuable thing, but a secondary property which derives from its other properties, which constitute its necessary, though possibly insufficient, condition. So, for example, a given plant is 'nutritious' for certain animals because it has a particular chemical composition. A certain thing is 'beautiful' because it has a specific shape and assortment of colours, etc. This path is adopted, for example, by formalist aestheticians when they claim that only so-called 'form' is of value in the work of art.[13] The second way of treating the problem via the first option consists in the thesis that value is that property of a thing in virtue of which the thing affects the recipient in a special way, in particular, it evokes certain feelings or gratifies yearnings in the person who comports with the thing having value. That is how the issue is represented as far as aesthetic values are concerned. In other cases one claims that a particular thing promotes a person's health or, conversely, is detrimental to it; and in the first instance it is beneficial, in the second it is harmful, and therefore 'bad'.

It is indeed well to distinguish in the object that on which its value depends (what makes up its necessary, and possibly sufficient, condition) from the value itself. But is whatever depends on certain properties of an object itself essentially a property*? Besides, even if that were the case, one would still have to be able to distinguish, amongst the many derivative properties [of an object], those that make up a value from those which are irrelevant in this respect. Thus, for example, the flow of electric current in the conductor which raises the temperature in the wire of a bulb and, by making it glow, subsequently gets it to light up depends on the difference in electric potential at two locations of a particular device and on the characteristics of conductivity. This temperature, this incandescence and the lighting are successively more remote derivative processes or states of the device that follow from its properties, but it is only that lighting which under particular circumstances becomes 'useful' to a human being, and this usefulness comprises the value of the appliance. But it is not a value *because* it is a 'derivative' characteristic of the device. Need not something thoroughly new be adjoined, if we may put it that way, to this matter of fact that the lighting is such a derivative property, something by virtue of which it first takes on the character of worthiness [*Wertigkeit*]? Some will perhaps reply that such is indeed the case, that the human being and his special needs, such as, for example, the facilitation of work that could not be done in the dark, need first be taken into consideration before that lighting could become 'useful', and thereby also possess precisely the value of 'usefulness'. Arguing in this fashion, however, we pass over to the second point of view, which links up worthiness with the given thing's particular mode of affecting the recipient, particularly the human being. But precisely on this account we undermine the thesis that the value ('usefulness') is a property of the (valuable) thing; for, the value first appears in the contact between a particular need of a human being and a device that stills this need. The value of usefulness, as one says, first 'emerges' out of this very appeasement of the human need. One could not therefore say that it is either a property of the thing, or a property of the human being, nor, finally, a property of the relation between human being and thing. In regarding 'usefulness' as the value of a particular thing, we have presupposed that the stilling of human needs is itself somehow valuable. 'Usefulness' as value is then something derived from another value, but is once again no 'property' of this other value.

An entirely different conception of the form of a value suggests itself at this stage, one that has already been repeatedly proposed from various sides. It is said, namely, that value is not at all a property of a valuable

*In the German, the word 'value' replaces 'property'. Tr.

object, but a certain 'relation' between the valuable thing and some other thing to which the former is somehow of service. This conception attains its greatest popularity where a human being, or even a human community, is that second thing. In such cases one sometimes speaks of a so-called 'social sanction' – which is supposed to confer value on an otherwise altogether worthless object. Starting from there, the way is already open for a general, relativistic value theory, which in the limit refutes altogether the so-called 'objectivity' of a value and asserts its 'subjectivity', be it either relative to a single human being or to an entire social group, whether large or small.

Without at all denying that there are values which in essence have at their basis a certain relation between appropriately matched objects, and even that values are possible whose matter is 'relational', we can still not concede that this is true of *all* values. For, not all values have a relational matter – it is impossible to assert this of either moral or aesthetic values. Moreover, even where at the basis of the appearance of a particular value a certain relation between the thing having value and the thing for which it has value is ascertainable, that does not mean that this value itself is a *relation*. The relation (as I have tried to show elsewhere[14]) has a certain special structure that cannot be ascribed to values (not even to those that have a 'relational' matter). We cannot say that, for example, something like 'charm' or 'grace', 'perfection', or 'nobleness' is some sort of relation – not even if it were possible to show that all these values spring forth from relations of one kind or another between suitably matched objects. Besides, that very (alleged) 'springing or issuing forth' of values out of these particular relations is a quite obscure issue. For it seems to be neither the consequence of a logical inference, nor something like a causal elicitation of an effect. And so, all the advanced hypotheses as to which form is really suitable to a value meet with serious doubts, and it could not be said that we are in possession of actual knowledge concerning this topic. All of these proposals leave out of account everything that seems to be characteristic and essential for a value: to begin with, its valuableness or 'worthiness' itself; and, in close connection with this, the fact that this worthiness allows a variation in ranking. In other words: one cannot speak about values meaningfully without conceding that it belongs to their essence for some to be 'higher' than others, and some 'lower'; and that consequently, some of them are more worthy of being realized and others less. The realization of a specific value can on that account be sacrificed under certain conditions for the sake of realizing some other, higher value. In this connection, it belongs to the essence of value that there is something about it which compels us to choose which of two values 'ought' to be realized when, say, the realization of both of them is not possible in a given context.

This, and a series of other circumstances which we shall presently discuss, inclines some authors toward the view that the value of something is indeed no self-sufficient object, and especially no thing, but that it comprises a certain entity (*entitas*) with a wholly *singular structure* which must be distinguished from all forms considered thus far, and particularly from the fundamental form that is characteristic of an object (even of an object which possesses a particular value, but is not itself a value). The structure of a value differs from the form of objects which are not themselves values in that moments appear in the value which do not and cannot appear in objects which are not values.

Further: a certain (categorical) form and a certain matter[15], as well as a mode of being in which this formed matter exists, can be distinguished in values (as it can generally in anything that exists). Yet 'valuableness' itself is already something which is necessary for every value, but is neither form, nor matter, nor mode of being, though in appearing in a value it entails a distinctiveness of the form of a value from the form of an object which is not a value. It also implies a certain special modification of the mode of being of a value.[16] Now, on the one hand, a certain 'rank' that varies in different cases is closely connected with worthiness, whereas, on the other hand, there belongs to it either a peculiar *positiveness* of some values or an equally peculiar *negativeness* of others. Some, for example Nicolai Hartmann, still distinguish a so-called 'power' of a value [*Wertkraft*[17]] which is supposed to vary in values of different kinds, for example be greater in moral values than in aesthetic ones.

Various authors try to give a more detailed account of these various moments discernible in the structure of a value, though we could not say that these analyses have progressed very far, something which is quite understandable in the light of the difficulty of the issues that crop up here. Thus Hermann Lotze having in mind the 'valuableness' of values affirms (as it seems to me) that values do not so much exist, as 'have significance' or somehow are 'in force' or 'hold sway'. In doing so he employed the expressions *gelten* and *Geltung*, which are very difficult to translate. The representatives of the South-German Neo-Kantian school (H. Rickert, W. Windelband, and others), and later also Max Scheler and N. Hartmann declared that every value conceals within itself a demand, as it were, for its realization, which modifies its existence in a special way. It was then said that a certain 'oughtness of existence' is characteristic of values (formulated in German by replacing '*Sein*' with '*Seinsollen*'*). In addition, this oughtness of existence is supposed to differ according to the basic kind of values. In the case of moral values this oughtness is, if we

* The English translator of Hartmann's *Ethics* employs the expression 'ought-to-be' as a translation of this word. Tr.

may put it so, 'absolute', which has the implication that failure to realize a moral value when the possibility of its realization obtains is the realization of a negative moral value (an 'evil'). It seems, on the other hand, that this kind of [absolute] 'oughtness' of existence no longer holds for, say, aesthetic values. Their non-realization when the possibility of their realization occurs does not yet seem to be an evil of itself, and in particular appears to be no moral wrong.[18] It cannot be denied that even in the case of aesthetic values a certain demand for their realization seems to appear; but the latter in a certain sense merely plead to be realized; they do not demand it in a manner that would burden us with blame were we not to heed their plea. We also rightfully say that if something is to serve as nourishment, then it ought to be 'nutritious' and not 'toxic'. And if something is to serve as a tool for something, then it ought to be effective in the performance of its function, and if, moreover, the end whose realization is served by the tool is itself positively-valued, then this tool 'ought' to be constructed; if, on the contrary, this end is 'evil', then the tool 'ought not' to be constructed. Both the value itself and the demand for its realization are here conditioned by some other value, so that this value is not *independent* in its valuableness from that of other values. This possible dependence of the valuableness of a value on other values is once again a feature that is characteristic only for the structure of values. This *conditioned valuableness* should not be confused with the so-called 'relativity' of values in its various possible significations, which have been elsewhere distinguished.* But even this relativity, wherever it appears in a value, is likewise a particular feature which has no place at all outside the realm of values, though it does not encompass the whole of this realm in any of its specific significations.

As we see, therefore, the value of something is a highly complicated formation, granting that the distinctions made above of the features or moments belonging to its essence are correct. This implies an entirely singular structuring of its form, which is distinct from the basic form of a self-sufficient object, from the form of a property, and, finally, from the form of a relation. The circumstance that a value is always a certain kind of *superstructure* built up on the basis of that whose value it is, plays a special role in its form; this superstructure, however, if the value is a genuine one, is not something alien in relation to the valued object, it is not thrust upon or added onto it from without, but emanates out of its very essence. But precisely because it can only *issue in this way out of the object which is its basis,* it is non-self-sufficient and derivative in both its form and mode of being. We say that the value 'accrues' to the object, but this accrual is a formal moment of it which is different from that which

** See "Remarks on the Relativity of Values", p. 119 in this volume. Tr.

appears in every property (characteristic mark) of something. Value also plays an entirely different role in the object than do either its properties or its nature. A property, with its matter, determines (specifies and completes) the object to which it accrues by virtue of its form, irrespective of how tightly this property may be bound up with the object's nature. The value of an object, on the other hand, is determined in its matter and valuableness by the properties, or perhaps nature, of the object, but at the same time, once it has been determined as a positive value, it confers upon the object a particular dignity, a certain wholly new aspect, which this object could never manage to attain without this value. It elevates the object above all objectivities that are devoid of value; the latter merely are, exist, but do not 'signify' anything.[19]

In this fashion we begin to acquire a certain insight into the peculiar structure of a value, but at the same time we have to realize that we cannot rest with simply singling out and enumerating all of these moments. Each of them is, after all, a source of new problems and would require a scrupulous analysis in order for us to clarify or give an account of what it really is. Only such an analysis could provide an account of the entire structure of a value in its most variegated possible modalities, and allow us to set forth and formulate the further problem concerning the interconnections and dependencies among the various moments of a value. Already, at the very outset of these considerations, it appears that these moments do not comprise some loose agglomeration or scattered multiplicity of separate items that are independent of each other. They are, rather, interconnected in various ways, in such a way that some play a leading role, as it were, while others are dependent on them and change in individual cases (variants of values) in conformity with them. A whole, complicated matrix of problems begins to surface, the possible solutions of which we cannot even divine in our current state of ignorance, and which it will be impossible to discuss here in any greater detail. But it appears probable that it is precisely the value-matter (or more particularly what I have elsewhere called the 'value-quality') which plays the leading role in the value and determines its other moments, including the rank of the value, its mode of being and conditioning by the object to which it accrues, etc. Here I shall try to sketch out some of the attendant problems.

Ad (3). Before attending to the mode of being of values, I still need to set one issue in order. Plato, as we know, considered values to be so-called 'ideas', that is certain extra-temporal, unchangeable entities – 'ideal' entities, as we say today. In the twentieth century, Max Scheler believed that values are 'ideas', or ideal objects and claimed that one can attain to a mathematical type of *a priori* knowledge of them. Alongside 'values' he also acknowledged 'goods' [*Güter*], i.e. certain individual (real) objects to which values were somehow supposed to accrue. But Scheler did not explain how certain ideal objectivities were supposed to appear as particular kinds of determinants of such individual objects.

Without being able here either to expound in detail Scheler's views on this matter or submit them to criticism, I must note that even though I agree to the existence of general *ideas of values*, the intrinsic content of which we can analyze in such a way as to gain certain general assertions concerning values, still, it is not these ideas that I spoke about in this paper when I employed the word 'value'. For I was at all times concerned with those peculiar non-self-sufficient entities that appear as bound up with individual, real objects, entities which are just as individual as those objects. Tying onto Schelerian terminology, we could say that a 'value', in the sense employed in this paper, is that ensemble of moments, which in appearing in a particular object brings it about that this object is not simply some thing, but that it is precisely a 'good' in Scheler's sense. These moments are individual, and possibly have their correlates in ideas of ideal qualities, but as entities they are just as different from these correlates as the shape of a square appearing concretely on a particular thing is different from the geometrical 'idea' of a square or the ideal quality 'squareness'. In saying that that set of moments owing to which a particular thing is a 'good' is a set of individual moments, I am not at all claiming that these moments are, or always have to be, real, or that they can only appear in a real object. There can be aesthetic values that come to light in aesthetic objects which are not at all real (are the intentional products of specifically structured operations of consciousness, of so-called aesthetic experiences), and even where they do occur as values of particular real objects (e.g. of a particular thing or human being, or human deed) they still need not on that account be themselves real. The problem concerning the mode of being of values rests precisely in our not having prejudged in advance that if a value is the value of something real then it must itself be real, or that if it is the value of some purely intentional object then it must itself be purely intentional. What is crucial at the moment is only that in posing this question I do not have in mind any ideal objectivities or ideas, but solely something which, in appearing effectively as a peculiar determination of some individual object, is itself individual, and makes this object into a 'good', in Scheler's sense, by virtue of its peculiar linkage with the object.

One can object, however, that the question concerning the mode of being of a value is formulated too generally, since it prejudges that all values – irrespective of their kind – exist in the same way. But it is highly probable that, say, moral values (of certain deeds or persons) may have a mode of existence different from that of artistic or aesthetic values, and still more, different from that of utility-values. This conjecture comes up because moral values accrue to human persons and their deeds, whereas aesthetic values apply to objects which are intentional products. But, say, a well constructed tool which is well suited for its purpose is useful, yet is at the same time a real object. It would seem, therefore, that its value of usefulness exists in the same way as do moral values. Nevertheless, both the utility-value of some tool and the aesthetic value of a particular aesthetic object seem to be conditioned in a different way, in their attachment to their bearer, than is a moral value. That is to say, both have for the foundation of their being, aside from the determinations of their bearers, some other additional object: in the first case the very thing to which we apply the given tool, and in the second case the subject apprehending a particular work of art in an aesthetic attitude. It seems to follow from this that the founding of these values in the objects to which they accrue is somehow more loose than in the case where the value has as the basis of its existence exclusively that object to which it accrues. It seems therefore that their mode of being is different from that of moral values.

As is apparent, we are here taking into account two different considerations by way of trying to clarify the mode of being of values. The first consideration is the mode of being of the value-bearer; the second is the way in which the value is founded in the object to which it accrues. In the first case it would seem apropos to state that a value exists in the same manner as its bearer: if the bearer is real, then so is the value; if the former is not real, then neither is the latter. In the second case, on the other hand, it seems instructive to suggest that a weakening of the bond between the value-bearer and the value has a debilitating influence, as I shall put it, on the mode of being of the value. Such a conjecture seems to be concealed behind the earlier mentioned argument against acknowledging the existence of those values which have turned out to be 'relative', thus more or less conditioned in their being by some object other than their bearer.

But are both these claims true? And does not the application of both to the discussion of the mode of being of values lead to contradictions?

From the first claim it would follow that only real values can accrue to a real object, and that if they accrue to it effectively then everything that is generally true of real objects in general is also true of the mode of being of these values. Thus, at least at first glance it appears that one and the same real object, say, a human being can be a handsome man (hence, a particular aesthetic value accrues to him), that he can at the same time be an honest and morally upright human being, and finally that he can be a so-called 'good father', meaning that he is capable of raising his children properly, that as a father, therefore, he is a useful member of his family. If we were to agree that aesthetic values which normally somehow accrue to aesthetic (non-real) objects cannot exist in the real mode, then we would have to deny the given man the value of handsomeness, and we would have to make a similar judgment concerning his value of being a 'useful' member of his family, which is conditioned not only by him himself, but also by the other members of his family to whom his modes of conduct are accommodated, and which would have to be real in some way other than is his value of being a morally upright man. According to the principle brought to bear at the beginning of this paragraph we would in this case have to deny the man the value of being a 'good father'.

Still other difficulties follow acceptance of the above assertion concerning the mode of being of values. Namely, all real objects exist in time: they are either objects which persist in time, or instantaneous events, or, finally, processes occurring in time. Can it be said of any value which accrues to a real object that it is either an event, or an object persisting in time, or, finally, a process? One can surely concede that values can *begin* to accrue to a particular object and that a particular event thereby occurs: the origination of a given value, or the inception of its accruing to something. We would surely also agree that a human being acquires certain values in the course of his life, by learning certain skills, for instance, by moulding a moral character, so to speak, in the face of life's travails, and the like. We would then perhaps be able to say that there can be a process of the *realization* of certain values. We would not however be able to concede that someone's being 'honest', 'fair', or 'brave to the point of heroism', and the like, are particular events or real processes occurring in the world, or in the given human being. But could we say that these values of the given person's character are objectivities that persist in time, that they therefore change in time just like the human being himself or any other thing whatever, that they acquire in the present a peculiar actuality of existence in order later to sink into the past?

We have said earlier that values are existentially non-self-sufficient in relation to that whose values they are, that is, to their bearers; and that they are also existentially derived from the properties of their bearer, or from an ensemble of properties belonging to two or more objects (for example, to a tool and the thing to which it is applied, to food and animal, and so on). In this respect, therefore they are different from objects persisting in time (in particular, from human beings and things). But it does not yet follow from these differences alone that the mode of being of values differs from the mode of being of their bearers, that they therefore cannot be real for this reason. For material things are also existentially derivative from other things from which they arose. And there are many non-self-sufficient moments in real objects (including each of the properties of such an object) to which we cannot, however, deny reality of existence on account of this existential non-self-sufficiency. And so also, we cannot on *that* account deny reality of existence to values, insofar as we were forced to impute to them such a mode of being, at least in the case of some of them.

Let us omit aesthetic values for the time being, whose 'realness' perhaps not all of us would wish to defend, since the circumstance that they appear on the basis of certain non-real objectivities does play some sort of decisive role here. One would perhaps like to assert at least that the value of a particular object cannot exist in a 'stronger' mode, so to speak, than that in which the object itself exists. But at the same time, the eventual non-realness of aesthetic values does not seem to be an issue over which it would be difficult to come to a consensus in view of the significance of these values and their role in man's life. On the other hand, the issue of the mode of being of moral values, as well as of utility-values, appears to be much more significant, and for various reasons more difficult, if we were to somehow equate their mode of being with the mode of being of aesthetic values. One would wish to somehow bring moral values closer to man's actuality, or that actuality in which the human being performs his deeds. It seems impossible to want to regard moral values as something that is found outside of time, such as ideas or objectivities of one sort or another. It appears unquestionable that the moral value of a particular deed (for example, the relinquishing of a certain good for the sake of another person, sacrificing one's own life in the defence of another human being or in the defence of a particular cultural ideal) *originates* at the instant of effecting this individual deed. The human being who has done this deed also first gains a certain merit at the instant of its performance, granting that this deed was not simply a purely mechanical reflex of his body. And there is surely also no denying that various kinds of values that a man 'represents' owing to his moral character, the talents and skills he possesses, his knowledge and experience, for example, are *annihilated,* ousted from being, the moment he dies or has a mental breakdown (for, even strong and noble men sometimes break down spiritually under certain conditions) even though these values continue to be 'credited' to him posthumously.

It is also impossible to eradicate from time utility-values of various sorts and significance. All so-called achievements of technology which depend on the construction of ever new devices, with the new capabilities inherent in them, bring forth the 'realization' of new utility-values, sometimes double-edged ones, in that they bring with them both benefits and harms. It must be said of all these 'benefits' and 'harms' that they arise at the instant of constructing the given devices and are annihilated concomitantly with the destruction of these devices, or at least along with their being put out of commission. When the given tool is 'broken', it *loses* its value. When its construction is 'perfected', even if only through the use of more durable materials, the utility-value, *ceteris paribus,* 'grows' or, to put it more precisely, a new value has been *realized*.

These are facts which, it seems to me, are difficult to refute. The difficulty, however, resides in the question as to what relation to time and to the actual object in which the given value is founded should be ascribed to the moral or utility value in the period of time between its realization and annihilation. Should mutability and transience in time be attributed to such values, as is the case with everything real, or should we concede that they somehow rise in their mode of being above this necessary transformability in time? Does the value of a deed pass in the same way as the deed which is performed; does it no longer exist after having been accomplished? Or does it abide, last somehow, even after the deed itself has already passed? Is it not altogether presumptuous to impute to values the applicability of the very same criteria that are appropriate to real, temporal objects, particularly those persisting in time, when values (in particular, moral values) are not temporal *sensu stricto,* somehow abide supratemporally, as it were, despite the temporal character of their originating and perishing?

This issue is important not only from a theoretical point of view; it is not a merely academic issue. Its resolution in one way or another holds implications for various human decisions and modes of conduct. It is connected with the problem of the responsibility of a human being for the deeds performed by him, responsibility at the very instant these deeds have already been accomplished and passed. Have they passed on along with their positive or negative value? How can one be punished or rewarded for something which no longer exists? But someone will say: the deeds and their values no longer exist, but the good or bad deed performed leaves on the person who has done it a trace of folly (hence, something negatively valued) or merit (hence, some actual, positive moral value). The human being *remains* a villain or hero; only then does punishment or reward make sense. He can be held accountable only if he is identical with the person who once performed the deed, and if at the present moment he still carries within himself the value of his folly or merit. Otherwise, he has the right to say: "I am not the one who performed that deed"; or, "I am today free of blame, I no longer bear within myself the negative value of the deed from that time. This negative value has gone by along with the instant in which my deed was consummated".

There is, of course, the idea of 'confession', according to which a confession constitutes a way of 'washing away' one's sins, of destroying negative values, about which it need be said that if it was necessary to have them 'washed away' and if this 'cleansing', this 'remission', were at all amenable to being accomplished, then these negative values somehow remained, continued to exist despite the lapse in time, despite the changes that have since transpired in the given person. With regard to this aspect, one would have to attribute to moral values not only the capacity of outlasting the lapse of time, but also the capacity of not succumbing, within this flux of time, to any changes in their nature or rank.

It seems that no form or variant of mode of being that is familiar to us (thus, neither ideal being, nor real being, nor purely intentional being (heteronomous being)) is fit to be ascribed to the way in which at least some values exist, and in particular moral values, given that the conditions of their 'realization' obtain.

Someone will say: "this is quite clear and natural", and indeed this has often been said by claiming either, as Lotze has done, that values do not exist, but 'hold sway' [*gelten*], have a peculiar 'significance'* [*Geltung*], or, as Rickert and other members of the South-German School of Neo-Kantians said, that values not simply 'are', but that they are characterized by 'oughtness to exist' [*Seinsollen*].

That is not, however, a satisfactory solution. For, something can 'hold sway', 'be in force' or have 'significance', if and only if it exists in some manner. Non-existence makes *Geltung* altogether impossible. One could then of course say: "values (in particular, moral values) not only exist, but have significance above and beyond existing", and the like. But is this 'significance' a closer determination (if we may say that) of their existence or is it something that is most intimately linked with the valuableness of a value?

The problem of *Seinsollen* is much more complicated. We can sensibly say of certain values that they 'ought' to exist in two different situations:
(a) when these values have not yet been 'realized', and
(b) when this has already been accomplished.

In case (a) we have to do with an 'oughtness' of existence which we can somehow read off from the intrinsic content of the idea of the given value (for example, fairness or civic courage). As far as a prospective concretization (ordinarily we say, not quite rigorously, 'realization') of the value is concerned, on the one hand, it need not, of course, necessarily come to that under the given conditions; but, on the other hand, the matter (quality) of the value dictates, one could also say 'demands', this concretization from those in whose power it lies to effect it. That 'ought-to-be' presupposes here that the value 'is not yet', and this

* Translators of phenomenological literature have most commonly rendered this word into English by 'validity' (Cairns) or 'counting as' (Findlay). The literal translation of Ingarden's Polish word in this spot is 'weight'. I follow his lead in note 19, above; in Polish, the word for 'significant' is in fact a cognate of the word for 'weight'. Tr.

roughly means that all will be 'in order' only when its concretization is consummated. In this case the 'ought-to-be' means something more than our expectation or anticipation of such a concretization. It means something more than it does when, in setting up a particular physical experiment and having established the conditions for the occurrence of a certain event or process we say, while attempting to effect these conditions: "process or event X 'ought' to occur under these conditions." Here, this only means that we foresee and anticipate the occurrence of the event as soon as the conditions we have established for it are realized. In the case of a particular moral value which ought to be realized in a given situation, we not only expect or anticipate that the deed realizing this value will be performed, but something more, namely, that everything *will be 'in order'* only when this realization has come about, in particular that the person who will perform this deed will be in order, that he will fulfill, as we say, the obligation that binds him (although it is at the same time the case that he does not *have to* fulfill it). This obligation stems precisely from that character of oughtness of bringing about (realizing) the given value in the situation at hand. The oughtness specified by the intrinsic content of the idea of the given value no longer obtains once the value has been effectively realized, that is as soon as the demand for its realization has been fulfilled. Should we say, in view of this, that once the value (of this type, say, a moral value) has been realized, exists, then its existence no longer bears upon itself any stamp which would somehow be the correlate of that oughtness, and in this respect does not differ in its existence from the existence of objects devoid of all value, that is from that of value-neutral objects? Yet, it appears that there is a difference here in the very existence of moral values as opposed to value-neutral objects. Perhaps someone may wish to see this difference as lying in the fact that a particular value's having been realized in a given situation is itself positively assessed, 'endorsed' as 'in order' or as 'appropriate', whereas the straightforward existence of a value-neutral object does not evoke such an assessment or acknowledgment. This would however represent a shifting of the problem. It *can* of course come to such an endorsement, but it need not; besides, the difference we are looking for is not to be sought in it. That something else is involved becomes evident once we realize that such an endorsement or acknowledgment can be either correct or incorrect. For it can only draw its correctness precisely from the fact that the effective existence itself of the value which ought to be realized is in itself positively valuable as the *fulfillment of this ought:* it is 'well', therefore, that there is a realization of the given value. This is presumably what Max Scheler had in mind when, as I have already mentioned, he asserted that the existence of a positive value is itself a positive value. But it seems that this statement goes a step too far. It is not that a new value emerges in this situation, but that the valuableness of the realized value somehow encompasses the existence of the value, or better put, it has one of its foundations in this existence, and so it stems not only from the matter itself of the value, but also from the effectiveness of its realization. In this case, not the *Sollen* alone characterizes the existence of values of this type, but indeed also the *fulfillment* of this *Sollen*.

Perhaps it will be easier to come to grips with that peculiar moment of the mode of being of moral values if we compare them with aesthetic values. I have already stated previously that these latter can never attain to that effectiveness of existence which holds of values realized in deeds, since they are always confined to the sphere of purely intentional being. But would the error reside only in our assigning to aesthetic values the sort of effectiveness of existence which apparently needs to be ascribed to moral values, and which is not attainable by aesthetic values? The error would surely reach farther. Aesthetic values would in such an event be equated, as I shall put it, with moral values as to the dignity of the latter; they would be equated with these in respect of a valuableness that does not at all accrue to them. The dignity of moral values goes counter to their being equated with either aesthetic or utilitarian values. Just as, to be sure, one would not agree to ascribe to truth values the same mode of being as to moral values, or such as is appropriate to aesthetic values. In the first instance that would amount to a promotion of their value, as it were, in the second to a demotion. We begin to surmise that the mode of being of values is somehow bound up with various factors, that is to say, with their own matter, with the type of their valuableness, as well as with the mode of being of the object to which they can accrue. Still, we do not know how to explain these issues in a satisfactory manner or to formulate adequately well-founded assertions. It also seems that in the diverse modes of being that we encounter in the domain of values we have to do with new modes of existence in comparison with those I have tried to circumscribe in volume I [§ 33] of *Streit*.

In conclusion, I must still note that I have only considered here how values of a particular basic type *can exist,* a manner stipulated for, or correlated to, the given type of values. I have therefore omitted the issue as to whether a particular value given to us *in individuo* in experience, and belonging to some fundamental type, does *really* exist in the given case, whether it is adequately grounded in the object which appears to be its bearer, or whether there is only a *semblance,* more or less founded, of its accruing to this object. We have to agree that not always when a particular man's specific deed is given to us as 'unselfish', or when some work is given to us as 'perfect' or 'full of charm', that such is actually the case, and that consequently separate investigations have to be undertaken concerning the manner of grounding the respective value in the object or in the circumstances in which it finds itself or, finally, in the conditions under which the value is apprehended. This is a sphere of entirely new ways of investigating the existence of a certain individual value for which the remarks sketched above – concerning solely the issue of a general coordination of a possible mode of being with a fundamental type of values – can have no more than an ancillary significance. These are the issues which are the subject of controversy whenever, say, art critics demand so-called 'criteria' of evaluation or where in court proceedings, for example, the guilt of the defendant in some definite case is at issue and the question arises whether the available circumstantial evidence is sufficient grounds for convicting the accused.

Ad. (4). The issue of the so-called 'rank' [*Höhe*] of a value affords equally serious difficulties. It is just as fundamental to a theory of value as the topics already touched on. Also, rank seems so obviously linked to the essence of all values that it is impossible to shun problems which arise in connection with it, even though to more than one reader the issue may appear so 'self-evident' and 'natural' as to dispense with a treatment of it.

What indeed seems to be self-evident is that every value has some definite rank of its worthiness, which is always a necessarily telling characteristic of that worthiness. It is less obvious, on the other hand, that when we have to do with two values, their rank is either equal or different, which in the latter case means that one of the values is 'higher' and the other 'lower'. Some would maintain, that this can only occur when both compared values are of the same basic type. If this condition is not satisfied, then neither of the cited relations obtains between the values. The very question as to whether one of them is higher than the other, or whether they are equal, is then deprived of any intelligible sense.[20] Because the concept of type of values can be understood in various ways there is the danger that values whose matter is different will be considered to be of different types, so that it would then be impossible to compare as to their rank any two values with different matter (different 'quality'). But even if we were more careful and confined ourselves to distinguishing only several basic types of values – as we have done at the beginning of this paper – we are forced to ascertain that even then there is a live tendency to compare as regards rank values of fundamentally differing types. We try, both in practice and in theory, to establish only, within a single type of value, whole series of values ordered according to rank. But even when we have to do with, say, a moral value and some aesthetic value, we sometimes ask which of them is higher. For there are at times situations whereby the realization of one of them hinders or even makes impossible the realization of the other and we have to choose which of them to realize. We also want to know, then, which of them is higher, in order to accord it the priority of being realized. This is connected with the sometimes pronounced postulate that if some two values cannot be realized simultaneously, then the lower value should be sacrificed in favour of realizing the higher value, assuming that there is altogether the option of choosing which of them is to be realized. There is also the quite widespread opinion that moral values are *generaliter* higher than aesthetic values, and the like. In that case, the elevation of some aesthetic value over some moral value and the realization of the former at the expense of destroying or not realizing the latter will, in conformity with that conviction, be burdened with a negative value, will be a 'wrong' in some sense.

There is no way of knowing, however, whether the thesis concerning the fundamental precedence of values of type A over values of type B should be understood in such a way that even a relatively low value of type A is always higher than any, even relatively high, value of type B, or whether it is to apply only to values whose status in both series of values, ordered according to their rank, is (at least approximately) the same. For this reason there is no way of knowing whether the mentioned postulate is applicable to every arbitrary pair of values taken from two different series, or whether it concerns only suitably matched values. In the first case, a postulate of this sort seems a little dubious in the least; in the second case, on the other hand, the feasibility of its application would presuppose the existence of, and familiarity with, a rigorous ordering according to rank of the values of the individual basic types. Even then it would be difficult to find those places that are, say, equally removed from the 'highest' value. Meanwhile, it would be difficult to point to even one such ordered series of values, though in various penal codes a varying severity of sentences is established for the different particular crimes. The severity of the transgression or wrong perpetrated does not however appear to determine exclusively the stiffness of the sentence. In many instances, when faced with two values of the same basic type (for example moral values), and especially in the case of two values belonging to different fundamental types, we are unable to tell which of them is higher and which lower, though we do have certain presentiments in this regard. These shortcomings stem from our not knowing in an adequately clear and precise manner what this rank, so ineluctably connected with the worthiness of a value, actually is. Nor do we know what it is that stipulates this rank, whether the value-matter, its mode of being, 'impact' [*Kraft*], or finally the 'oughtness of its existence'. It may well be that this oughtness is functionally dependent on the rank of the value, and the rank is functionally dependent on the value-matter. But what attests to this actually being the case? After all, it is a widely held opinion that the rank of a value does not at all depend on its matter, nor on anything that can be distinguished in the value itself and which characterizes it immanently, but that it depends on extraneous circumstances – among others, as has been frequently claimed, on recognition by man, who wants to dispose over the given valuable object, or on the social opinion reigning during a particular period of time in a particular cultural milieu. The number of objects having similar value (for example, the amount of so-called merchandise on the market) and the extent of demand at a particular time are likewise supposed to influence the rank of a value. In these diverse views concerning what determines the rank of a value there shines through the opposition between the absolutist and relativist theories of values, or more accurately, only one form of that opposition.

According to the 'absolutists', the rank of a value and the value itself should first of all be distinguished from the 'price' which is assigned to a valuable object under certain circumstances. It is in fact the price, and not the rank of the value of the particular object, which depends on the just mentioned factors and varies in accordance with their change. The rank of the value, in contrast, is univocally and invariantly specified by its matter, and only by it, and remains constant through price changes. The price, we say in many instances, 'corresponds' to the value; if it is disproportionately high relative to it, we say that the given object was 'overpriced', if it is low, we say it was 'underpriced'.

Further, the absolute rank of a value which is determined by its matter should be distinguished from the relative rank which follows from the comparison of valuable objects in a particular manner. This especially applies to the utilitarian values of the various kinds of technological products, when as a result of the appearance of higher quality merchandise, the merchandise thus far available, which does not yet have this quality, looks to be 'worse' in comparison with the new product. Its relative value is diminished in relation to its absolute value. From the point of view of its utility it continues to be just as valuable, since it provides for the same needs as before, but it is worse because it does not satisfy new needs which set higher standards. The relative rank of the value of a particular object is variable, depending on what other objects of the same type have materialized, but this variable relative rank comes into play first of all in the case of utility-values and it is at least questionable whether it occurs among values of any other fundamental type, such as moral values. Finally, the absolutists will say, both the relative, comparative rank of a value and the price ('worth') of a valuable object *presuppose* the existence of an absolute rank of a value which is exclusively specified by its matter. This absolute value-rank is independent of being recognized, of vogue, of need and its relation to the available number of objects having the same kind of value, and the like.

The 'relativists' of the brand in question will say, however, that differences among values as to rank pertain exclusively to relative, comparative rank or are reducible to a difference in 'worth' which is determined solely by the factors already mentioned.

The controversy is not easy to settle precisely because it has not been adequately clarified what the rank of a value is, which is after all at first glance only a closer, as it were, but nonetheless necessary determination of the valuableness of a rank. It is necessary because without it that 'general', as I shall put it, valuableness would not be possible – general, because this valuableness has to appear in every value of any type whatever, but at the same time requires in each particular species of values augmentation by 'rank', different in each individual species and different still in individual values. General valuableness is here a generic moment, as it were, whereas rank is a moment that within certain limits differentiates the species of values, and ultimately even the individual values within the same species.

Some researchers attempt to resolve this problem by setting up criteria for the rank of values.[21] But the very search for such criteria attests to the fact that the rank of a value is not sufficiently transparent either intuitively or through some other mode of experience. That is why we have to search for indices outside of value-rank itself that would allow us to identify that rank. It is quite characteristic that, in the criteria he had set down, Scheler does not at all appeal to the matter of the values whose rank he tries to establish with the aid of the criteria, but to entirely different concerns, such as the durability [*Dauerhaftigkeit*] of values, the foundedness of certain values in others – whereby lower values are supposed to be founded in higher ones – and even to something like the degree of gratification which accompanies the realization of a particular value (!). It is also unclear whether these criteria are only supposed to be the means for *identifying* the rank of a value or the factor on which the value-rank is functionally dependent. This last would certainly open the way to a relativistic resolution of the problem of value-rank. Irrespective of how the criteria laid down by Scheler are to be understood, they are at any rate something other than the value-rank itself, the elucidation of which was my immediate task. Recourse to them cannot therefore be helpful in solving the problem that has occupied us here.

Ad. (5). The next problem I still wish to consider here is the so-called 'autonomy' of values. It will have a different look for each different type of values.

All values are, as I mentioned, existentially non-self-sufficient in relation to the object to which they accrue. At the moment, however, we are concerned with a different kind of self-sufficiency or non-self-sufficiency of certain values, that is to say, that of one value with respect to another or that of one value-type with respect to another value-type. The question arises whether there are values that can appear in an object *without* the simultaneous and necessary concomitant appearance in that self-same object of some *other* values of the same or another basic type. A value which is distinctive in this way – if such exists – I call an 'autonomous' value, whereas a value which appears in an object if and only if some other value of the same or another type appears in it at the same time, I call 'non-autonomous'.[22] In this connection, we have to stress that it is exclusively the quality (matter) of the value which decides its autonomy or non-autonomy in the sense defined. It is this quality which necessarily demands the co-appearance in the same object of some other value that is strictly well-defined in its matter, or at least in the type of this matter. There can however be reasons for two values having to appear together in a single object without this following from their respective qualities. It may happen that the conditions for realizing value V_1 in object O are of such a kind that they can occur in it if and only if some other conditions also obtain, whose consequence will be the emergence of value V_2. I would then say that V_1 and V_2 are *derivatively* non-autonomous.

But what purpose does this sort of distinction serve? The question concerning autonomy or non-autonomy has been repeatedly raised, under the address of specific values, in the annals of art theory or aesthetics since Plato's times. Plato, for example, claimed that there exists a highest 'idea', which according to him was at the same time the highest 'good' (value); this was the idea 'Beauty-Good' *(kalokagathia),* whereby the one could not appear without the other. But similar assertions were at times pronounced considerably later, under cultural conditions that were already wholly altered and when philosophical currents were dominant which had nothing in common with Platonism. This was most often done by art critics, in particular literary critics, who carried on disputes as to whether 'beauty' can appear in a work of art if values of some other kind do *not* appear in it at the same time. This other kind of value on which they made the 'beauty' of the work dependent varied according to circumstances. It was most frequently demanded that the work of art contain some sort of moral values, that it portray in the represented world people endowed with such values or depict conflicts revolving around realizing them, whereby a work was considered 'beautiful' if some high moral value triumphed in the conflict. There were also critics in an opposing camp who considered, say, a literary work to be 'beautiful' only if it exhibits in the represented world precisely the negative moral values such as evil, crime, cruelty. This meant that the work is 'realistic', and this 'realism' was most highly valued from an artistic point of view, with the proclamation that only such a work was 'truthful'. In other quarters it was decreed that a work is not valuable, in the sense of a particular aesthetic value, unless it displayed certain social or political ideals in the represented world, for example, the patriotism of its heroes, and the like. The reproach of so-called formalism which was frequently advanced in the past several decades – a reproach which concealed a number of diverse motives – relied precisely on the refusal to assign autonomy to strictly aesthetic values.

On the other hand, the slogan of so-called 'art for art's sake' – again, interpreted in many different ways and stemming from a variety of motives – had at its basis the clouded conviction that aesthetic values are in general autonomous in the sense set forth here and that failure to acknowledge their autonomy is what in artistic practice most frequently leads to the situation that wholly different values, having nothing to do with art and beauty, are considered as the only important ones in the work of art, and that the latter exercises its function only when it caters to those other values. Truth, especially so called historical truth, vital truth, etc., was held by opponents of the 'art for art's sake' slogan to be not only indispensable but the proper aesthetic value of a work of art, so that here it came not only to a rejection of the autonomy of aesthetic values but even – according to the proponents of the above slogan – to a dissembling substitution of values of one type in place of values of another type. The conflict was then waged not over the autonomy of aesthetic values, but over what makes up the 'true' aesthetic value.

The basis of these squabbles, which so frequently appear in history and which are ordinarily characterized by each side refusing to yield to the arguments of the other, is first of all an inadequate account of the specific character of the generic matter of aesthetic values, on the one hand, and of moral values (or any other), on the other hand. The failure to bring the peculiar qualities of values to a clear intuitive grasp and to the conceptual determination connected therewith, is the source for the use in these conflicts of words lacking a precise and fixed meaning, so that the parties do not know over what these disputes are in fact waged. But just the illumination of the specific qualities of the values in unfailing intuition is not enough; it is in addition necessary to glean the non-self-sufficiency of certain value-qualities, to realize that they are necessarily inseparable within the framework of a single whole – that is, to acquire a particular insight into the *a priori* interconnections between these values. Only systematic investigations of the most diverse value-qualities – carried out on a wealth of material – can lead here to a clarification of the issues.

But one more thing may be the reason that it is so difficult to reach agreement in the given controversies. In the everyday practice of comportment with values of this or that type, in the struggles waged for their realization or elimination from human life, there occurs sometimes a certain *falsification of the very experience* of values. Not only do we sometimes hold erroneous views concerning this or that value, not only do we employ muddled and ambiguous concepts, but what is worse, we sometimes sense values erringly and our emotional reactions to them are improper. We react, for example, with an aesthetic emotion where moral values emerge or, conversely, we react to aesthetic values appearing in a work of art, and which are not identified in their own character, with an indignation that is appropriate rather to negative moral values. Where it comes to that, it becomes extremely difficult to communicate with the proponent of a different view, for there is lacking a common basis of experience. One has first to try and somehow reinstate the called-for experience, to neutralize the deception stemming from the falsification, which of course is often unattainable.

We need to distinguish the issue of the autonomy or non-autonomy of values from an issue which is sometimes confused with it, that of the dependence or independence of values with respect to other values appearing in the same object, or sometimes even only appearing in the same field of experience or in temporal proximity. At issue is the fact that in some cases the matter of value A is subject to certain special modifications as a consequence of appearing in object O together with some other value B. We then say that value A is dependent in its matter on value B. Something similar happens here to the well known fact of the simultaneous or sequential contrast among colours. Here, modification of the matter can be bilateral, that is to say the qualities of *both* concomitantly appearing values are slightly modified, without destroying each other. But it can also be the case that the matter of one value will emerge with a much greater liveliness and distinctness when some other contrasting value appears simultaneously with it. So, for example, in certain works of architecture the symmetrical distribution of masses can constitute an aesthetic value, but the appearance of some unsymmetrically situated particular can underscore even more the symmetry governing the work. It may also be that not the matter of the value, but its valuableness or rank becomes modified by the appearance of some other value which harmonizes or clashes with the former. One could also interpret this phenomenon by saying that it is not the rank of this value which suffers modification, but that this valuableness does not impose itself on the observer with the same intensity as before, that, as we sometimes put it, it does not 'address' the recipient with its due force. The serene lyricism of a new situation that follows some very tragic scene, for example, does not attain its due expressiveness or manifestation in its peculiar value because the force of the tragic events and its resonance extinguishes the mood of delicate serenity, and the like. It may well be just the opposite, and it would require special studies to show how the one and the other are possible – this would of course have to be done through changes in frequently minute and hardly noticeable details, which nonetheless have a great significance for modifications in the mutually dependent values.

The modifications which values undergo by appearing together can be not only mutually dependent on each other, but can stand in a distinct functional dependence. Various possibilities open up here for transformations within the structure of the value itself, possibilities which would have to be more closely investigated in order to grasp their diversity and limits. We are here talking about dependencies between various moments within the structure of one and the same value. Whoever holds that it is matter that is the fundamental factor in the structure of a value will surely expect that a particular modification of this matter has to entail correlative modifications in the valuableness of the value, in its rank, in the oughtness-character of its existence, and the like. These expectations may however be premature, and too schematically or generally conceived. For it is perhaps the case that these issues fare differently for different types of values, and that there is a greater independence between the various moments of the structure of a value in one type than in another, so that not every modification in the matter of a value implies a change, no matter how slight, in, say, the rank of that value. Various surprises can confront us here, and only probing experiments, so to speak, with various assortments of values appearing in a single work – experiments in which creative artists necessarily engage in their artistic practice – can move us a step closer toward exposing this issue of the dependence or non-dependence of values on each other, an issue which is so crucial in all realms of values. At the present moment all these issues loom before us as only provisionally outlined *tasks,* for the execution of which our current knowledge is insufficient.

The autonomy and independence of a value could extend so far, in certain instances that owing to its matter it could not only exist as the sole value of the given object, but would, moreover, either not allow the realization of *any* other value in the same object or object-complex, or forbid at least some of them. There would then obtain a relation of absolute *exclusion* between value A and value B or all other values. This would be, one could say from a different point of view, a case of a peculiar *intolerance* of the given autonomous value with respect to other values. Such intolerance could be 'moderate', as it were, if value A did allow the emergence in object O of some other value B, but the appearance of A and B in the same object would entail the phenomenon of *discord* – in music, so-called 'dissonance' – that is the appearance of some *negative* value. This phenomenon of intolerance in its multifarious forms and consequences must also become the object of separate investigations.

Ad (6). In conclusion, it still remains for us to touch on the relation or connection between value and the object to which it accrues, in particular the issue of its 'founding' in the object. This is perhaps the most important issue with which values challenge us, and the most difficult. A thorough discussion of it would require a separate treatise, so I shall confine myself to some remarks, and the analyses carried out in my other papers may serve to amplify what I say here. This problem, frequently referred to as the *problem of objectivity,* assuredly looks different as to particulars for the different basic types of values and should not be solved in a single stroke for all values in general, but separately, relative to the values of each individual type. In the sort of general considerations here set forth it can only be a question of the *possible* ways in which particular types of values can be founded in the objects to which they appear to accrue. But exploration of the question whether in some individual case a particular value is really founded in this or that way in the object for which it is a value cannot be confined to the results of those general investigations; it must reach to the factual attributes of the given object and take account of all the circumstances in which the value appears in the given concrete instance.

I mentioned before that every value is existentially non-self-sufficient with respect to the object whose value it makes up, and that it is existentially derivative from its properties. Such is indeed the case if the value *exists* effectively. But its appearance on the object as basis may be deprived of *fundamentum in re;* it may only be a deceptive illusion that it truly accrues to this object. A value is non-self-sufficient in its general structure, that is to say it requires a certain basis for its existence. It exists if some object can be found which is capable of appeasing this non-self-sufficiency by supplying for its basis such properties as would be sufficient for the concretization of the particular quality of the value. As an augmenting factor which removes the value's existential non-self-sufficiency, this object is at the same time that which offers the necessary condition for the concrete coming into being of a value with the given matter (quality). To ascertain, therefore, if a value of a certain type (for example a definite charm) has a sufficient and necessary foundation in a particular object, we have to seek out those properties which, in appearing in this object, necessarily *imply* the appearance *in concreto* of the given quality in the given object. Contemplation of this situation has two aspects, or, if one prefers, falls in two phases. In the first, fundamental and general one, we are concerned with the question of *which* properties must be realized in an object that would be at all suitable as bearer of a particular type of values in order that they may serve as an adequate foundation for the manifestation (disclosure) of a value with some definite matter (quality) (such as, for example, a value from the domain of aesthetic values, the value of 'charm' or 'fairness', or a particular variant of 'beauty'). In other words, we need to search out a sufficient and necessary correlation between a certain assortment of properties of a possible bearer and values with a given determinate quality. Whoever does not believe that such essential correlations between qualities (or manifolds of qualities) obtain and are discoverable in a secure manner, has prejudged from the outset that value-qualities appear on objects in a 'hit-or-miss' fashion, that there is not, and cannot be, any effective founding of a quality (whether specific or general) in the object on the basis of which the value exhibits itself. Expression of assent to that sort of prior conviction would be just as unsound and dogmatic a solution to the problem as adopting the opposite stance that some such necessary interconnection between value-matter and a possible multiplicity of properties of a particular object obtains in each and every case. Only through a detailed analysis of cases in which a value with a definite matter appears, an analysis of which properties of an object in which it appears 'entail' it, are in a necessary, essential interconnection with it, and to what extent possible changes in this assortment of properties change the value-matter or altogether annihilate the value as a consequence, is it possible to determine what endowment (if any) of the object a given value corresponds to, what necessary and sufficient grounding in these properties the value demands and can be indulged in its demand. To be sure, such investigations are taxing and have to be carried out on many variegated examples, and only in the course of time can they lead to the acquisition of secure positive results. Without them, all positive or negative solutions concerning the possibility or impossibility of founding values in objects are devoid of scientific value. They are the dogmas of skeptics or the dogmas of optimists. But if someone asks me what today's (1964) status of the investigations into this problem is, who is actually in the right here? – I shall reply: this is precisely one of those things about which we still do not know anything today. The bare beginnings of this sort of research can be glimpsed in the individual domains (ethics, aesthetics, theory of economic values, etc.).

This general question is of course fundamental, and the most important, but it does not take care of everything. If someone asks us what aesthetic values show themselves to us in an aesthetic contemplation of one of Rembrandt's self-portraits (e.g., the one in the Frick Gallery in New York) or, say, Chopin's Sonata in B-minor, and whether the aesthetic values which are manifested in these works and discovered by us are effectively founded in the works of art – then those general considerations could indeed be of great help to us, but they would not release us from an individual examination of how things stand with precisely the given work and the aesthetic object which is, or can be, constituted on its basis. That is the question in which so-called art 'critics' are primarily interested, but one for which they are for the most part unprepared; aside from the fact that they are possibly endowed with a special sensitivity to the manifested values, and therefore able to single out value-qualities that are disclosed to them in comportment with the work in a much more mature and subtle manner, they are generally not in a position to investigate whether these values are *cum fundamento in re* or whether they are merely conditioned in their manifestedness by the subjective modes of the observer's behaviour, though these values no doubt show themselves on the given work's 'visage'. Here lies the sphere of the possibility of grounding the evaluation of the values of a particular work. Here also we leave the terrain of general considerations belonging to the theory of values in general or to the theory of values of some special type, and pass over to specialized knowledge about art or knowledge about morality, and the like. At this point I have no intention of meddling in these questions. My only intention was to indicate the theoretical foundations of this sort of positive knowledge about art or morality, and the role which general value theory or the theory of a particular type of value can play for this positive knowledge about art or morality. And I wanted to make myself at least roughly aware of what essential deficiencies or shortcomings are today still contained in this general value theory.

Notes

[1] The problem of the so-called 'relativity' of values is discussed in a separate paper. [See p. 119 in this book. Tr.]

[2] Some researchers simply state that values are qualities (see, for example, Herbert Wutz, *Zur Theorie der literarischen Wertung,* Tübingen, Hopfer, 1957). That, however, is an improper oversimplification of the matter.

[3] In other qualitative spheres this difficulty is sometimes overcome by appealing to numerical or quantitative differences which are correlated to quality differences according to some principle, as, for example, in the realm of colour, different colours are correlated with different frequencies of light waves. This, however, is more like going around the difficulty than overcoming it. Besides, can something like this be done in the case of qualitative differences between values?

[4] This 'reduction' of A to B is ordinarily understood to mean that A = B. But this is in fact false in the case I am discussing.

[5] If by 'aesthetic attitude' we understand that attitude in which cognitive acts of a special kind can be effected, acts which enable us to grasp aesthetic values directly, there is as yet nothing false in this, provided that we now, in turn, explain what kind of acts these are which apprehend values. It is worse, however, when we hear that aesthetic values, for example, are just those values which are 'pleasing' to us, or which afford us this or that delight.

[6] The acceptance of such an assertion is supposed to be an expression of scholarly prudence of researchers, the manifestation of that attitude which refuses to permit any 'metaphysics'

which 'hypostatizes' special entities where nothing of the sort exists (where there is nothing more than subjective behaviour of one kind or another).

[7] For example, Max Scheler, "Formalismus in der Ethik und materiale Wertethik", in: *Jahrbuch für Philosophie und phänomenologische Forschung,* vol. I, 1913, pp. 412 ff. [*Formalism in Ethics and Non-Formal Ethics of Values,* trans. by Manfred S. Frings and Roger L. Funk, Evanston, Northwestern U. P., 1973, pp. 13 ff.; all subsequent references will be to the English translation. Tr.]

[8] For this reason, reism should, for the sake of consistency, reject the existence of all values, and should not discourse on 'good work'. [The reference here is to T. Kotarbiński's *Traktat o dobrej robocie,* whose reism purportedly admits the existence of things [*Dinge*] only. – Tr.]

[9] Of course our discussion here concerns value *in concreto* and *in individuo* and not some ideal object or idea (as Plato would have it, or in the 20th century, Max Scheler). I shall return to this issue below.

[10] I have tried to demonstrate this assertion of formal ontology in my book, *Der Streit um die Existenz der Welt,* vol. II,1, Tübingen, 1965 [*Controversy over the Existence of the World*].

[11] G. E. Moore has pointed them out, designating this conception as the error of so-called 'naturalism' in value theory. Cf. *Principia Ethica,* (Cambridge, 1903).

[12] See, for example Herbert Wutz, *Zur Theorie der literarischen Wertung* (Tübingen, Hopfer, 1957).

[13] It is not important at the moment what meaning they attach to this instance. That is a highly complicated issue. What is crucial in all this, is that they treat 'form' as a property of the given object.

[14] See R. Ingarden, *Streit,* vol. II,1, ch. XII.

[15] I have tried to elucidate the form and matter in the sense here in question in ch. VII of *Streit,* vol. II,1, and have called them 'form I' and 'matter I' in order to distinguish them from other meanings of these terms. I also employed the term 'analaytic form', introduced by Husserl. He had not, in fact, distinguished the many varied meanings of the term 'form', but he enabled the reader to gather which meaning is at issue by pointing to specific instances of the form involved.

[16] For the interim, we have only said about this mode of being of a value that it is existentially non-self-sufficient with respect to what possesses it and, moreover, that it is existentially derivative, be it merely from certain properties of whatever has the value, or from the properties of some other objects.

[17] See N. Hartmann, *Ethik* (Berlin, W. de Gruyter, 1949), 3rd ed., p. 276 (*Ethics,* trans. from the 1st ed. [1926] by Stanton Coit, New York; Macmillan, 1932, p. vol. 2, p. 51)

[18] Max Scheler (*Formalism,* p. 82) pronounces a series of what he believes to be *a priori* laws for *all* values, such as: "The existence of a positive value is itself a positive value" or "The non-existence of a positive value is itself a negative value", etc. Disregarding the fact that such generally formulated assertions lead to a *regressus in infinitum,* it seems to me that these assertions are not applicable to all values precisely because the oughtness of their existence is not of the same kind in all of them. [In place of 'existence' of a positive value Ingarden has 'realization'. – Tr.]

[19] The sense of 'significance' which comes into play here is extremely difficult to define without reverting back to the value and its valuableness. The French existentialists, for example, have it in mind when they speak of *'signification',* whereby it is *not* a matter of the 'meaning' that characterizes every word that has a sense.

[20] Monroe C. Beardsley, for example, is of this opinion in his book *Aesthetics. Problems in the Philosophy of Criticism,* New York, Harcourt, Brace, 1958.

[21] Max Scheler does so, for example, in his *Formalism.* In reference to this, we should not forget that Scheler belongs to the 'absolutists', at least as far as moral values are concerned. Cf., *ibid.,* p. 87 n.

[22] These terms have an entirely different meaning in my ontological terminology. But I employ them in reference to the just defined variants of values because it has become commonplace in value theory, as well as in the theory of art, to use these words to denote the designated differences between values. Besides, they are applied quite according to custom, without due explanation of what is actually at issue.

An Analysis of Moral Values*

Let us review the main results of the previous lecture. I tried to establish a series of necessary conditions for some conduct or fact to have a moral value. They are actually the conditions for the realization of the kind of value which characterizes some human virtue or conduct as moral. There were six such conditions in all. The question came up, however, whether all of them taken together provide a sufficient condition for some value to be of a moral nature. That issue was left open. Let us then first of all recall these six conditions (there was still another, whose necessity was not really settled).

1. In every situation where it makes sense to speak of a moral value, an alert, acting subject must participate in the realization of this value, and 'in functioning as the subject' of his action [*Handeln*], this conscious subject must fulfill some further conditions. That is to say, the subject must guide or direct his action, while at the same time recognizing certain facts – in particular, certain values. Both presuppose not only the existence of the subject of action, but also his conscious awareness.

2. Some sort of conduct must be effected by the conscious subject, conduct in a very wide sense of the word, which could also be covered by the expression: some sort of behaviour by the subject. In a special case this will be some active doing, that is an activity that changes something in the world.

3. Values must somehow come into play when this conduct is placed within the context of a more encompassing situation. To the question as to what sort of values these have to be, I answered that they can be of various types. They can be values related to matters of life and death, economic or, more generally, utilitarian values, cultural values, and the like, but I do not exclude the possibility that these can also be moral values. I carried out my analysis within the scope of the problem of fairness. Being fair involves some sort of judgment or the appropriation of some sort of values to someone; these values can be extra-moral just as well as moral ones.

4. There has to be accountability on the part of this alert subject who behaves in a particular manner. There can be no question of any fact or

* This article represents a revised transcript of the 14th in a series of lectures on ethics delivered at the Jagiellonian University on Feb. 20, 1962.

behaviour, in particular of any deed, falling under the category of moral values, without the presence of this accountability. Accountability, for its part, requires the fulfillment of certain conditions for its realization. Some sort of conscious awareness of the acting subject belongs among these conditions, along with his self-identity, which needs be preserved in the course of an action that may extend over a period of time. Responsibility weighs on the subject even after the action has terminated. And in order to be able to weigh on him, his self-identity must have been preserved. Sometimes we speak of a collective responsibility. There were times in European culture when such a notion was operative. There was collective responsibility in the guise of clan law; the whole clan was responsible for any one of its members. In such a case, irrespective of how many accountable subjects there are, there ultimately exists some super-ordinate collective subject, and this too must retain its self-identity if any of this is to make sense.

5. The fifth necessary condition, in my opinion, is the freedom of decision and conduct. Freedom must of course be maintained in the course of executing the decision, that is during the subject's behaviour, in the course of some prospectively carried out activity and its performance. The subject must also have the option of withdrawing from an action he has already initiated. Once someone is uninvolved, so that from a particular moment on everything runs its course independently of him, he ceases from that instant to be responsible. But if he is to be responsible, if his being morally responsible is to come into play at all, he must be free to behave as he wishes.

6. The sixth point is the thesis that the person himself, the 'I' governing in this person, must be the source of decision and the basis of responsibility in the course of executing the given activity. Not only the making of the decision comes from the person, but also *backing* it in the course of its implementation. This is not to be regarded as some peripheral, external or only physical source of behaviour. The subject's behaviour ought to have its starting point in the very centre of his whole psycho-physical organization.

These six points seemed to me indispensable for some activity or act to be at all able to fall under the category of a positive or negative value in a moral sense. I then touched on two more issues. One of them was the absence of a conflict of interest. I was careful here, and said that this was essential and necessary for realizing the moral value of fairness. A self-seeking fairness is at least suspect. If someone were fair in his own interest, he would actually be partial; his fairness is then without moral value. I asked, however, if disinterestedness is in every case a necessary condition of morally worthy conduct, or whether it plays such a role only in the case of fairness. That remained a question.

I touched on yet another issue, namely, what is the proper subject or bearer of values. There are three theories relative to this matter, which ask whether the bearer of values is a person, or the person's volitional act, or the conduct itself. I tried to answer this question by discarding such a formulation of the problem. I stated that we should not insist on either (a), or (b), or (c), but should reckon with the possibility that perhaps some combination of these factors is the bearer of moral values. It may well also be the case that one kind of moral values accrues to the person, another kind to the act of volition, and still a different kind to the conduct. This whole matter demands a more thorough analysis, but not until we have a well-advanced orientation regarding the variegated types of moral values. Having assembled these points, I posed the question whether all this taken together is a sufficient condition for some conduct or, more generally, fact to have a positive or negative value in a moral sense, or whether something else must still be added. And I left this issue open.

Since I considered all these matters in reference to the problem of fairness, I would like to raise the question (as an issue that cannot be ignored, and which should be resolved in the construction of a theory of justice, as well as in a general analysis of moral values), whether under all the cited conditions the very 'fairness' (for example, of a particular conduct, which *is* fair in a positive sense) does not bring into the set of conditions a certain 'plus' which decides that the realized value is to be counted among moral values. It is the matter [*Materie*], the qualitative determination of 'fairness' – the 'justness', if I may put it so – that would, with the remaining conditions having been satisfied, make the particular value take on the imprint of value in a moral sense. I shall not substantiate my decision here, but I do believe that *such indeed is the case.* Fairness itself, as the fairness *of* something, is a peculiar quality or assortment of qualities which, among other things, implies a specific feature for moral values. This claim would require a separate demonstration which I cannot give here, but I do want to underscore in passing a particular significance of such a decision. In making it, I am endorsing a certain special standpoint in ethics, namely a position that historically has taken on the title of a *'material'* ethics, i.e. a non-formal ethics of *content* which recognizes moral values to be qualitatively determined. In the case under consideration, fairness *as such* is a certain *qualitatively* defined determination of the value of a particular decision or conduct. And this qualitativeness is of such kind as to bear this worthiness within itself.

The tendency away from material ethics, i.e. from an ethics which sees moral values in certain *qualitative determinations* of human deeds and which considers these very values as specifically determined, has sedimented since the time of Kant. Instead an edict to do *formal* ethics was pushed, an ethics that does not investigate which modes of conduct are indeed worthy, but rather simply establishes certain formal conditions for conduct to be of moral value. A discussion of what these formal conditions are, what the basis of this so-called formal ethics is, and of its theoretical sources exceeds the bounds of my present considerations. I shall only mention that the Kantian categorical imperative has, among others, this formal character. The Kantian formalist position later solicited strong echoes; many people were, and still are to this day, of the opinion that only formal ethics is scientifically cogent and viable. Yet there are doubts as to whether such a stance is correct. I cannot here discuss the merits of the case in substance, but only raise the issue by suggesting that there is also a different attitude or standpoint in ethics. At any rate, I am only taking the stand that the specification of justness of a given conduct, or of its value, must still be added on to all those necessary conditions on which perhaps the consummation of a conduct having a (positively or negatively) valued moral determination depends, in order for us to have a *full complement* of conditions not only for the realization of moral values, but also for specifying their *unique* matter.

We know that 50 years ago Max Scheler came out against Kant's formal ethics and opposed to it a 'material ethics of values' [*Der Formalismus in der Ethik und die materiale Wertethik mit besonderer Berücksichtigung der Ethik Immanuel Kants. Halle,* 1913–1916]*. He carried out a noteworthy critique of Kant's formalistic standpoint. However, in constructing his "material ethics of values", he reached certain conclusions that, I believe, still have a formalistic character. In particular, to the question of what kind of deed is morally valuable, Scheler replies that a deed is positively valuable morally if in the course of the conduct:

1. a correct assessment has been made of all values which in their very nature do not belong to the category of morality, and
2. in the case of conflicting values, a higher value is chosen to be realized over a lower one.

More precisely, if we have two values, A and B, that are comparable, that is belong to the same category of values (both are, for example, utilitarian values), and if we are able to demonstrate that value A is higher than value B, and we behave appropriately in preferring value A over value B, so that in view of this we realize value A while foregoing value B, then this conduct is morally worthy. The moral worthiness of a deed depends on an accord between the value selected for realization and the hierarchy among values that are morally neutral in their matter,

* In English as *Formalism in Ethics and Non-Formal Ethics of Values,* trans. by Manfred S. Frings and Roger L. Funk, Evanston, Northwestern U. P., 1973.

especially when there is a conflict in which the realization of A excludes the realization of B. If we know that B is a value lower than A, and is prospectively negative, but realize it nevertheless, our conduct is morally bad. Positive moral value accrues to a conduct which does not bring in its own, new value-determination, but depends on correct *"Vorziehen"*, as Scheler says, i.e. *giving preference to value A over value B,* and on realizing it even in possibly unfavourable circumstances. If we have to choose between two systems of procedure, for example two systems for regulating rivers, and one of them is advantageous to farming, while the other beside accomplishing the same realizes some *additional* economic values, for example is favourable to the construction of an electric plant, then the latter offers a higher economic value. In view of this, we decide in favour of the second system and put it into effect. Scheler would have to say that we proceeded here in a morally worthy manner because we chose the higher value and are realizing it. And whoever would institute the worse system of regulation would *ipso facto* have to be committing a morally bad deed. – But I will say that this conduct is in either case *neutral* from a moral point of view. One is not a morally better person for having realized a higher rather than a lower economic value; perhaps one is smarter or more efficient from a social perspective, or more resourceful because one organizes social, or economic-technical, life intelligently, etc. But what does morality have to do with any of this? The straightforward reduction of the problem of the moral worth of conduct to certain relations among values does not seem well-founded or sufficient. Some sort of supplementation would surely appear to be called for here. If, for example, the engineer were to choose the less effective system of regulation because instituting it would bring him personally certain material gains, to the detriment of the overall national economy, then we would perhaps not charge him with stupidity but he would appear to us in a poor moral light. Some kind of need for this sort of addendum should be shown for the various values of a moral nature. It seems to me that in the case of, for example, the problem of fairness, it is not merely a matter of choosing the higher value over the lower and of realizing it, but, moreover, it needs to be investigated whether fairness itself, whether the 'justness' of conduct as such has a specific value, is a specific value-quality, in particular a value-quality that is decisive for a man as a moral subject. A specific quality emerges here, a determination of my conduct, which as such, in and for itself, falls under worthiness in a moral sense. Thus, I go a step further relative to what Scheler has done; and I am not the first to do so. Anyway, at the moment I am only concerned with contrasting the various standpoints possible in ethics.

Let us therefore consider for the time being how things stand with fairness. There are those six necessary conditions for being able to arrive at values in a moral sense; let us attach to these that specific quality of the worthiness of fairness as such, and ask if by somehow adding up all this together we come up with a sufficient condition for recognizing some fair conduct as being *morally* worthy, whether the 'moralness' of its value is thereby sufficiently guaranteed.

This is a difficult issue and I do not wish to settle it quite yet, since we are not adequately prepared for that. I would first like to consider the following point: let us say that we managed to find the conditions that have to be fulfilled in the case of fairness; but we were concerned with acquiring certain *general* conditions that are necessary not only in this case but also in various other instances of human behaviour, of whose moral worth we are *prima vista* convinced, correctly or not.

I began to discuss the matter of demarcating moral values from others by citing a series of the most diverse examples of merits or virtues, or modes of conduct which appear morally worthy. This collection of examples was not of course exhaustive, and couldn't be such, since I still do not know the range of what can be a moral value in a positive or negative sense. And I shall not know that as long as I have not resolved the issue in terms of content, of what the 'moralness of a value' is, of what is a 'moral' value. As a result, the various instances I have mentioned here were just so many examples which in the final reckoning may prove imprecise. At any rate, I know of no ethical system that would say: here is a complete set of moral values; all these, and only they, are moral values in a positive and negative sense. Being aware therefore of the tentativeness of the whole discussion, I have to return to the material brought up earlier and ask how the six cited conditions fare in the other cases of human conduct about which I spoke above. Are these conditions applicable to the given cases, or not? The decision here can have a twofold undertone: Either we say that we already know that these six conditions suffice to determine a situation in which a moral value may be involved, and should they not obtain in the given instance then the example in question does not belong within the realm of moral values; or we can say that if the confrontation of these six conditions with a certain special case produces discord, that is, that there is no doubt in our mind that heroism, for example, is a moral value, or that courage is, but the six conditions do not suffice in relation to these, or that one of them turns out not to be necessary, then something has to be changed in these conditions. In the second approach to this issue we shall rely on our obscure, but nevertheless firm, intuition, on the conviction that such a value, such a situation is indeed unquestionably of a moral nature. In view of this we shall have to correct our previous theoretical commitments. At the moment I am not leaning in either direction; I am allowing the possibility of both prospects. This is an attempt to gain conceptual resolutions that can be carried through only on the basis of concrete material and not on the basis of some sort of 'it-seems-to-me' adopted in advance. Naturally, I cannot accomplish this here in a systematic manner and arrive at final decisions, since this is an introductory course, but even within its framework I would like to move as far as possible in the direction of attaining to some kind of resolution. In today's lecture I shall discuss some selected examples.

Let us begin with so-called 'courage'. Ordinarily we say that courage is some property or feature of a man's character. We say: "that's a brave man." But what kind of argument do we resort to when it comes to verifying such a statement? We then say that someone behaved courageously in this or that situation. Thus, someone's courage can first come through in some conduct or, to put it differently, it can fist be constituted through conduct. A man can learn courage, he can mouled himself into becoming a brave person. It is precisely upon cases of realizing courage that I would here like to focus attention and to discuss. There are two distinctly different situations involved. There is the one in which there is a particular physical threat, sometimes a menace to life, but always with regard to our bodily individuality, a certain danger which is somehow imminent. Our behaviour is gallant in the face of such physical jeopardy, of 'military' jeopardy when we are able to guard our post, if we fulfill our obligations under such a threat. We say that a man who conducts himself in such fashion is distinguished by some particular courage or gallantry. But courage is not simply being bold in the face of something impending. It is also a matter of someone persisting in an activity which for some reason he must perform, during the *course* of which he must face the threat of physical pain, or wounds, or death. If he has succeeded we say that his behaviour was courageous. The second case is one where weathering a threat is entirely unrelated to physical jeopardy, to the danger of pain or being crippled or dying, but where there are other dangers present: moral ones. We are then dealing with so-called 'civil' courage, civil 'daring'. This, in turn, is a certain 'sticking to one's guns', whether in connection with certain convictions or in relation to certain values or through a commitment to be truthful, etc., in a situation which may involve some threatening consequence of our conduct. We are not vulnerable physically, but rather somehow spiritually, if we do not summon up that steadfastness, that civil courage. For the harm that threatens us may be the loss of our career, for example, a failure in some life's endeavour, worse working or living conditions, or something of the sort. If, on the other hand, we are prepared to face up to such undesirable changes in order to maintain our stand or defend values of whose importance we are convinced and whose preservation others wish to prevent, we do so in respect of a wholly different threat, which possibly inheres in the realization of a wrong – the threat of a negative moral value within ourselves. If we succumb, if we do not get up the courage to remain steadfast in the point of view we have adopted, then we have performed a deed which we ourselves feel to be deplorable; we commit some sort of treachery relative to our very own convictions, relative to our own allegiances. That is the looming danger which we wish to avoid. We are then exposed to various sorts of harms – loss of social position, fortune, sometimes even freedom or life – but despite this we stick to our attitude of avoiding a 'wrong' in the sense of a betrayal of our own ideals, even though the perpetration of these wrongs could bring us practical benefits, that is certain positive gains for our psycho-physical being. These are situations which involve the courage of human conduct, be it in the face of physical threats or spiritual threats of tempting corporeal benefits or gains of everyday life. To analyze this matter thoroughly would require further discussion, but it seems to me that what I have said already illumines quite well the situations involving *brave* human conduct, be it in a rather physical sense, or in the sense of so-called civil courage.

Let us now ask whether the conditions I spoke about when discussing fairness are satisfied in the case of courage of our conduct, in this or that context, in the situations we have roughly outlined here. The first point was the participation of a consciously aware subject. If conduct is to merit the assessment of 'brave conduct', and this assessment is a clear case of imputing a value to it, then it is clear that without the participation in the behaviour of an alert subject there can be no talk at all of any 'praise' or 'blame' in connection with his brave or cowardly behaviour. Only when someone is consciously immersed in the total situation and, well aware of what is going on and of the risks involved, nevertheless consciously conducts himself in precisely this way rather than some other, can we speak of courage or of its opposite. Suppose someone is not brave on the face of it: he behaves fearfully, in a cowardly fashion, but he does so in a situation where conditions prevent him from being fully aware of his action – he is not then 'without courage' in a moral sense. There are people with a nervous constitution such that in the face of physical danger they become short of breath, simply 'freeze', their blood pressure rises rapidly, etc. Such a person simply loses cognizance of what is happening, becomes disoriented and runs. We would say that he in fact behaved in a way ungallantly, but we have to come to his defence: his participation throughout the course of the event as a fully aware subject of action was very minimal because he has such a feeble body. We shall say that he must first be cured, that he has to be given a better heart, a better nervous system, and that perhaps then he would be capable of being brave. He would like to, but cannot, because his body is weak and not amenable to such activities; place him in a different situation and he will prove to be a very brave man – not indeed on the battlefield, since his participation as an alert subject of action is here precluded. But put him in a situation where he is called upon to defend certain of his beliefs, certain values; he will then valiantly summon the courage and steadfastness to uphold his views, no matter how great the effort to get him to change his mind. This man has, we shall say, civil courage. But such is the case only when his participation as an aware subject of action has been realized, when he is simply in command of those external conditions that would allow him to react cognizantly, and not as previously when he finds himself in a panic, when his 'heart is in his throat', blood pressure rises, etc. The participation of an alert subject in some conduct therefore appears to be necessary in order to be able to reasonably speak of the 'courage' of someone's behaviour, or of its contrary.

Secondly, some sort of *conduct* by the alert subject must be going on here. We are not talking about some state, but about conduct, this or that kind of behaviour. A man is not inactive in a physical or mental engagement, but exhibits certain modes of behaviour of a purely physical or mental sort; in the latter case by making some decision, for example, or by sticking to some conviction or other. These are also particular *activities* of his, just as the fair assessment of others' virtues or sins and a fair decision as to who is and is not right in a dispute, were particular activities. There, activity was also confined to mental activities, but they were necessary for being able to arrive at a just action. They are here in the same way a necessary condition for being able to end up with courageous, or cowardly, conduct. It seems, therefore, that the second condition has to be satisfied if there is to be talk of civil courage or of bravery in a physical battle.

Third condition: Some values connected with this conduct must come into play, meaning that certain positive values will be realized through this conduct, or they will not be realized because something is missing in the conduct that would enable them to come about. Or, finally, it is a matter of realizing negative values, that is 'bad' rather than 'good' ones, through this or that conduct. In the case of fairness it was necessary to take into account some sort of values and their realization; there, indeed, the values of 'good' were dealt out, someone was alloted, accorded this or that value, etc. It does not seem to be any different with issues of a man's brave or cowardly, non-courageous, behaviour, be it in situations having the character of a physical fight or those from the realm of spiritual matters. In either case, the very decision to be brave, to want to behave courageously, has sense only if this or that value is realized in the course of the relevant behaviour or if its realization depends on the latter. Which value? That, to a certain degree, is a matter of indifference, though not entirely. But if the conduct in which we were to display our courage did not involve *any* values at all, the issue of courage or cowardice in this behaviour, in this conduct where danger lurks, would be somehow senseless or would be some sort of courage for the sheer feat of being brave (bravado!). That is the situation that comes up, for example, in certain *quasi*-sports events. I understand that there is ample opportunity to draw educational benefits from the pursuit of sport, in the sense that it serves as a stimulus for instilling in man diligence in a particular direction, ambition for fortifying endurance in the face of trying circumstances which need to be overcome. However, the moment sport transforms into foolhardy acrobatics, the whole thing loses sense for me and the heroism of jumping from a very high trampoline appears to me senseless, for why be brave in this sense, why be daring for the sake of such foolishness? It is no good to anybody at all, unless some considerable economic values are involved, for example to get a sizable sum of money to flow in for organizing these 'games', but then it is surely a pity to waste these daring and brave human beings for such ends, and their courage has no moral value. And there are such completely senseless competitions, for example in collecting match-boxes. People get pleasure, for example, from being able to build some other objects out of them. Why, perhaps some person may be inclined to say of someone that he is very courageous, that he is prepared to expose himself to any risk just to be able to win a first prize – in stamp collecting for example. My reaction to that would be that it is very funny. This conduct gives rise to certain situations which are altogether neutral from the point of view of any value whatever. If, however, that person tells me that that collector is very brave because he exposes himself to various dangers or sacrifices in order to be able, later, to sell his stamp collection for a great deal of money – and finance with it the most wonderful hospital in all of Poland, I begin to understand that something like that may have something in common with bravery: one is then struggling not over the trading value of stamps, but toward realizing the value of bringing aid to ill or unfortunate people. If the latter is not the case, the endeavour is no different from a bet over swallowing a frog.

If bravery is to be situated within the realm of moral values, then the conduct in which someone's courage is manifested or realized ought to be such as to create or destroy some essential value. What value? That is a good question. It can be an extra-moral value, for example a high economic, social or cultural value, just as well as the realization of a moral value for a person thanks to someone else's brave conduct. It can also be a vital value: human life belongs to these. If someone is brave in saving a human life, then here the rescue of that life is such a value, especially if it is achieved at the risk of one's own life. Such courage takes on the distinct brand of a moral value. It seems to me that the third condition must also be satisfied if courage is not simply someone's showing off, but is to fulfill the function of realizing a value of a moral nature.

The fourth point is the issue of the subject's responsibility for his conduct, the necessity of which we have ascertained in the case of fair conduct. It appears that this condition is also in force for courageous or cowardly conduct. Someone's brave or cowardly behaviour charges the agent with responsibility. He becomes accountable for either the positive value of his bravery or for (the negative value of) his cowardly behaviour. And if the conditions are lacking for being able to assume and accept or bear responsibility, then brave or cowardly behaviour loses the stamp of a value in a moral sense. If someone behaved in a way that outwardly looked like very brave behaviour but it occurred under conditions that absolved him of responsibility for it, then there is no moral virtue in it for him; his action has no value whatever, it is meaningless. For let us assume that it was a reflex action, or that it was effected without the understanding that the realization of certain moral values depends on this action and was simply corruptible behaviour – someone wanted to gain something for his 'brave' behaviour, for the sake of ambition, to improve his living conditions, for a reward, etc. Such behaviour is not at all brave, because this someone was not duly responsible in it, he was lured by things which compelled him to merely purportedly courageous actions. And this issue, bound up with responsibility and the conditions for its being operative, is tied up with yet another matter which has already come up in the case of fairness, the issue of disinterestedness. Someone's brave behaviour (in one sense or another) can claim to be a bearer or realization of some *moral* value if and only if it is at the same time disinterested, if it occurs without conflict of interest on the part of the acting person, if it is not a vehicle for bargaining or bribery: thus, only if someone is brave because he believes that the good fortune of other people depends on his courage, sometimes the fate of an entire community, and not because he wants to get a decoration, for example, or become famous. If, however, he manages to avoid fear only for the latter reasons, and overcomes his weakness because he wants to gain something for himself on that account, then the courage of his conduct is either morally neutral or even morally deplorable. Disinterestedness, therefore, comes into play here in regard to the realization of the morally positive value of being brave. Self-interest, on the other hand, is that factor which goes into effecting the negative value of a courage which gives the semblance of being something positive. We could go a step further and state that if the conduct is self-serving then there is no bravery in the strict sense; there is only some physical feat or mental toughness, but not bravery in the sense of moral virtue.

Fifth point: is the freedom of deciding to be brave an essential condition for a person's brave behaviour to have value in a moral sense? Can we say that someone's bravery, for example, in military conduct, can be the bearer or realization of value if that conduct is compulsory? Can we say that a soldier (or equally someone in civilian life in cases of so-called 'civil courage') realizes a moral value with his (presumably) brave behaviour if he has no freedom of choice? It seems to me that the most outwardly heroic behaviour has no meaning from a moral point of view if it occurs under duress, let us say under the threat of facing a firing-squad for cowardice. Therefore, freedom of decision on the part of the person who behaves courageously seems to be a *conditio sine qua non* for the bravery of his behaviour to be the realization of a particular moral value. And we are not talking about freedom through the course of the decision itself, but also in backing up this behaviour, that is in maintaining his position despite impending dangers. Freedom of decision must be sustained, at least in the subject's consciousness, throughout a whole manifold of varied behaviour. For the time being it has to remain an open question whether this freedom is realizable in other respects, with respect to the problem of so-called determinism, etc. This problem, too, will still be discussed, namely: what are the possibilities concerning not only the phenomenon of freedom, but also the realization of it for people under certain conditions (in particular, the conditions under which, in a causally ordered world, we in fact live).

The last point is the issue of the source of decision and the basis of our upholding it in the course of brave behaviour. In the case of fairness, we said that the source of this decision, if the fairness, the conduct is to be morally valuable, must be the *centre* of the person and not just some irresponsible states 'floating about' in him, states which are not his doing, not 'his' in the strict sense of the word. It appears that it is precisely in matters tied up with brave conduct, when we get up the courage to stick to our convictions, that making the decision in the very *centre* of our ego to behave in just this way is, despite all arguments to the contrary, perhaps most characteristic of courage in civilian life. The special dignity of the high class of moral values adorns this courage of sticking to one's opinion, for example, to one's evaluation, fair conduct, etc., only because this decision, perseverance, even doggedness, are most intimately bound up with the person's centre. And so also this sixth condition, that the source of decision and sustenance of behaviour has its place in the person's centre, is necessarily retained in the case of courage if courage, physical or mental, is genuinely to belong to the class of moral values. If courage of conduct stems from an assimilated discipline, from a mechanism of habit in which the human ego takes no part at all, then this courage, which might even be to some extent socially positive, has no moral value.

In conclusion, I wish to touch on the adequacy of the given six conditions (plus disinterestedness) in the case of so-called 'honesty'. Honesty is an example of a virtue in a moral sense that accrues to a person or to an instance of some sort of moral value in conduct. Sometimes we say that something is the 'honest' or 'dishonest' conduct of a person in a given situation. Well then, we have to come up with an account of what is at issue in the case of 'honest' behaviour, once again in a preliminary fashion, or: of what makes a man honest. We call a man honest when he behaves in a special way in certain situations, so that honesty indeed begins to be a feature of his character at a particular moment; if this feature were not realized in any conduct of his, there would be no basis for asserting of him that he is truly honest. In the statement that someone conducts himself honestly or dishonestly there is contained implicitly an evaluation – in the colloquial or popular sense that suggests imputing to something or someone some sort of value-trait, positive or negative. When, however, do we say that someone behaves 'dishonestly'? The matter is complicated, and I do not know if I am not mistaken here, but it seems to me that in the first place someone behaves dishonestly who is somehow false in his conduct. That is to say, he behaves in a certain way because he really wants to effect a situation different from the one he claims to be the target of his conduct, or he pretends with his conduct to want to achieve a different situation from the one he is really aiming at. In this way, some sort of falseness of conduct, of behaviour, is directly connected with dishonesty; the falseness arises not so much in someone's speaking, as in his making pretense with his behaviour of wanting to attain some end that is different from the one that he really wants and is reaching for. There are still two possible cases involved here: the first is that the situation which someone really wants to effect with his conduct is somehow negatively valued, is something bad, and pretends to strive for a different situation, one which bears the stamp of some positive value, that, to put it briefly, someone wants something bad but behaves as if he wanted something good. This is no longer just falseness of behaviour, and therefore dishonest conduct, but this dishonesty is further compounded by the fact that what we really want to accomplish is something negative and we pretend, make appearances, that the goal of our conduct is positive. But another situation is possible, when someone behaves 'dishonestly' in the sense that, as before, he falsifies his conduct in a particular way by wishing to achieve situation A, yet pretending to aspire to situation B, but where the situation he really wants to reach is no worse than the one he pretends to aim for, and perhaps is even better; however, the conditions for realizing it (A) are such as to preclude its realization without producing the semblance of striving toward the situation (B), which is *de facto* of lesser worth. In this second case the behaviour is also dishonest, but we absolve ourselves of it because what we want to achieve is, despite everything, better than what we would have attained through honest conduct. This is a situation in which a physician sometimes finds himself. He has to behave dishonestly, in a certain sense, toward his patient – for the good of the patient. When the patient asks about his prospects for recovery, for example, and the doctor knows that they are nil, that the situation is hopeless, should he tell him so honestly, or should he behave so as to make it appear to the patient that it is otherwise? The situation the physician wants to achieve is different from what he lets on. He'll say that everything will be well; but what he really wants is to keep the patient's spirits up, with the aid of dishonest means. It is an important question whether we ought to ascribe a moral value to that conduct, and if so, what value? At any rate, those ways of behaving are wholly bad which contain that fundamental falseness and which consists in aiming at realizing a *negatively* valued situation while pretending to pursue a *positively* valued one. These are the one-hundred-percent bad, dishonest modes of conduct. Honest conduct evades the falseness I spoke about, and at the same time evades bad goals, doesn't aim at negatively valued goals. Still a third factor belongs to honest conduct: it should stem from right motives, i.e. it should not be conditioned by negative motivations. If for someone it emerges out of self-serving, egoistic motives, and is 'honest' in the sense of not making false pretenses while at the same time aspiring to something good, yet its ultimate motivation does not have as its target the realization of the value of honesty, but rather the realization of his own gain – then such conduct, too, is not fully honest. It will not be fully honest until even these subjective considerations for one's own benefit are excluded, and until we are exclusively oriented toward realizing some positively valued situations with the aid of unfalsifying means.

I do not know if this conception of honesty and dishonesty is satisfactory. It may well be that it still calls for a good number of second thoughts and many improvements, but perhaps what I have said will suffice to serve as a point of departure for deliberating whether the previously enumerated conditions are, and have to be, satisfied also in this case, if honest conduct is to be valuable in a moral sense. Perhaps the reader will ponder over this. And perhaps the reader will also consider whether honest conduct, too, is one of the conditions for enabling other moral values to be realized. Does not honesty, too, belong to what determines or co-determines the sense of the 'moralness' of values? That would get us a step closer toward solving the problem which concerns us here.

Some Words Concerning Fruitful Discussion*

Freedom of discussion? – Why, yes, of course. That is a necessary condition of all progress in science, and an equally essential factor in all cultural and social development. Surely there is no need to write anything more about it.

Still, if the discussion is to be essentially fruitful, its freedom cannot be purely formal, cannot consist merely in the fact that one does not beset the discussion with any external, formal obstacles. Fruitful discussion must be characterized by other essential features. First of all, it must emanate from the genuine, inner *need* of all the participants, and must be conducted under observance of their *inner* freedom. This inner freedom is borne of the absolute earnestness of thinking, of honesty toward oneself and of striving, undaunted by any circumstances, to attain to an explanation of unexplained matters, matters which are sometimes dogmatically accepted on faith or on the strength of authority. It is borne of the need to check accepted assertions or nurtured beliefs through critical, unbiased research.

But inner freedom is genuine only when it is unmitigated (which I shall explain presently), and when it allows us to overcome all our blindly nurtured attachments to certain ideas or values. I said it has to be unmitigated; that means it has to relate not only to the individually or socially accepted statements of others, but also to our *own* assertions, already acknowledged as true and well-grounded, or even to the beliefs cherished by us. When we are truly free internally, we are always prepared – and manage successfully, to a greater or lesser extent – to suspend our own beliefs, assertions and even preferences, in order to initiate discussion in full readiness to acknowledge the view of *another* and not just with the inclination to belabour our own opinion. Where this readiness to retract our own assertions and accept our opponent's position is lacking, discussion is hampered from the first moment and is carried on rather for show or to assuage our own ambition than to reach the truth *together* with our theoretical adversary. The readiness to suspend our currently held assessment of the position or stance of the other is here of especially decisive significance. Without suspending this assessment we are not truly inclined to hear out the arguments of the

* From *Przegląd Kulturalny* [Cultural Review], November 1961.

other, nor to understand why someone else acknowledges some assertion that we deem false, and opposes one that we espouse. The first condition of a genuine and truly free discussion is the accurate and faithful understanding of another's thought, prior to arriving at its eventual rejection or acceptance. Gaining independence of our own intellectual habits and, especially where philosophical discussions are at issue, being first of all emancipated from the automatism of our own language, from our own conceptual apparatus, play a crucial role in all this. It is indeed the indispensable key to undertaking the attempt and the (sometimes considerable) effort to understand the language and conceptual apparatus of another. The multitude of so-called national languages, and especially of the specialized academic languages of the particular philosophical groups and schools, the power of getting used to employing only our own language, the disinclination to think in any other language – all these are factors contributing today to the creation of solid walls between individuals and communities of various types (scientific, artistic, cultural, religious), walls which make it more difficult, if not utterly impossible, to reach mutual understanding in regard to many theoretical, and what is worse practical, issues. What is supposed to be the means to communicating and to obtaining agreement on the same assertions turns into a sometimes unbridgeable barrier. Moreover, it is not only an obstacle to communicating with other people, but also to reaching to a reality seen and linguistically articulated by someone else. Thus sticking obstinately to one's language, one's own way of understanding and evaluating is that very lack of inner freedom which makes illusory every attempt at discussion between human beings.

In science, and especially in philosophy, the willingness to become somehow acquainted with someone else's position in its original form is the very first condition for liberating ourselves from our own prejudices and biases, but it is at the same time the first condition for the right to demand that *our* position, like that of the other, be understood and thought through in an equally free manner. There is no free discussion as long as this condition has not been fulfilled. In other words, there can be no question of realizing a truly free discussion as long as there is no *spirit of collaboration – on equal terms and with equal earnestness and effort* – in the acquisition of knowledge or in getting free of one's own errors; and until such time all discussion is actually superfluous, since it is merely sham discussion. Only when all sides are prepared to consider in common strictly impersonal propositions, when the identity of whoever advocates them or discovered them plays no role whatsoever in the discussion, when, therefore, we are all free with respect to the assertions discussed or ideals considered – only then does it make sense to engage in discussion.

After all, the need for discussion and its essential function have their origin not in the desire or craving to have one's own position on any matter whatever acknowledged as valid (though it is true that many discussions unfold for this very reason), but in the limitations and frailty of the creative, and in particular the cognitive, powers of a single man. It also frequently has its source in the awareness of our *one-sidedness,* often so inevitable since it follows either from the type of our talents and abilities or from our preferences, which so frequently transform that one-sidedness into *partiality,* into an absence of inner freedom. Discussion is precisely what is to serve for overcoming these human frailties, discussion which is a search for help from others, a check on what we ourselves have managed to attain and a supplementation to what we have not been able to acquire with our own efforts. And it is precisely in this function of mutual assistance or collaboration that discussion should and can attain that freedom which we all ought to demand as the right of man and, at the same time, as something which alone could yield a discussion which is fair.

Index